This Book
Belongs To

Lynn Searl

This Little Light

This Little Light

Beyond a Baptist Preacher Predator

and His Gang

by Christa Brown

Foremost Press
Cedarburg, Wisconsin

Published by Foremost Press
www.foremostpress.com

ISBN: 978-0-9818418-3-0
ISBN-10: 0-9818418-3-X

StopBaptistPredators.org

Dedicated to clergy abuse victims whose voices have been silenced. Silenced by shame. Silenced by the false instruction of religious leaders. Silenced by church shunning and bullying. Silenced by church contracts for secrecy. Silenced by suicide.

Contents

Introduction

As a kid, I was sexually abused by a Southern Baptist minister in Farmers Branch, Texas. The decision to write a book about it did not come easily. Why in the world would I choose to speak publicly about something so unspeakable?

The answer is because the story goes beyond the personal. The story is about an institutionalized inertia that cloaks evil behind a veil of denial and leaves countless kids at risk.

Southern Baptists are the largest Protestant denomination in the land, and yet they have no denominational system of oversight for their clergy. Even when things go terribly wrong, denominational leaders typically wash their hands of the problem and invoke Baptists' congregationalist structure. "It's up to the local church," they say.

So, unlike other major faith groups, Southern Baptists have no denominational system for responsibly assessing clergy abuse reports or for even keeping records on abuse reports. They have no denominational system for removing credibly-accused clergy child molesters from ministry or for even warning people in the pews.

These are dreadful safety gaps for a faith group with 43,000 churches and 101,000 ministers. Clergy predators can readily exploit the lack of oversight, moving church to church without anyone tracking them.

The minister who abused me has been publicly named in news articles, TV coverage, and court documents, but I have chosen not to use his real name in this book. "Eddie Dunagan" is a pseudonym. This story isn't about him. It's about all the rest of what I encountered in Baptist-land. The blind-eyed do-nothingness of the many was ultimately far more damaging than the dastardly deeds of the one.

If you're a parent in a Southern Baptist church, and you're wondering who Dunagan really is, then perhaps you will begin to understand the problem. No one in Southern Baptist circles is keeping systematic records on such men. Dunagan himself could move to another town and start work in a Baptist church tomorrow, and there would be no system to stop him.

"Eddie Dunagan" has never been convicted of any crime in connection with any of the events described in this book.

In *all* faith groups, most credibly-accused clergy child molesters have never been convicted of any crime. This reality is a big part of the reason for why other faith groups have established their own denominational review boards. Though review boards can't throw such men in jail, they can at least prevent them from using ministerial trust to prey on kids. But Southern Baptists don't bother.

I have changed the names of many other people in the book, but they are all actual people. I have *not* changed the names of most denominational leaders.

If change is to occur, I believe it will happen only when people stop seeing the problem as "just a few bad apples" and start seeing how the barrel itself enables the rot. Baptists need to demand accountability from their leaders.

This is a true account of events as I remember them, but as with most people, my memories are imperfect. They have been affected not only by time, but also by trauma.

The last thing I want is to be viewed as a victim. Some of my memories are so unthinkable that they long rendered me mute, but my life has also been marked by immeasurable grace.

I hope that, by sharing my memories, it may help others to reclaim their own memories with a new understanding that the shame does not belong to them. I also hope this book may serve as a tool to help Baptists themselves reforge their faith group into one that fosters clergy accountability.

Part One

A Church Girl

I am alone
my shadow runs back into me to hide
and there is not room for both of us
and the dread.

W.S. MERWIN,
"Second Psalm: The Signals"

1

The Minister's Mustang

After church, we would pile into the minister's Mustang. It was a '66 stick-shift, and one of us always had to sit in the middle and scrunch up our knees in between the bucket-seats. He would crack a joke about how he was going to put his stick between our legs.

We giggled. All of us. None of us ever knew what to say. He was the minister, and we were just giggly girls.

I think that's how it started.

I look back and see how lurid that was. But as kids, we didn't see it. If anything, we felt cool.

None of us smoked. None of us drank. We were church kids. So what we did to feel cool was pile in the car with the minister and laugh at his jokes. In hindsight, cigarettes and alcohol would have been a lot safer.

On my 16th birthday, I babysat all day for the Ganzer kids, and when their mom got home, I headed over to the church parsonage on my bike. Eddie Dunagan, the youth and education minister, had invited a bunch of girls from the church to a sort of impromptu birthday party. I was excited. The last time anyone gave me a birthday party was when I was seven.

I stopped off at Gussie Field park on the way. It was just a few blocks from the parsonage, and I had a long-standing bond with a tree there. Several years earlier, I had promised I would climb that tree every year on my birthday. . . . forever and ever. So I stopped off, climbed up, and soaked in the sound of the woods. Then I went on over to the parsonage.

It wasn't much of a party. There wasn't any cake, and we didn't play croquet like Eddie said we would. Instead, he brought out a football.

Over and over again, I wound up face down on the ground with Eddie on top of me. He was about 8 inches taller than me, and weighed a lot more, but somehow he couldn't manage to just pull the flag.

It felt awful. He was all over me and always slow getting off me. But I didn't want to be a wuss. Besides, everyone else seemed to be having a good time. I didn't want to whine.

Is that when I became prey? Is that when it started?

I look back and search my memories, but I still can't quite figure out exactly when it started.

The kids in the youth group used to play Twister. Though he was older and bigger, Eddie often played too. Somehow, every time my turn came, Eddie would step in, and the next thing I knew, he would be all over me. Maybe that's when it started. Maybe that's when I went from being just a church-kid to being sexual prey. But of course, it was just a game.

Maybe it started when I used to practice the piano in the sanctuary. He started coming in to talk to me. I didn't really mind, but it made it hard to get in my practice time. Besides, the reason I liked playing in the sanctuary was because I liked the solitude and the full whole roundness of the sound going into the stillness. So after a while, I just quit practicing at the church as much.

Maybe it started on Easter Sunday when I was 15. I didn't have a new Easter dress like other girls, but I put together my sister's white skirt with a red, white and blue top. It was an outfit that looked more like the Fourth of July than Easter, but at least I had some new shoes.

It was the first time I ever wore high heels, and I was wobbly. Eddie laughed. "You'll learn," he said. Then he told me how good I looked and how he really liked what high heels did for a woman's legs. I blushed. But I was so embarrassed about not having an Easter dress that I was mostly just glad that anyone had even noticed me.

Maybe it started when my dad had back surgery. Eddie offered to let my sisters and me sleep at his house while my mom stayed overnight at the hospital. Three of us slept in a double bed with my youngest sister in the middle. Did he leer at me while I slept? Or worse?

Was there ever anything at that church that was just good and clean and wholesome? Or was every bit of it some piece of the minister's set-up for sexual abuse?

Every memory I have is tainted – every Sunday School class, every retreat, every Bible drill, every camp-out, every mission trip, every choir trip, every revival, every Vacation Bible School, every prayer group, every ping-pong game – all of it.

2

Family Troubles

It was another day of curses and yelling, of sending us all to hell and calling us every name in the book, and of teaching us all a lesson. Who knows what started it? Maybe he couldn't find the TV guide.

I was trying to drown it all out with some Rachmaninoff.

Things had gotten a lot worse since my dad's back surgery. It didn't go well, and he was constantly popping pain pills. He couldn't sleep much. Even when he did, his combat nightmares kept all the rest of us awake. Worst of all, he hadn't been able to go back to work. For my dad, that was like a death sentence.

Over the sound of my piano pounding, I could tell this one was going to be bad. Why couldn't Sarah just keep her mouth shut? She was living back at home with us while Ronnie was in Viet Nam, and since she was a married woman now, she seemed to think she could yell back at Dad.

But Sarah was screaming, not yelling. Mom was screaming too. Dad was growling.

I stopped my piano pounding and looked in the den.

Dad had one elbow locked around Sarah's neck. He was choking her. Sarah had stopped screaming and her face was turning red. Mom and Jane were trying to pull Dad off. Faye was cowering in the corner.

Frozen in place, I took in the scene. Then suddenly, I did the unthinkable. I ran to the phone in the back bedroom and I called the police.

There must have been a thousand fights under our family's roof, and no one had ever before called the police. Even as I did it, I couldn't believe I was doing it. It was a sort of out-of-body experience, with one part of me dialing the phone while the other part watched, saying "You'll be in trouble now."

I stepped back to the edge of the den and yelled that the police were on the way. Dad let go and skulked back to his bedroom. Sarah took a deep breath. All of them looked at me like I must be crazy.

By the time the police arrived, things seemed calm. No one had much to say, including me. By then, we were all in our usual mental mode of wanting to pretend it never happened.

The police didn't make much effort to sort it out. They asked which church we went to. When we told them First Baptist, they called up our pastor, Brother Hayden.

He came right over and set right to work praying for us. Then Brother Hayden sat at our kitchen table and talked about what a fine Christian family we were and about what an example we set in the community.

"Think about others," he said. "Think about how they'll feel if they learn that the police were called to a family like yours." He looked straight at me when he said it.

I was stunned. My father was choking my sister, and I'm supposed to worry about what people will think?

But he was our pastor. His glare made me shrink in my chair. Why in the world did I pick up that phone?

Brother Hayden said we shouldn't talk about it, and he promised he wouldn't tell anyone about it either. He admonished us to pray and to take care of our family problems privately. "That's the biblical, right way," he said.

He told my mom that she should try harder to be a good helpmate for my dad, to not make him angry, and to support him. My mom was still crying, and she didn't say much. None of us did. We just listened to Brother Hayden, and when he was done praying and talking, we thanked him.

A couple hours later, I left to go to the church for my piano lesson. We all acted as though nothing had happened. In my family, it just got lumped in with all the rest of the big pile of stuff we never talked about.

3

Moving In on the Prey

"I heard the police were at your house, Christa."

It was Eddie Dunagan, the youth and education minister. I had just finished my piano lesson and was getting a drink at the water fountain in back of the sanctuary when he came up behind me. I managed to swallow without choking, but I didn't know what to say. I knew it was wrong of me to have called the police.

Eddie said he wanted to talk to me and told me to come into his office.

I sat there and started bawling. I had never talked about my Dad's temper with anyone, not even my closest friends. But Eddie asked questions, and I answered them, and he seemed to care. In some ways, it was a relief to talk about things.

Eddie said he wanted me to come talk with him every Sunday, in between my piano lesson and the start of choir practice. But he said not to tell anyone. "It would probably just make your parents mad if they knew you were talking about them."

That made perfect sense to me. Besides I wouldn't have told my parents anyway. They had way too many other problems than to worry about me.

Weeks went by. I liked the attention, and I began to feel more and more comfortable with Eddie.

After church youth events, he started taking me home last. He would drive around in the dark and talk about all sorts of things. Mostly I just listened while he talked about what great things he was going to do for God. But sometimes he veered onto other topics.

Once he told me I reminded him of Barbarella.

Then he showed me a picture of the movie poster with Jane Fonda. I didn't know what to say. I just giggled.

"Did you go to see this?" I asked. "I mean . . . what kind of movie is it?"

He looked at me and laughed. "It's about sex in space, and it's a really good movie."

Even in the dark, I'm sure he saw me blushing because then he started lecturing me about how sex was a gift from God.

"There's no need for you to get all nervous about it."

But I *was* nervous. That was probably the first time I had ever heard the word "sex" spoken out loud, except for during health class at school.

After that, he started reading to me sometimes from the Song of Solomon. He told me that I too had "doves' eyes," and a neck like "a tower of ivory."

When he started talking about "breasts like clusters of grapes," I was embarrassed to even hear the word "breasts" spoken out loud. But I didn't know what to think. After all, it was in the *Bible*. It was God's word.

4

Obsession

The church bought Eddie a new station wagon so he could carry around more kids. Everyone liked Eddie a lot and our youth group was growing fast.

There at First Baptist Church of Farmers Branch, we were flat-out having more fun than kids at the other two Baptist churches in town. Eddie said those churches were stuck in old ways. We were going to be the ones bearing witness to the *joy* of living in Christ Jesus.

It seemed as though our joyfulness was working. New families were joining our church, and every Sunday, the pews were packed.

After the first football game that year, Eddie drove a bunch of us kids home in the new station wagon. Since I was on the school drill-team, I was still wearing my Lionette uniform with its tasseled white boots and sequined cowgirl hat.

As usual, I was the last one left in the car.

He drove out on a dark road near the Addison airport and pulled over. He said he just wanted to talk to me a little more.

"Do you know what 'obsession' means?" he asked.

Then he proceeded to explain the word, and told me he was obsessed with the idea of kissing me. I didn't know what to say.

I had never been kissed by anyone. Until just a few weeks earlier, I had a full mouth of metal. I hadn't even hardly thought about kissing anyone, and I doubt anyone else had ever thought about kissing me. I was a goody-two-shoes nerd, and I wasn't exactly what anyone would call "pretty." No one had ever even looked at me with any interest, or maybe I just hadn't yet learned to notice it.

I suppose some other girl might have thought me a bit dense. But that would have been some other girl. I didn't have a clue.

What I remember is how much I wished that I didn't have my Lionette uniform on. My legs were so white they practically glowed in the dark, and my thighs suddenly seemed enormous. I tugged at the short skirt, but it didn't do any good.

On top of that, my hair was stringy and sweaty. I was drenched. That's how it is with Texas football. At the start of the season, there's so much sweat flinging around on the field that the grass gets watered without any rain.

I just kept sitting there, feeling my sweat and looking down at my legs.

Finally, he asked me directly. "Will you let me kiss you?"

"No."

But I didn't want to hurt his feelings. So I tried to soften it.

"You're like an uncle to me or maybe a big brother. I just don't understand."

"Silly goose."

That's what he sometimes called me.

"I can see you aren't ready. Go home and pray about it. We'll talk again."

After that night, he asked for a kiss on every ride home. "What would be the harm in just one kiss?" he kept asking.

It didn't make sense to me, but I never had a good enough answer to his question. Finally, I said "Okay." I thought one kiss was all he wanted, and then we wouldn't have to keep talking about it, and that would be the end of it.

But it seemed so weird that I tried to set some rules.

I had never been on a date. I had never even held hands with anyone. But I had heard other girls talk about "making out" in their boyfriends' cars, and I knew I didn't want it to be anything like that.

So I insisted that he couldn't kiss me in the car and that we had to be standing up. I guess I thought that would make it more formal.

He just laughed and drove out on a road near the Addison airport.

There in the dark, with me standing against that blue station wagon, he proceeded to kiss me. But he didn't stop. He kissed me again and again, all over my face and neck. I pushed at him, but I was trapped between the car and him, and neither one of them was moving.

He started licking me. Licking me! Licking my face, my eyes, my mouth. I stood frozen.

"It's all right," he whispered in my ear. "Nothing's happening. There's nothing wrong with this."

Then he told me how much he loved me and how long he had waited for me and how much he had prayed about me.

5

With God as a Weapon

After that first night, church events often ended up with him driving me out on a dark road. Or sometimes he would circle back to the closed-up church and take me into the sanctuary. It always seemed wrong to be there. But he said the love we shared was sacred, and so the sanctuary was the perfect place.

Sometimes when a new family joined the church, Eddie would recommend me as a babysitter and tell them how good I was with his own young son. Then whenever someone hired me, he would badger me to put the kids to bed early, and he would stop by. Once he even told me to move the clock forward so that I could fool the kids into going to bed sooner. And I did it.

One weekend, he drove a bunch of us girls out to Hardin-Simmons, a Baptist school in Abilene. We drove back late at night, and he put the seats flat in the back of the station wagon so Jane, Barbara and Donna could lie down and go to sleep. I stayed in the front seat.

He drove with one hand on the wheel and one hand messing with me. I was terrified one of the other girls would lift her head and see something. But he just kept shushing me.

So many times I tried to understand.

"We're already married in God's eyes," he proclaimed. "It's preordained."

"But you're already married to Patsy."

"Christa, God has predetermined that we are to be together. It's already written in His plan, and He will make a way for it to happen. Your task is to live by faith and to stop fighting it. His ways aren't our ways, and it's not for us to try to understand."

He told me about how men in the Bible often had more than one wife and even had concubines. I knew that was true, but I still just didn't understand.

"I've prayed long and hard about this, Christa. God wants you to be a helpmate for me. He wouldn't make me feel this way if He didn't intend for you to be with me."

Then he said the three words I could never argue against.

"It's God's will."

That was what he said over and over again, week after week after week.

He often combined it with one of his favorite verses, which he always said with a preacher-style roll on the "know."

"We *know* that all things work together for good to them that love God and who are called according to his purpose."[1]

Then he would launch into a mini-sermon.

"Christa, you should know this by now. You're called of God, and this is your predetermined purpose. You need to start trusting that God will take care of it and will make all things work together. You have to live by faith. You have to trust that it's all part of *His* plan."

I was stubborn and kept trying to understand. But he said it was sinful of me, and he admonished me.

"Lean not unto thine own understanding," he quoted Proverbs.[2]

Dozens of times, that verse rang in my ears.

God was testing me, he said, and God wanted to see whether I would continue to insist on my own way, or whether I would be willing to trust in Him and "live by faith."

"Think of Abraham – think of Moses – think of Noah. Do you think what God wanted made sense to them?" He pointed out how God was able to use these men in great ways because they had the faith to do whatever God wanted even when they couldn't understand it.

He threw in Mary, too. "Where would we all be if Mary hadn't trusted God even when her special role was something she couldn't understand?"

I thought about that one quite a lot. I wanted to serve God, and it's certainly true that faith is the very essence of things not understood. I kept trying to ponder it all in my heart, just like Mary did.

I loved God and wanted only to do whatever God called me to do. My faith was pure, true and absolute. Ultimately, I believed it all, every bit of it. My one and only heart's desire was to know God's will and do God's will.

Nevertheless, as things escalated, I would still reflexively balk sometimes. I couldn't tell him that he had bad breath, and so I would just try to turn my face away. But then there was all his poking and probing. And sometimes he bruised up my breasts. It hurt.

1. Romans 8:28 (KJV).
2. Proverbs 3:5 (KJV).

His touch wasn't caressing. But of course, back then, I didn't know that because I didn't have any idea what a caress would feel like. It's not as if I had any basis for comparison. It's only in looking backwards that I realize how brutish he was. At the time, I just figured it was what men did.

Besides, whenever I balked, he would invariably chastise me with "Oh ye of little faith."[3]

He always told me that I would get used to it and that it would get easier.

Most of all, I worried about making sure I stayed a virgin. Even though Eddie insisted we were already married in God's eyes, I had it in my head that I needed to stay a virgin until we were married here on earth. Somehow that seemed all-important to me at the time, but I wasn't actually sure what counted as "having sex."

Eddie explained it to me. He said that what we were doing didn't count. "It's only sex if it can make you pregnant," he said, "and that's not going to happen."

I felt foolish for being so frightened. I should have known that what we were doing wasn't really "sex."

Eddie also explained to me about my hymen. In fact, that was something he seemed to have a fascination with, and he talked about it quite a lot. Eddie said that as long as what we were doing didn't tear my hymen, I would still be a virgin and so it was okay.

Somehow that made sense to me at the time. But of course, before Eddie explained it, I didn't even know what a hymen was. I don't think we covered hymens in health class.

Eddie explained a lot of other things to me.

"God gave us all sorts of ways to show our love for one another," he said. "All of these other ways are good ways that God gave people so they could show their love before they're actually married."

He said they were the steps that would teach me to become a good wife, and that he was training me for the time when God would make a way for our marriage here on earth.

Whenever I was compliant, Eddie always ended things by telling me how much God loved me.

I yearned for those words: "God loves you, Christa."

Sometimes I sang hymns in my head. My favorite was this one:

---

3. Matthew 8:26 (KJV).

Have thine own way, Lord! Have Thine own way!
Thou art the potter, I am the clay;
Mold me and make me after Thy will,
While I am waiting, yielded and still.[4]

That was pretty much me, "yielded and still," and waiting for God to mold me to His will.

Eddie always said that God had chosen me for something special. I guess I really wanted to believe that. Doesn't every kid want to think they're special?

Besides, who was I to question a man of God? It wasn't my place. My role was to be submissive.

He said it was all part of God's plan, and that God would bless me forever for putting my faith and trust in Him.

So, like the good Baptist girl I was, I deferred to male pastoral authority. It was the biblical way. "Obey them that have the rule over you, and submit yourselves, for they watch over your souls."[5]

I guess you could say that, sip by sip, I drank the Kool-aid.

As time went by, I began to actually *feel* special. I thought I was downright lucky to have been chosen by God for such a special role as the helpmate for a great man of God who would do wonderful things for God. I began to sing "I surrender all" with a new fervor: "All to Jesus I surrender, Lord, I give myself to Thee; Fill me with Thy love and power, Let Thy blessing fall on me."[6]

When Eddie stressed the importance of keeping my special role secret, he said it was because others were less mature in their faith and wouldn't understand. With juvenile arrogance, I felt proud to be a more mature believer.

---

4. Adelaide A. Pollard, "Have Thine Own Way, Lord," (hymn with music by George C. Stebbins).
5. Hebrews 13:17 (KJV).
6. Judson W. Van DeVenter, "I Surrender All," (hymn with music by Winfield S. Weeden).

6

Following the Rules

I tried hard to be a good helpmate, but somehow, I was never good enough.

"Christa, you aren't supposed to just be a chunk of wood," he complained.

"What should I do?"

"Well, move around. Move your arms. Don't just lie there."

So I would move my arms. But I was just trying to follow instructions. "Step number 7: Move arms."

I was like a mechanical doll.

In the beginning, I used to clench my teeth, but he told me not to and instructed me to let my mouth open a little. "Step number 4: Part lips and don't clench teeth."

Once I decided to take out my orthodontic retainer ahead of time, before meeting him. I thought it would make me prettier and that he would be pleased. He wasn't. He wanted me to still have my retainer in my mouth when he saw me, and then for me to take it out in front of him. To me, that seemed gross, but it was what he wanted. "Step number 2: Leave retainer in mouth."

One time, I spent some of my babysitting money on perfume. It was a big expense for me, and I picked it out real carefully. I thought he would be pleased. I was wrong. He was infuriated and told me to never wear perfume again. "Step number 3: Don't put on any perfume."

Eddie always complained that I needed to relax. He said he was learning about hypnosis in a counseling class at Southwestern Seminary, and he thought that might help me.

"Help me with what?" I didn't have a clue.

I thought the hypnosis thing seemed like a game and I just went along with it. That's what I did about almost everything. I went along. I tried to do whatever I was told and always hoped it would make me pleasing in God's eyes. "Step number 9: Relax."

I tried to get all the steps right and I tried to follow all the rules, but I still managed to mess up.

When I cut my hair, it made Eddie so angry. He said I should have asked his permission.

I felt so deflated. My new haircut wasn't really all that short. It was still chin-length. It was how other girls wore their hair. But he hated it.

Right after he yelled at me about my hair, I left to go to a weekend Girls' Auxiliary convention. Southern Baptist girls from all over the state met together to pray and sing and worship. We slept on mats on a gym floor in Brownwood.

There in that high school gym, in the midst of all those other sleeping girls, I whispered my secret to my best friend, Brenda. I was so worried about how upset Eddie had been over my haircut that I broke down and told Brenda about it.

"Oooohhhh . . . just like Judy and Paul," she exclaimed.

Brenda was talking about the prior youth minister. Paul wound up marrying Judy Powell, a girl in the youth group. Brenda and I were 8th graders back then, and Judy had just graduated from high school. Like all the other girls in the church, we thought the "Judy & Paul" story was *sooooo* romantic. It was the biggest wedding our church ever had, and probably every girl there imagined herself in Judy's white dress.

"If Eddie says it's God's will, then it must be God's will," contended Brenda. "You shouldn't doubt him."

Of course, Brenda never seemed to doubt much of anything. One time in Training Union, when I asked about how Mary could have been a virgin, Brenda started crying right out loud. She was afraid I wasn't really saved, because a person of true faith would never ask such a thing. "The Bible says it and I believe it," wailed Brenda. "Don't you believe it too?"

Brenda was practically hysterical, but every eye in the room was staring at *me*. I looked at all their faces and knew there was only one thing to do. I back-pedaled off the question and reassured everyone that my salvation was secure.

Now it was Brenda's turn to reassure me about Eddie.

"Somehow God will make it all work out, Christa. He has a plan. You just have to have faith."

Those were the words of wisdom from my best friend, a born and bred Southern Baptist 15-year-old girl. Her father was a deacon.

Brenda also told me that I made a mistake cutting my hair. She couldn't believe I hadn't thought to ask Eddie's permission. "You've got to apologize and make sure he knows you understand how wrong it was and that you won't do it again."

Of course, I made Brenda promise she would never tell anyone about anything I had said. If she did, Eddie would be even madder than he was about the haircut.

7

Still a Virgin

After I cut my hair, things got more bizarre. Once, he spit on my chest – a big wad – and then he rubbed it around on my breasts.

He laughed at my disgust. "What's the difference whether it's inside my mouth, or out?"

I never had a good answer for most of the things he asked.

Sometimes, he would hold my head so tight that I couldn't move. If I choked or gagged, he would just laugh. He said I would get used to it. So I just tried to slip into my own little cocoon inside my mind.

If I balked, he would chastise me. "Oh ye of little faith."[7] My ears rang with that verse, and I always felt ashamed whenever he said it. I didn't want to be a person of little faith. I wanted to be a person of great faith.

There were a couple times when I couldn't breathe. I was afraid I would pass out and wondered if I might die. But I never did.

More and more often, he seemed angry. He started telling me that I was the "serpent" and "Satan's ally." He said I had allowed Satan to enter in and that I was a temptress who had seduced him into sin. He told me he was praying to God to have strength against me.

I didn't know what to think. To hear Eddie talk, I actually had the real live Satan right there inside of me. I was terrified. I felt as though I had opened the door to hell, and Satan had taken up residence within me. Worst of all, I didn't know how to get Satan out of me.

I started waking up at night screaming. I woke up the whole girls' cabin one weekend at a church youth retreat. Eddie managed to hear about it from one of the women chaperones.

"Just a nightmare," I said.

It was all so confusing. There were other times when Eddie was still sweet. He would tell me about how special I was and how "God would find a way" to make it all work together for good. I wanted to believe that.

---

7. Matthew 8:26 (KJV).

On Valentine's Day, Eddie left a rose and a gold "Christa" pin inside my school locker. Sue was standing right next to me when I opened my locker and saw them. But when she asked who my admirer was, I just shrugged. I left the rose in my locker until it totally dried up and I never wore the pin. I couldn't imagine what I would say if my mom asked where I got it.

Then there came the day when Eddie took me to the parsonage while his wife, Patsy, was out of town, visiting her mom with their son.

Eddie pulled a couple beers out of his refrigerator. I was shocked.

"But we aren't supposed to drink," I said.

"Silly goose."

"But it's against our religion. I don't understand."

"Christa, I've told you before. Some of the rules are for lesser believers. They're meant to protect them. Without rules, lesser believers might go down the wrong path. But for more mature believers like us, God's grace opened up an infinite world of freedom. We don't have to worry about all those rules."

I tried to ponder it, but I didn't understand. He kept shoving the beer into my hand and insisting I drink it. I didn't want to. It seemed wrong. But finally I took a sip. It tasted awful.

He laughed. "You need to drink more," he insisted. "It's a taste you have to get used to."

When I kept pushing it away, he finally got so frustrated with me that he went in the kitchen and poured the beer in a glass. "It'll taste better this way."

So I sipped it again, but it didn't taste any better. He kept shoving the glass back in my hand. But mostly I just pretended to sip it while he kept guzzling from the cans.

The next thing I knew, I was naked on the bed on my stomach. His voice was behind me in my left ear. I couldn't move.

"Don't worry. You'll still be a virgin."

8

Satan's Ally

After the beer-drinking episode, Eddie went back to telling me about how I was harboring Satan, but now he was relentless. He said I had seduced him and that I was a terrible temptress.

One day he called me into his office and made me kneel. I cried and cried there on my knees while he stood over me. He prayed long and loud, beseeching God to cast Satan from me and to cleanse my soul.

His praying went on forever. My knees ached. My tears became a torrent.

At one point, I sat my butt onto my heels and collapsed prone with my head and hands on the floor. But Eddie stopped his praying and chastised me.

"Christ hung on the cross for your sins. You can at least manage to stay on your knees for repentance."

I only cried all the more. But I straightened my body and pulled myself back up onto my knees.

When Eddie finally finished praying, I didn't feel cleansed. I felt low and evil, as though I should slither away on the ground.

I went home and did my own praying. I prayed like I had never prayed before. I prayed without ceasing. I begged God to keep me safe from Satan. I begged for forgiveness.

I didn't know how I had let Satan inside me. I didn't mean to.

When did it happen? How did it happen? I didn't understand.

I prayed and prayed and prayed, but it didn't do any good. I was utterly and completely alone and empty. No longer was there any Spirit beside me or within me.

Before all this, God had been my constant companion, a presence as real as any physical being. But now, even God had turned away from me.

Everything went dark inside me. The darkness was like another living creature. It breathed with me and through me. It was always there – every hour, every minute, and every second. I didn't have a clue how to make the darkness leave me.

Questions without answers filled my mind. Since I didn't know how I had let Satan in the first time, how would I keep Satan out the next time?

Since I didn't realize I was harboring Satan before, how could I be sure that I wasn't still continuing to harbor Satan?

I was someone who had harbored evil. I had seduced a man of God. I had allowed Satan to live within me. What kind of person was I?

Whatever the answer, I was absolutely certain that I would burn forever in a literal hellfire. With full vividness, I remembered all of the pastor's pulpit-pounding sermons about the endless pain, the wailing for water, and the searing of flesh. I could practically feel the flames on my skin – and I knew it would last forever, and ever, and ever, and ever.

I was terrified.

9

Going to Hell

At my next piano lesson, I sat there in a stupor staring at the music.

"Are you all right, Christa?"

"Yes." I put my hands up on the keyboard and looked again at the music. It was nothing but black and white. Meaningless. I looked out at the sanctuary. It all seemed to spin.

There I was seated at the grand piano in the church sanctuary, and I couldn't play a note. I tried to look at the music. I tried to focus. But my hands started shaking.

Then my whole body began quaking. It was no use.

The tears started coming. I couldn't stop.

My piano teacher was the church music minister, Jim Moore.[8]

"I think I'm going to hell." I choked out the words in between sobs. "I'm going to hell. I harbor Satan."

Brother Moore just looked at me and said it might be better to talk where it wasn't so open. He took me into his office, shoved a box of kleenex in front of me, and told me to calm down. He was sure it couldn't be as bad as I thought.

Under Brother Moore's questioning, I told him I "had an affair" with Eddie.

"Will I go to hell?" I pleaded for an answer. "Isn't there some way I can make everything right again?"

Brother Moore asked me to tell him exactly what I had done with Eddie.

I looked at the ground. I stayed quiet. I didn't know what to say or how to say it. I prayed for the earth to open up and swallow me whole. But it didn't.

"What exactly did you do?" he demanded again.

---

8. Affidavit of James A. Moore, filed 9/27/2006 as Exhibit A to Rule 11 agreement in Cause No. 05-06465 in the 192nd Judicial District, Dallas County, Texas.

"Everything but . . ." I whispered.

I hoped that would be enough and that Brother Moore would understand what I meant – that I was still a virgin.

"All right. That's good. Have you told anyone else about this?"

Again, I prayed for the earth to open up. I knew I had done wrong and had to admit it.

"I told Brenda, just Brenda."

"It'll be better if you don't tell anyone else," he instructed. "It will be easier that way."

I readily agreed, and I promised that I wouldn't tell anyone else.

"Am I going to hell?" I asked again.

"No, Christa. Just leave it in God's hands."

The next week, I went to my piano lesson as usual. I acted as though nothing had ever happened, and Brother Moore never again spoke to me about it.

10

God's Biggest Test

On a Sunday morning a few weeks later, Brother Hayden announced from the pulpit that Eddie would be leaving to go to First Baptist Church of Tyler. I sat there stunned, and wondered what had happened.

"I'm so sorry," I blurted out as soon as I saw Eddie. "I couldn't help it. I don't know why I told Brother Moore. It just came out. I didn't mean to make you lose your job. I didn't mean to make you leave. I didn't mean to do anything. I'm so sorry."

"Christa, this is a good thing for me. It's a bigger church. It's a bigger salary. I'll be in charge of all their children's programs. It's a great opportunity. I can do much bigger things in this church."

Then he told me that it wasn't just because I had talked with Brother Moore. Someone in the congregation had written an anonymous letter to Patsy, telling her about me. He wondered if I had any idea who it might be.

"I'm so sorry Patsy found out," I said. "I never meant to hurt you."

"Don't worry. I'll be fine. When Patsy got back from visiting her mom, we got down on our knees and prayed together. I cried, and we both cried, and we prayed, and we cried some more. But God is good and God has forgiven me. Patsy has forgiven me too, and now God has given us this great new opportunity. We're looking forward to it together. 'All things work together for good to them that love God'."

I stared at him, struggling to find the words to ask what I needed to know.

"When will *we* be together?" I asked. "You always said that we would be together someday and that it was all part of God's plan. I don't understand. When will it happen? HOW will it happen if you move away?"

"It will happen, Christa, but it will happen in God's time. He'll make a way."

I just stood there, while he kept on talking.

"This is God's very biggest test for you, and you have to be willing to live by faith. God is testing whether you'll keep faith or not. So you just go on and live your life, knowing that it will all work out, and then one day, it will. All things work together for good to them who love the Lord."

"But *how?*"

"Christa, love is patient. Love endureth all things. I don't know how this will happen, but God does. He has pre-ordained it and He already knows the when and the how. You have to put your trust in God on this. Just go on living your life and wait for this to happen in God's own time. One day when you least expect it, you'll look up and I'll be there. God will bring us back together, and then we'll be together forever."

I pondered his words and decided that I would prove my faith worthy and that I would pass God's test. I would wait.

11

The Last Assault

"You need to apologize to Patsy."

"What? I can't talk to Patsy. What would I say?"

"You'll feel better if you do, Christa. You sinned, and now you need to repent. You seduced me, and now you need to ask Patsy's forgiveness."

"Please don't make me talk to Patsy. I don't know what to say."

"I've already arranged it, Christa. She'll meet you in my office. It's the biblical way. She's entitled to confront you with this transgression, and you need to confess your sin against her and ask for forgiveness."

Like a beaten-down dog, I went to Eddie's office at the appointed time. Patsy was inside, standing with her arms crossed. She was about 8 months pregnant.

I looked around at that room where so much had happened. I felt sick and began to cry.

"I'm so sorry." I must have said those words twenty times, but Patsy just kept glaring at me.

"It was all my fault." That was what Eddie had told me to say. And hearing the words from my own mouth, I knew they were true. It was my all my fault.

I begged Patsy to forgive me. I blubbered and begged, and then begged some more.

Patsy showed no emotion.

"I'll pray for you," she finally said. It was a stonily delivered line, as though she had said it before. Her voice didn't waiver.

Then she told me to leave, and I stumbled out the door, blinded by my tears and hoping no one would see me.

The next Sunday was Eddie's last day at the church. Brother Hayden praised him mightily from the pulpit and talked about how blessed we all were to have known such a great man of God. After the service, everyone stood in line and shook his hand and hugged him. I did too, acting as though nothing had ever happened.

Then there was a big pot-luck supper in the reception hall, and everyone put out their casseroles and jello-molds.

Several weeks later, Brother Hayden announced from the pulpit that Eddie and Patsy had a new baby girl. Everyone said "Praise the Lord."

After the service, Brother Hayden pulled me aside and said he was praying that I would rededicate my life to Christ.

So I did.

The next Sunday, in that sanctuary where I had marched into Vacation Bible School, where I had walked down the aisle for Girls' Auxiliary coronations, where I had played hymns for countless services, and where I had lain on the floor with the minister, I went forward to the front and told Brother Hayden and the congregation that I was rededicating my life to Christ. I hoped it would make the darkness leave me. But it didn't.

So at school the next week, I gave up my Lionette uniform and quit the drill team. I was a good high-kicker, and I had always been near the center of the field, just one away from the 50-yard line. I loved being a Lionette, and I hated quitting. But I decided Brother Hayden might be right about it after all.

There had been many a Sunday evening service when he had preached against dancing and short skirts and immodest ways. Sometimes the dancing prohibition got a sermon all its own, and sometimes it got lumped in with sermons on other sins like drinking, smoking, cussing, and card-playing.

Whenever Brother Hayden preached about dancing, he always looked directly at Maggie and me. Maggie was a Lionette too, and we usually sat together in the back corner of the sanctuary. Brother Hayden would glare at us and raise his voice and shake his fist. We knew he thought we were sinful for parading out there on the football field in our short skirts, but we just ducked our heads whenever he started in on it.

Maggie was often my prayer partner, and we had talked together about it and prayed about it. Since we never got any message from God that we shouldn't be Lionettes, we stayed with it and ignored Brother Hayden.

But things were different now.

I had rededicated my life to Christ and I needed to be certain that I was doing everything exactly right. Dancing with the Lionettes was the only thing I could think of that I had done wrong. It was my one act of rebellion. So I thought it might have been how I opened the door to Satan.

But quitting the Lionettes didn't wind up making any difference. The dreadful darkness stayed with me.

One night, I lay awake listening to Jane talk on and on about how much she loved Dale. Jane was only one year older, but she always had a knack for taking a know-it-all attitude toward me, her know-nothing nerd of a younger sister. Matters of the heart were no exception.

"You wouldn't understand," she finally said. "You've never even held hands with anyone."

"But I do understand," I fired back. "I love Eddie, and we're already married in God's eyes."

"What? What are you talking about?"

There in our dark bedroom, I proceeded to tell Jane about Eddie and how he had promised that God would join us back together someday.

After I spilled my guts, she had only two words.

"You slut."

The words hit me harder than any body blow she had ever thrown, and she had bruised me up quite a lot through the years. No one ever stopped her, and Jane had always been tougher, stronger and angrier than me. I had always been the shy, quiet sister. Growing up with a severe speech impediment, I learned that I got less stares if I didn't talk much, and the lesson had stayed with me.

As soon as I heard the venom in Jane's voice, I knew I had made a terrible mistake in spilling the beans about Eddie.

"Please don't tell anyone," I begged her. "Don't tell Mom. Please. Promise me."

"You stupid slut," she spit the words again. "But I won't tell."

I rolled over and tried to merge myself into the wall. I choked my sobs into my throat, and I stayed quiet.

After that night, I didn't speak of it again . . . not for decades.

Part Two

A Wife

In a dark time, the eye begins to see.
I meet my shadow in the deepening shade.
I hear my echo in the echoing wood –

Dark, dark my light, and darker my desire.
My soul, like some heat-maddened summer fly
Keeps buzzing at the sill. Which I is *I*?

THEODORE ROETHKE,
"In a Dark Time"

12

The Dream

I am paralyzed. I can't breathe. I am held in place by a weight I can't see, and I sense a shadowy presence. I am filled with terror, but I can't cry out. Desperately I try to bring forth sound from my throat, but nothing comes out. Unable to move, unable to scream, and suffocating, I have died a thousand deaths in that dreaded dream.

Sometimes, Dan manages to wake me up. He senses a slight twitching or hears a guttural sound, and he knows I'm inside the nightmare.

I am always so grateful to be awakened. If I could, I would never ever sleep. Too often, sleep opens the door to a place I don't want to be.

Some times are worse than others. When I first met Dan, it was almost as though the nightmare invaded my waking world as well.

I was crazy about Dan from the get-go. But the closer he got, the more terrified I became.

Lots of people are afraid of relationships. But for me, it was cold, stark, unimaginable terror.

Sometimes, in the middle of the night, I would run out of his apartment. I ran to Stacy Park where I would wander, listening to the trees and the creek. Finally, I would find a bridge and sit under it in the dark. With my knees folded up against my chest, I would wait for the waves of nausea, rage and terror to pass.

Often, Dan would awaken and go out in the dark to search the park for me. I could hear him calling my name, but I seldom answered.

Of course, Dan knew every nook and cranny in the park. He was the one who first introduced me to a lot of those trees. So he usually found me whether I answered or not.

Then he would sit down beside me and try to soothe me. He would talk to me as though I were a wounded wild animal, which I guess wasn't far from the truth. Dan didn't know what was wrong with me. Nor did I. But in the dark of the park, understanding was irrelevant. What mattered was only the sound of his voice.

Later, when we lived by the coast and Dan worked graveyard shifts, I would sometimes go out alone on moonless nights and scream into the ocean. Somehow, it would calm me in the same way that the trees and creek had calmed me in the park.

I screamed until my voice gave out. I screamed until I was depleted.

There at the ocean's edge, my screams became one with the sound of the crashing waves.

The waves brought my screams immediately back to my ears, but transformed them. Sometimes the waves took my screams and made them even louder, as though the ocean itself were roiling in rage beside me. Sometimes the waves took my screams and allowed them to simply join with the cosmic chorus, as though they were an accompaniment to the ocean's own endless music.

Whatever the ocean's response, I would keep screaming until I could scream no more.

I didn't have a clue why I was screaming. I only knew that I needed to scream and that, when I stood in the dark at the ocean's edge, the screams came forth from within me.

13

The Voice in the Air-Conditioner

The harder I tried to stay with Dan, the more my head began to split in two. Voices, sounds, and smells – they haunted me. Sometimes I wasn't 100 percent sure which ones were real and which ones weren't.

It reminded me of when I used to hear a voice coming through the window air-conditioner. That was the summer after Eddie left Farmers Branch and moved to First Baptist Church of Tyler. It was the summer of my 17th birthday.

My sister Sarah had moved back with her husband, and for the first time ever, I had a room to myself. I thought it would be great, but then the air-conditioner started talking to me. I could never quite make out what it was saying, but it was definitely a voice – a garbled voice.

The more I tried to figure out what the voice was saying, the more terrified I became. What if it was Satan? What would he tell me to do?

I was afraid of not knowing what the voice was saying, but I was even more afraid of knowing. After all, I had already harbored Satan before, and now here he was talking to me in my bedroom.

Finally, I told my mom about the voice in the air-conditioner.

"Oh Christa, don't be silly. There's no voice in the air-conditioner."

"But I'm hearing something. It's there."

"Christa, there's no voice in the air-conditioner."

"Please, Mom." I pleaded with her. "Just stay in the room with me one night. Maybe you'll hear it too."

"Christa, there's no voice in the air-conditioner. I don't need to stay in the room with you to know that. Now I don't have time for this. I don't want to hear anything more about it."

So that was the end of it. I didn't talk about the air-conditioner voice again.

I don't remember what happened to the voice. I don't think I ever cut the air-conditioner off, because that unit helped to cool the rest of the house, and I was supposed to leave it however my dad set it. As I recall, the voice just stopped after awhile.

But now, here I was, at age 25, and something just as weird was happening again.

Eventually, I became a guinea pig for a psychiatrist's toolbox of psychotropic pharmacology. I hated taking drugs, and I didn't like the psychiatrist at all, but I was in graduate school, and the only psychiatrist I could afford was through the student health center. So I couldn't be choosy.

In hindsight, I figure he may have saved my life, but at the time, I just hated him. I kept going anyway because I didn't want to risk the alternative.

A couple years before meeting Dan, there was a morning when I woke up lying in my own vomit. I felt only surprise at finding myself alive and disgust for being so inept. I couldn't even manage to properly kill myself off. There was nothing to do but clean up the mess.

I knew I didn't want that experience again.

Besides, I was crazy about Dan, and I didn't think he would stick with me if I wasn't making a serious attempt to get myself straightened out.

Mostly what I talked about with my psychiatrist was family stuff. After all, "dysfunctional" would be a compliment for the family I grew up in. So, family history provided plenty of fodder for talking.

But my psychiatrist went through a spell when he drove me nuts. He kept asking questions that seemed to suggest I may have been a victim of incest. It infuriated me.

"No! Nothing like that ever happened!"

I told him that over and over again, but he just wouldn't let it go. He asked me about my memories of uncles and cousins and whether I had memories of sitting on anyone's lap.

"Why do you keep asking this stuff?" I demanded.

He said that a lot of my psychological manifestations were consistent with incest victims.

"Well maybe I'm messed up in the head, but that doesn't mean I'm an incest victim."

I was adamant. "Nothing like that ever happened to me."

14

A Stockholm-Syndrome Sort of Bond

When Dan wanted me to move in with him, I began to really flip out. There was no way I was going to get that connected to anyone. The closer he got, the more scared I got, and the more I pushed him away. A couple times, I ran away and stayed away.

My two older sisters got married in our childhood church, but I couldn't even imagine the possibility of a wedding. Not there or anywhere. I had a dozen reasons in my head for why I would never get married. But mainly, I just didn't want to talk about it. I didn't want to think about it.

I couldn't even put words on it. I had no clue what I was afraid of or why I was acting the way I did. Dan was wonderful. But I was terrified. Absolutely terrified.

Finally, I decided that I might feel freer to commit to Dan if I let Eddie know that I wasn't going to keep waiting for him. I wish I could remember how I came up with such a bizarre notion.

Did my psychiatrist suggest it? I don't remember ever talking about Eddie with the psychiatrist. But he once asked me to write 20 pages about my life, and I may have put in a sentence or two about having an affair with the youth minister.

So maybe the psychiatrist noticed it, and maybe he planted in my head the notion of talking to Eddie. Maybe the psychiatrist thought that, if I saw Eddie, it would trigger some realization or understanding on my part.

But maybe not. Maybe I just came up with the notion of seeing him on my own. I don't remember.

What I do remember is thinking that, if I saw Eddie, it might help me make a whole-hearted commitment to Dan. I wanted to clear the decks and tie up all the loose ends. I wanted to make sure there wasn't any tiny corner in my brain that was holding anything back. I wanted to make sure I wasn't being tentative in any way.

I also remember thinking that I owed it to Eddie to let him know. I didn't have any feelings for him, or at least I didn't think I did. But

35

given how we had left things, I wanted to tell him honestly and up-front that I wasn't waiting for God to reunite us. I felt like I should tell him that to his face.

How I could have ever thought that I owed him anything is something I'll never understand. It's crazy. And yet, I remember thinking that.

Decades later, my therapist explained it as a sort of Stockholm-syndrome type of loyalty.[9] But I didn't have a clue about that at the time. I just knew I needed to talk with him.

So I wrote to him at First Baptist Church of Tyler, and said I would like to talk with him in person. I asked him to tell me a time when it would be convenient.

He phoned me right away and said that he was flying into Dallas for a conference and that he could meet with me at the Dallas/Fort Worth airport. He gave me his flight number and the time, and told me to meet him there.

I drove a couple hundred miles from Austin to Dallas, and I waited for him at the airport. I had him paged. He never showed up. Finally, I gave up and drove home.

Eddie called me a few days later and said that he was going to be in Austin and would like to visit with me at my apartment.

When the time came, I waited. This time, he showed up. As soon as I opened the door, he stepped quickly inside and launched into a long prayer.

I don't know what I was expecting, but it wasn't that.

I stood there listening to his prayer, and my mind went blank. I thought there would be something to talk about, but suddenly I was frozen. No feelings. No nothing. Just frozen.

When he was finally done praying, I found it almost impossible to speak. I couldn't get words out. My voice was gone. I felt in a fog.

"Why did you want to see me?" he asked.

"I wanted to see you with the eyes of an adult." That's what I said. It was a line I had rehearsed ahead of time. But where was that adult? What became of her? I was acting like a scared child.

"I figured it was just something simple like that," he said. "Patsy was afraid, but I told her there was nothing to worry about."

---

9. Dr. Patrick J. Carnes describes this sort of "Stockholm Syndrome" as a "trauma bond" that can give rise to "insane loyalties." Abuse literature, he explains, "is filled with examples of ongoing abuse followed by profound loyalty extending years and decades." Patrick J. Carnes, *The Betrayal Bond*, at pp. xix, 34–35 (Health Communications, Inc. 1997).

"Afraid? What was Patsy afraid of?"

"Afraid of you."

"Why?"

"Oh, forget it. I don't know what she was afraid of. Patsy just gets funny ideas sometimes."

I felt so befuddled that I never invited him to sit down. I didn't even offer him a glass of water. He stayed only a few minutes. He wanted to know what I was studying.

As he was leaving, and already outside the door, he suddenly asked, "So did you ever find out who sent that letter to Patsy?"

I stared at him blankly. "I figured it was Connie Griswell," I finally said.

He glared. "It wasn't Connie."

That's when I heard it. The anger. The voice.

"How do you know it wasn't Connie?"

"Connie would never have done something like that." He was spitting his words now. "I knew Connie, and Connie wouldn't have done that."

I took a step to the side. He walked toward his car, got in, and drove away.

Part Three

A Mom

From behind a thin cloth
a blaze of straw pretends to be the moon.

There are those who destroy soul growth
by using sacred symbols in their talk.

> RUMI,
> "Bridge to the Soul"
> (translation by Coleman Barks)

15

Opening the Box

When Emily turned 16, I began to think about the person I had been at 16. It wasn't anything dramatic. I didn't think about it all at once. But little fragments began to seep into my consciousness.

It was as though I suddenly noticed a dusty box at the far back of the top shelf in the darkest corner of my storage-closet brain. I began to give little glances at the box from time to time.

The box had a label, but it was scarcely readable. Finally, after a few sideways looks, my curiosity got the better of me. I brushed away some of the dust and saw what it said: "Affair with minister."

I remembered slapping that label onto a super-heavy box many, many years ago. Then I hoisted it up there and shoved it to the back as far out of sight as I possibly could. But now all these years later, I had noticed it again. The box was still there in the darkest corner of my brain, just where I left it.

Whenever it caught my eye, I didn't let my gaze linger. It was as though the box was electrically charged, and if I looked at it for too long, I would start getting short of breath. So I would just glance and then avert my eyes.

I kept thinking about how I would feel if I learned that Emily was having an affair with one of the trusted adults in her own life. Of course, there wasn't any way to imagine Emily having an "affair" with a preacher because we never went to church. Through the years, I had simply done a home-school version of Sunday School.

But there were plenty of other trusted adults in Emily's life. She spent endless hours with her coach and hung on his every word. What if I learned that she was having an "affair" with him?

I knew I would be outraged. I wouldn't call it an "affair."

Was the label on my dusty box wrong?

If it was Emily, I'd be sick with worry. I'd be trying to figure out what to do and where to get good counseling and how to help her.

Every time I thought about it happening to Emily, I started crying. It took me a long time to figure out that I was really crying for myself – for that naive 16-year-old girl that I myself used to be.

About that time, an article in the newspaper caught my attention. It was about Rob Gianni, a man who was sexually abused by a priest when he was 15. Rob had studied for the priesthood himself, but then got married and became an attorney instead. He worked for a Catholic diocese, helping it handle a string of priest abuse claims and negotiating to send the accusers away with as little as possible.

Then one day, something about one woman's story gripped him, and Rob found that he couldn't put his own memories back in the box. He could no longer pretend that what happened to him as a kid didn't matter. Rob eventually sued the diocese, and the news article was about the settlement of his lawsuit.

Over and over again, I read that article. I couldn't let it go. Rob was a teenager when it happened. He wasn't a 7-year-old; he wasn't a little kid; he was 15. Yet he was calling it "abuse." I didn't know what to think of that. If what happened to Rob was "abuse," then I guess what happened to me was "abuse."

Was the label on my dusty box all wrong? Should it have been labeled "abuse" instead of "affair"?

So many things about Rob's story troubled me. Clearly, he wasn't some bad kid. He was a good kid. Like me, he had been a leader in his church youth group, and his faith was a vital part of who he was. Yet there he was, with his picture in the paper, and he was calling it "abuse."

After pondering Rob's story for months, I finally picked up the phone and called the diocese where the article said he had worked. The person on the phone said Rob wasn't there any longer.

So, I tracked Rob through the directory of Texas attorneys, got a number for him, and eventually picked up the phone again.

"Hi Rob. This is Christa Brown. I'm an attorney and I saw the article about your lawsuit. I've got a situation that's sort of similar and was hoping I could talk with you about it."

Rob was generous with his time and listened to me for quite a while. But finally, he interrupted.

"Christa, are you talking about a client of yours or are you talking about yourself?"

I paused. I took a breath.

"I'm talking about me."

I barely whispered it, and immediately I choked. Rob waited me out.

"I'm sorry. This is the first time I've given voice to this."

Rob was compassionate and understanding. But in hindsight, I see what a bizarre conversation it was. I tried to detach myself and put on my professional hat and act like it was just a routine phone call with another lawyer. Meanwhile, Rob put on his "almost-a-priest" hat and assumed a ministerial role.

Finally, I got to the heart of what I wanted to know. "I was 16," I said. "It's not as if I tried to run away, and I figure I was old enough to know better, wasn't I? How do I let myself off the hook? I mean . . . why wasn't it just as much my fault as his?"

I hated asking that, because it sounded as though I might be blaming Rob for what was done to him. And I wasn't. Not at all. But somehow I figured I was different. I was raised to take responsibility for my own actions, and I was old enough to know better, and now I just needed to understand why what happened to me was different from what happened to Rob.

Rob didn't take it personally. He just gave a huge sigh. "Christa, you're at the very beginning of this journey, and you're going to need a lot of help along the way. For starters, you should spend some time looking at the SNAP website. Some articles there might help you."

I had never heard of SNAP, but he explained that it was the Survivors Network of those Abused by Priests. I told Rob I wasn't Catholic, but he said SNAP was about any kind of clergy abuse. Every time I heard him say the word "abuse," I cringed.

"You really should get some counseling about this," Rob said.

"Oh no, I'm fine. I don't need any counseling or anything like that. I'm just trying to understand things a little better."

Rob just gave another sigh.

16

First SNAP meeting

I didn't need counseling. That much I was sure of. Besides, counseling was something that cost money. I would figure this thing out by myself.

So I launched myself onto the SNAP website[10] and read everything there. Then I ordered some books, and read a lot more.

When Rob called to tell me about the SNAP meeting, I said I'd try to go, but I knew I wouldn't. I'm a loner by nature, and this sounded like some sort of group therapy thing. I didn't want to go sit and talk with a bunch of people.

But Rob had been so kind, and he called back on the day of the meeting to make sure I was going. So I said I would.

I got in the car and drove over. I went in the building. I peeked in the room.

Then I turned away. I didn't want to sit in that circle of people. I figured they probably all had problems of some sort, and I didn't. I was fine.

But Rob saw me and guessed who I was. He stepped out and called to me as I was walking away. So, I acted as though I had just been hunting for the right room, and I went in with Rob and sat in the circle of chairs.

Rob started talking, and told a bit of his story. Then the circle went to Miguel. And then it went to Barbara. She talked about her son, Eduardo, who had committed suicide. As a mother, I heard her great pain, and I felt the weight of all that she had lost. I thought of her son, and I thought of my own precious daughter, and then I thought of the girl I used to be.

If anyone had ever done to my daughter what was done to me, my fury would know no bounds. Thinking of it as a mother made me weep for the young girl that I myself once was.

---

10. www.SNAPnetwork.org

44

That was when the dam inside my head began to break, and the murky waters started flooding in. I just couldn't hold it all back.

I thought about waking up on the floor in that stench of vomit. I thought about all the weeks I had planned it. I thought about all the months when deciding to kill myself was the only thing that made sense. I thought about the enormous, incomprehensible pain of that time, and how the infinite darkness of it stretched on through the years, and how desperately I had wanted it to end.

Was this what that was about? Was it all connected to that church I grew up in? Suddenly I knew that it probably was.

I felt gratitude and grief inseparably mixed. I was alive in spite of everything, and I felt so grateful for the goodness of my life and for the wonder of my own glorious daughter. But I felt an equal measure of grief for the girl I used to be and for all that she went through all alone.

And I felt grief for Barbara's son, who didn't make it. His suicide was successful. All I could think was "But for the grace of God, it could have just as easily been me."

All of the pent-up anguish and pain swept over me like a tsunami.

The circle continued around, and in every person's story, I heard little pieces of my own life. I knew we shared something terrible.

By the time the circle came around to me, my mind was reeling. I managed to choke out just 8 words: "I was sexually abused by a Baptist minister." After that, my whole chest clamped shut. It was as though my mouth had a mind of its own, and it refused to speak what my brain was trying so hard to bring forth. I opened my mouth again, but no sound came out.

As I struggled to breathe, Rob quietly said, "Thanks for sharing, Christa," and he moved on around the circle.

17

Dan's Wail

I didn't know it then, but I had crossed over a line, and there was no going back. Though I didn't attend another SNAP meeting for months, my mind kept churning.

Rob and Miguel called me, trying to get me to come to another meeting. But I said I was fine, and of course, I was busy.

"It won't be like it was with you," I told Rob. "I've got proof. My situation is different."

By then, I had looked at the Southern Baptist Convention's online registry of ministers and had seen that music minister Jim Moore was still there at First Baptist Church of Farmers Branch. I was elated. That would make things easy. Moore knew what Dunagan did, and he wouldn't lie about it. So there wouldn't be any problem. I just needed to figure out the right way to bring it up.

While I worked at mustering my courage, I kept reading. Every book and article I saw talked about the trust issues that are so typical for clergy abuse survivors. Basically, they just don't. They don't trust *anyone*, including themselves. It makes it tough to build relationships.

I thought back on all the over-heated arguments that Dan and I had in our earlier years. We had a lot of them. We fought long and hard and often.

Nowadays, I can't even begin to remember what all our fights were about, but at the time, I always thought they were about something important. And I always thought I had really good reasons to be so angry.

Strangely, regardless of what they were about or what I thought they were about, a whole lot of our arguments ended in the same way. Dan would finally wail at me in frustration: "What in God's name do I have to do to make you trust me, Christa? What will it take? Huh? Will you just tell me that? What will it take?"

That wail of his never made sense to me when I was in the middle of hearing it. If anyone had ever asked me, I would have certainly said,

"Well of course I trust Dan." But the truth was that I didn't. I didn't trust him. I just didn't realize it.

Dan saw it. He knew it.

But I didn't.

18

The Church Threatens Me

"Please give him another chance," I pleaded. "He was always an upright, good man. He's raised a daughter of his own by now. When he's had a chance to think about it, I'm sure he'll do the right thing."

John had phoned up music minister Jim Moore for me.

I figured Moore had probably felt bad about it all these years and wished that he had done things differently. I figured he would be glad to hear from me and to know that I was okay. I was certain he would want to help me.

Well . . . .almost certain. I wanted desperately to talk with him, but I didn't want to make the first call. I was afraid.

John kept phoning Moore at the church. He left a half-dozen messages saying that he was calling about one of Moore's former piano students, Christa Brown. Moore didn't return the calls. Finally, John managed to get Moore's cell phone number and reached him that way.

Moore said he remembered me, and he immediately acknowledged that I had told him about having a sexual relationship with the youth and education minister, Eddie Dunagan.[11] But then he got nervous. He wanted to talk to a lawyer before saying anything more. He told John he could call back in a couple weeks if he wanted.

John thought it was pointless. But after I pleaded and pleaded, he called Moore again.

"What's to be gained by going into this now?" demanded Moore.[12] He asked it repeatedly. "What's to be gained?"

"She's got no business bringing it up," he told John. "Nothing good can come of it. There's nothing to be gained. The statute of limitations has run."

"Besides," Moore continued, "it was a consensual relationship."[13]

---

11. Affidavit of J. Sadler, Cause No. DV05-05669M in the 298th Judicial District, Dallas County, Texas, C. Brown v. First Baptist Church of Farmers Branch and James A. Moore.

12. Affidavit of J. Sadler, *supra.*

13. Affidavit of J. Sadler, *supra.*

John reminded Moore that I was below the age of consent,[14] but Moore said he wasn't talking about technical "legalities."[15]

"She's got no business talking about this."

When I heard what Moore had said, I sat and cried. There he was again, just like all those years ago, telling me that I shouldn't talk about it.

Moore had spent his career as a high-school choir director.[16] How could he imagine that a full-grown trusted adult could have sex with a kid, and that it could somehow be "consensual"? Would it be okay with him if one of the other teachers at his high school had done that to a kid? Would he keep it quiet for the teacher and say it was "consensual"?

Would he call it "consensual" if a minister did to Moore's own daughter what was done to me? Or to his granddaughter?

I pondered all of it and none of it made any sense. He was my childhood piano teacher. He knew what kind of kid I was. How could he call it "consensual"?

After that, I told Donna Dean that I wanted to go ahead and make a written report of my abuse to the Baptist General Convention of Texas. Commonly called "the BGCT," it was the largest statewide Baptist organization in the country.[17]

I had been so excited when I found Donna online. She herself had reported a minister's sexual abuse to the Baptist General Convention of Texas, and when nothing happened, she kept talking about it until they finally put together a committee to address clergy sex abuse.[18]

---

14. At that time, the age of consent in Texas was 18. Act of April 2, 1918, 35th Leg., 4th C.S., ch. 50, 1918 Tex. Gen. Laws 123 (renumbered as article 1183, effective September 1, 1925), repealed by Act of September 1, 1973, 63rd Leg., R.S., ch. 399 § 3(a), 1973 Tex. Gen. Laws 991 (which lowered the age of consent to 17 for incidents post-1973).

15. Affidavit of J. Sadler, *supra*.

16. In more recent years, James A. Moore has been a director of choral activities at a Baptist university in Texas.

17. By the time this book is published, the Baptist General Convention of Texas may be called the Texas Baptist Convention. It began the process of considering this name change in 2008. Ken Camp, "Texas Baptists elect Lowrie, defer name change proposal," *Associated Baptist Press*, November 11, 2008. (Of course, a name change won't alter the organization's tragic history of mishandling clergy abuse reports.)

18. Affidavit of D. Dail, Cause No. DV05-05669M in the 298th Judicial District, Dallas County, Texas, C. Brown v. First Baptist Church of Farmers Branch and James A. Moore; *see also* Dee Ann Miller, "The Collusion Act of the Southern Baptist Convention and Clergy Sexual Abuse," *TakeCourage.org* [http://www.takecourage.org/updatesbc.htm].

Of course, it was about that same time when Southwestern Baptist Theological Seminary was hit by scandal. The chairman of its board of trustees resigned amid allegations that he had sexually abused two women who went to him for counseling.[19] It got a lot of press in the Dallas/Fort Worth area, and so that too may have prompted the BGCT to put together a committee.

Donna had gone before that committee and addressed them in person.[20] I didn't know Donna. I had never met her. But I read about her online, and since she herself had reported clergy abuse, I felt safe telling her about what happened to me. I knew she wouldn't judge me.

As an attorney myself, I had a lot of attorney friends and acquaintances. But I couldn't imagine talking with any of them about this sordid thing in my past. What would they think? Would they ever refer another case to me? Would they think I was psychologically unbalanced? I figured it was better to talk to a stranger than to anyone I actually knew.

But Donna and I didn't exactly get off to a good start. She looked at what I had written in my letter, and then called me.

"How did you get my name? What do you know about me?"

It seemed like a pretty abrupt start to the conversation, and she sounded a little angry.

"I saw something about you online. I think it was Dee Miller's website," I said. "And then I looked up your name in the State Bar directory."

"Do you know that I myself was sexually abused by a Baptist minister?"

"Well, I can't remember exactly what the website said, but yeah, I think I figured something like that had happened."

"Do you know my perpetrator?"

"Well . . . no. I have no idea. I mean, I really don't know anything except what I saw on the website, and I don't even hardly remember exactly what that was."

---

19. Marv Knox, "Seminary chairman quits amid sex charges," *The Baptist Standard*, October 14, 1998.

20. Affidavit of D. Dail, Cause No. DV05-05669M in the 298th Judicial District, Dallas County, Texas, C. Brown v. First Baptist Church of Farmers Branch and James A. Moore.

"My perpetrator is the pastor at First Baptist Church of Farmers Branch."[21]

"Oh."

"You didn't know that?"

"No. I can't believe it. You mean he's the pastor right now?"

"Yeah. You didn't know?"

"No. I'm sorry. I didn't mean to upset you."

Finally, we smoothed things over. She couldn't believe it any more than I could. How was it possible that, in the whole state of Texas, I had managed to contact a woman who was claiming that she was abused by a pastor in the same cursed church I had grown up in?

There were thousands of Baptist churches in Texas. Hundreds in Dallas County alone. This couldn't be mere coincidence. So I figured it was a flat-out miracle. God would make something good come of all this.

Even as I thought that, I cringed. I always hate it when my brain goes down that "God will make something good of it" path. But I couldn't help it. My brain tends to go down those paths all on its own. I guess they're more like ruts.

At first, the only thing I wanted was for Donna to tell me who the best people would be for me to talk with at the Baptist General Convention of Texas. I thought I would just send a short letter, and I hoped Donna would give me the names of exactly who to send it to.

But Donna thought I should file a more extensive report. She said that more details would make it more credible, and she gave me a copy of the BGCT's policy booklet called "Broken Trust." It said the BGCT looked for "substantial evidence" in considering clergy abuse reports. So Donna said "substantial evidence" was what I needed to show them.

As a lawyer, my instinct was to reject the notion of giving them so much information. But this wasn't a lawsuit, and Donna insisted it

---

21. The report alleged "sexual abuse and sexual exploitation" by the pastor of First Baptist Church of Farmers Branch. Affidavit of D. Dail, Exhibit to Plaintiff's Response to Nonparty's Objections to Subpoena in Cause No. DV05-05669-M in the 298th Judicial District, Dallas County, Texas, C. Brown v. First Baptist Church of Farmers Branch. The church characterized it as "misconduct" rather than "abuse." *See* Dee Ann Miller, "The Collusion Act of the Southern Baptist Convention and Clergy Sexual Abuse," *TakeCourage. org* [http://www.takecourage.org/updatesbc.htm]. Though not applicable at the time, under current Texas law, it is a felony for a clergyman to use his position as spiritual advisor to sexually exploit another person, regardless of the other person's age. Tex. Rev. Civ. Stat. Ann. § 22.011(b)(10).

would have more of an impact if I told them more of my story. So I accepted her guidance and paid her a few hundred dollars to help me with making a clergy abuse report to Baptist leadership. Because Texas Baptist leaders knew Donna and because she had testified to their committee on clergy abuse, I hoped that having her name on my report would implicitly convey to them how much I wanted to try to handle this within the Baptist structure.

It was only a couple months, but the time went by slowly while Donna prepared a 25-page written report. I was so anxious. I just wanted to send something off and be done with it. Once it was done, maybe my head would stop churning. At least that's what I thought then.

Donna sent the report to the chairman of the deacons at First Baptist Church of Farmers Branch, to First Baptist Church of Tyler where Dunagan went next, and to various officials with local, state and national Southern Baptist organizations.[22] The report made clear that another Baptist minister, Jim Moore, had substantiated my story.

So no one had to do much work to know the truth of my report. All they had to do was call up music minister Jim Moore. He might characterize it as "consensual," but whatever wrong label he stuck on it, that didn't change the fact that Moore knew Dunagan had sex with me when I was a girl in the church youth group. His words confirmed that.

My abuse report didn't ask for any money other than two years' worth of counseling. I didn't think I needed counseling, but I asked for it anyway as a matter of principle. When I saw that the Baptist General Convention of Texas provided a standard two years' worth of counseling for clergy sex abusers – to restore them to ministry[23] – it only made sense to me that they should also provide counseling for the victims of clergy sex abusers.

---

22. Sent by certified mail, with return receipts, to: Bobby Welch, President, Southern Baptist Convention; Mike Floyd, Chairman of the Deacons, First Baptist Church of Farmers Branch, Texas; Wm. Jan Daehnert, Director, Officer of Minister-Church Relations, Baptist General Convention of Texas; Charles Wade, Executive Director, Baptist General Convention of Texas; Ken Hall, President, Baptist General Convention of Texas; Garry L. Hearon, Director, Dallas Baptist Association; Jim Richards, Executive Director, Southern Baptists of Texas Convention. Sent by regular U.S. mail to the Chairman of the Deacons, First Baptist Church of Tyler, Texas. (Because Baptists have a buck-stops-nowhere system, each of these men might conceivably say that the problem simply wasn't his responsibility. Therein lies the problem.)
23. Christian Life Commission of the Baptist General Convention of Texas, *Broken Trust* at p. 36 (circa 2000).

I also asked for a written apology, press statements in the cities where Dunagan worked, and some sort of enduring symbolic gesture as a sign of the denomination's concern for clergy abuse victims and as a focal point for awareness of the problem. I thought my request was so positive in nature.

But the church didn't see it that way.

The church responded with a letter threatening to seek "recourse" against me if I pursued the matter.[24]

I couldn't believe it. I thought I had played out every possible scenario in my head, but in my wildest imagination, it never occurred to me to think my childhood church would threaten to sue me. Why? How? On what basis?

It didn't make any sense to me. They knew what I was saying was true. Music minister Jim Moore, who knew about the abuse when I was a kid, was still right there. But instead of doing anything about the minister who molested me, the church was threatening ME.

I felt as though a bomb had exploded in my head. It was a sort of preemptive strike, and it was very effective. The church seemed determined to knock me out fast and swift. For a while, they did.

I curled up on my bed and cried. For days and weeks, I could hardly move.

Donna called. She wanted me to press forward, but I couldn't. I was immobilized.

She pointed out that it was only the church that had responded with so much hostility. The letter from the Baptist General Convention of Texas had thanked me for sharing my experience "in a way that will benefit and protect others."[25]

That only made the church's over-aggressive response seem all the more puzzling. Obviously, I hadn't done anything to prod such aggression because the Baptist General Convention was thanking me and saying I had reported the abuse in a good way.

Of course, how could they possibly have said otherwise? My report followed the guidelines of their own policy booklet, *Broken Trust*.

That was when I first began to get a glimmer of the fact that the BGCT's policy booklet was just words on paper. Nothing more.

---

24. Letter of August 9, 2004 from attorney on behalf of the First Baptist Church of Farmers Branch, Texas, and music minister James A. Moore.
25. Letter of August 3, 2004 from Wm. Jan Daehnert, Director of the Office of Minister-Church Relations, Baptist General Convention of Texas.

Why would the church threaten to sue me? Every day my head ached from churning over that question. I kept trying to look under it, around it, beside it, and through it. But I never could figure it out and I couldn't answer it. Still, there it was: a threat.

All I could think about was how much my life would hurt if I pressed forward. I didn't want to spend any part of my life fighting off some trumped-up claim of the church. For what? And how much would it cost me before it was over?

If there's one thing I know as a lawyer, it's that truth and justice do *not* always prevail. And trying to get to justice could sometimes cost more than justice might even be worth. And what if the church actually won on whatever ridiculous trumped up claim it made up? Would I lose the money I had set aside for retirement? What about the money we had in our daughter's college fund?

Besides, move forward with what? All I really wanted was some acknowledgment of what happened. Was I going to put everything on the line just for that?

The Southern Baptist Convention in Nashville had written back, saying that it had no record Dunagan was still in ministry anywhere.[26] So at least I didn't need to worry about him pulling the same biblical con-job on another kid. That made it easier for me to think about just walking away.

But still, day after day went by and I accomplished nothing. Nothing in my law practice. Nothing in the way of housework. Nothing in the way of exercise. I could barely move. Even getting out of bed seemed like wading through quicksand.

Donna kept calling me, but I didn't return her calls. I didn't know what to do. So what was there to talk about?

I thought I would be able to get back to normal if I could just stop thinking about it. But I couldn't.

One fact kept turning over in my head. Donna had told me that the church's attorney, Phil Waller, was the same guy she herself had dealt with eight years ago when she made her own clergy abuse report to the Baptist General Convention of Texas. They wanted her to sign an agreement saying she would never speak of it again, with the

---

26. Letter of July 26, 2004 from attorney James P. Guenther on behalf of Dr. Bobby Welch, President of the Southern Baptist Convention; *see also* Bob Allen, "Southern Baptist leaders challenged to get tough on sex abuse by clergy," *EthicsDaily*, September 27, 2006.

condition that, if she did, the church could sue her for damages.[27] Donna didn't sign it.

A couple years later, when she spoke to the Texas convention's committee on clergy sex abuse, she told me that attorney Waller was sitting in the room.

So it was clear that Waller wasn't just some rogue attorney representing a single church. He was the attorney who had long represented the largest statewide Baptist organization in the country, the Baptist General Convention of Texas.

Suddenly the whole thing looked like a slick sort of good cop/bad cop routine. The Baptist General Convention of Texas had sent back a nice letter, saying "thank you" for telling us about this in such a good way. Meanwhile, their own long-time attorney had written a letter threatening to sue me, but had written it on behalf of the church.

Waller's threatening letter was also written on behalf of Jim Moore, the music minister who knew about Dunagan's abuse of me. That really took my breath away. There I was, thinking that, after all these years, my old piano teacher would want to do the right thing and help me, and instead, Moore was threatening to sue me.

On a day when the fog lifted a bit, I sent off an email to Dee Miller, a former Southern Baptist missionary who had been sexually assaulted by a fellow missionary.[28] When she tried to report it, she herself was put "on trial," and even though two other alleged victims were minors, the perpetrator was able to continue as a Baptist pastor, and no one stopped him. Dee was originally from Texas and her website[29] revealed that, in Baptist circles, she had been talking about clergy abuse for about 12 years.

So I asked Dee whether the name Phil Waller meant anything to her. It did. She too had encountered Waller way back when she herself was trying to talk with people at the Baptist General Convention of Texas.

That's when I began to wonder how many others there had been. How many other clergy abuse survivors had this Baptist attorney slapped right back into silence?

In my report, Donna had asked the Baptist General Convention

---

27. Dee Ann Miller, "The Collusion Act of the Southern Baptist Convention and Clergy Sexual Abuse," *TakeCourage.org*, [http://www.takecourage.org/updatesbc.htm].

28. Bob Allen, "Former SBC missionary speaks out for victims of clergy sex abuse," *EthicsDaily*, October 16, 2006.

29. [www.takecourage.org].

of Texas to provide "crisis guidance" to the church. That was one of the services it talked about in its pretty little policy booklet.[30] It said it would provide "crisis guidance" to churches confronted with clergy sex abuse so that they would have the expertise and resources of the BGCT for assistance in knowing how to appropriately respond.

Suddenly I saw what "crisis guidance" really meant. The Baptist General Convention of Texas sent out its own long-time attorney to help the church clean up the problem. And the way he did it was by threatening suit against the victim. Meanwhile, the high-honchos at the BGCT simply sat on the sidelines, smiling and acting nice.

On paper, "crisis guidance" for churches may have looked like a good idea, but in actual practice, it seemed more like a pathetic joke or something even more sinister.

Waller reminded me of "Mr. Wolfe," the Harvey Keitel character in *Pulp Fiction* – the guy who "takes care of problems." If a clergy abuse survivor started making any trouble, statewide Baptist leaders would send out this Mr. Wolfe–like guy to make sure the mess got cleaned up. Their Mr. Wolfe–like guy would scrub it, whitewash it, spin it, and make it all go away. He was good at what he did, and just like Mr. Wolfe in the movie, he did it with a surreal air of pseudo-civility.

But of course, if anyone actually pondered what was getting whitewashed – clergy child molestation and child-rape – then it would turn their stomach. I figured that was why the Baptist General Convention of Texas kept "Mr. Wolfe" at the ready. He took care of such problems, and that way, the Baptist bosses could wash their hands of it and not have to personally contemplate the ugly realities of it too much.

I started staying awake at night. Whenever I closed my eyes, I could almost hear their weeping. Was it the weeping of people hurt in the past? Or was it the weeping of people who would be hurt in the future?

Maybe I was hearing my own long-ago weeping. I couldn't tell.

I started taking sleeping pills. Most of the time, it didn't help. I stayed awake.

How could I imagine that I was the only one? How many other victims had been sent right back to their quiet corners of shame by the intimidation tactics of this lawyer who worked for the largest state-wide Baptist organization in the country?

That question literally haunted me. How many others?

---

30. Christian Life Commission of the Baptist General Convention of Texas, *Broken Trust* at p. 36 (circa 2000).

19

Getting Past Their Nose-Thumbing

I was still stuck in my "I don't want anyone who knows me to know this about me" frame of mind. So I wrote letters to a couple lawyers who had handled some Catholic priest abuse suits, but they were lawyers who didn't know me, and I didn't mention that I was a lawyer myself. The proper thing to do would have been to call them up and schedule an appointment. But I couldn't even bring myself to do that. Writing words on paper was still a lot easier than getting words to come out of my mouth.

They both wrote back that the statute of limitations would present too great a hurdle. They couldn't help me. One of them suggested that I contact the Baptist General Convention of Texas and the Southern Baptist Convention. He was certain they would want to know about this minister.

"Yeah, right," I thought. "That's what rational people simply assume."

But I myself was still in the process of learning that there's nothing rational about how Baptists handle clergy sex abuse.

With enormous embarrassment, I finally contacted a trial lawyer friend, and shared with him the abuse report that Donna had sent to Baptist leaders for me. I hated letting him see this terribly ugly thing about me. I hated showing this weakness. But he took it in stride.

Craig was a decade younger than me, and once upon a time, he had looked up to me as a sort of mentor. Now it was my turn to look to him for help. I knew that, before it was all over, Craig would wind up seeing that I wasn't nearly the sort of "in control" person that a lot of people imagined me to be.

"I need some bargaining leverage," I told him. "Not a lot, just a little."

Craig was extremely sympathetic, but he knew the same thing I knew. The odds were stacked against me for any sort of lawsuit. Too much time had gone by, and Texas courts were not flexible with exceptions to the statute of limitations. Dallas courts were some of the least flexible of all.

"But I can't just walk away and let them treat me this way," I said. "How many others do you think they've done this to?"

Craig didn't have any experience with clergy abuse cases. But he had worked with me on a lot of cases over a lot of years, and he never doubted the truth of my story. Though he didn't know what to do about it, he could see that I needed some help.

"I've got nothing to negotiate with unless I can at least hold forth the possibility of filing a lawsuit. If they aren't at least a little bit worried that I'll file a lawsuit, they're just going to thumb their nose at me. They've made that clear. They've shown their game plan."

"What about the bigger organization, Christa? What's the Baptist equivalent of a diocese?"

Craig was Catholic and so thinking about a diocese-type of organization was his instinct. It's also the instinct of a good lawyer to look for a line of responsibility. You look for the supervisors who knew or should have known about wrongdoing – those who could have prevented it or stopped it.

"Baptists aren't like that," I told him. "They claim each and every church is independent. It's not totally true, but that's what they claim. If we tried to sue the bigger organizations – the state or national organizations – they'd pull out the biggest canons they've got with a First Amendment issue, and there's no way I can afford to fight that kind of battle."

"So, do you hear yourself, Christa? You know this isn't a good lawsuit, don't you? I mean, you tell me. You're the guru. You're the one who's so good at figuring out creative strategies. What do you imagine is going to happen here?"

"I know, Craig. I would never recommend that any trial lawyer take this case. But it's not frivolous. It's just a loser."

Craig agreed with me, and he knew the same thing I knew. Even if we filed the lawsuit only against the church, if it went on for too long, it could be a huge money-loser. Craig was also worried about what it might do to me psychologically.

I didn't say so, but I was worried about that, too. I wasn't sure how much I would wind up digging in my heels for the long haul. I knew that, if I filed a lawsuit, the church would probably win on a summary judgment based on the amount of time that had gone by. But I also knew that I could appeal that, and could do the work myself, and could force the church to spend a lot of money on attorney fees by the time I dragged it up to the Texas Supreme Court.

Of course, if it came to that, I would wind up spending a lot of money myself, not to mention a whole heckuva lot of time.

I had won enough high-profile cases on appeal that I figured, if Waller checked on me, it might cause him just a bit of concern. But probably only a little bit. I wasn't fooling myself. I could drag things out and I could make some strong arguments. But they were arguments that would probably still lose. I knew that. Texas courts weren't likely to see their way around the statute of limitations, and I knew that as well.

But I also knew that I didn't want to let them treat me like dirt. I wanted the church to own up to what had happened. I hoped that just having a good trial lawyer on board with me would be enough to nudge them toward treating me with decency.

So Craig and I worked out a deal where I would front the costs and do a lot of the legal work myself. Craig would act as an intermediary for negotiations and would put his name on court filings if it came to that. We both hoped it wouldn't.

Craig knew that it wasn't about money for me. That was obvious. If it were about money, I would have walked away, because this looked like a good chance to lose a lot.

What I really wanted was some sort of reconciliation. Reconciliation with what? I wasn't sure. With my faith? With the church? With the people? With a part of myself? I didn't know.

In any event, since Craig could see that my goals were different, he didn't make any threat of a lawsuit or any demand for money. Besides, we both knew that any lawsuit would be a lousy one. Like so many things about the law, it had nothing to do with truth or justice. It had to do with a legalism – in this case, the statute of limitations.

Another problem was the fact that I had already given them so much information. Though he was always diplomatic in asking about it, Craig couldn't quite figure out why I started out the way I did. There was no getting around the foolishness of my having given them a 25-page report.

"Christa, why in the world did you give them so much? They already have the biggest chunk of virtually everything they could want to know, and they didn't even have to work for it. They didn't have to take a single deposition or spend a single dime to find out most of what they might need. Meanwhile, you haven't gotten a shred of information from them. We still don't even know where this guy lives. Why did you put yourself at such a disadvantage?"

"I know Craig. It was stupid. Donna said it was the thing to do, and I went along with it. I read their policy booklet, and it seemed nice enough, and I thought it meant something. I thought they would want to do the right thing. I never imagined that they would take what I sent them and try to use it against me. And even in my wildest dreams, I *never* imagined that they would threaten to sue me."

"Christa, I'm not trying to make you feel bad about it. You're obviously feeling plenty bad enough. It's just a little unusual and I was trying to figure out if you might have had some off-the-wall sort of game plan."

"No. No game plan. I wasn't thinking about it that way. I wasn't planning on having a lawsuit."

"Well, hopefully we still won't. Maybe we can just set up a time to talk with them. Let me see what I can do. I know you need to have some peace of mind on this."

20

Seeking a Symbolic Gesture

Craig wrote a couple letters and placed some phone calls. Church deacons and leaders at the Baptist General Convention of Texas agreed to meet with me. They put it off and rescheduled a couple times, saying it was to accommodate a deacon's schedule. But finally, we had a definite date.

At my expense, Craig and I flew to Dallas to meet with them in a conference room at the airport. All they had to do was drive a few miles across town. Yet, not a single deacon from the church actually showed up for the meeting. No minister showed up either. Only the church's lawyer was there, Phil Waller.

I was heartbroken. They wouldn't even do me the courtesy of sitting across a table from me and hearing my story. That hurt.

But I went ahead and talked with the three men from the Baptist General Convention of Texas: Jan Daehnert, Sonny Spurger and David Nabors.

Things were cordial. I wanted to try to put them at ease and let them hear my voice so that they would see I wasn't a threat. So I immediately shook their hands and thanked them for meeting with me. I started right in and told them straight-up that I had no interest in any kind of lawsuit.

"I'm a lawyer myself," I said, "and so I've got a good idea of what a lawsuit would entail. I don't have any illusions about it."

They were looking at me intently.

"I think it's precisely because I *am* a lawyer that I'm trying to come up with some *alternative* way of dealing with this. I don't want a lawsuit. What I want is to try to make something good come out of this ugly thing. That's what I'm looking for, and I hope you'll help me with it."

Both Jan and Sonny had buttery, pastoral voices. They said they had talked with lots of other people like me and so they knew how terrible it was when a minister did something like this. They sounded as though they really cared.

"I think I'm one of the lucky ones," I told them.

By then, I had been to enough SNAP meetings that I believed it was true. I had plenty of problems in my twenties, but things had smoothed out for me, and I wound up with a loving husband, a strong and enduring marriage, and a dynamite daughter. It was so much more than what I had seen with many other clergy abuse survivors whose lives seemed to never get back on track.

I told Jan and Sonny how important it was to me that they try to do something to reach out to others. "There's so many who are so hurt. They're out there."

"Oh we know, we know," Sonny said. "We know what this does to people. We talk to them all the time."

I thought the meeting was off to a good start and decided to keep plowing.

"Look, you all need to know what this lawyer you've got is doing to people. It just isn't right to have a lawyer who threatens to sue people when they try to report abuse."

I pulled out Waller's letter and held it out to them. "This is what he does, and I just want to make sure you know about it."

"Oh well, that's the church, Christa. They're separate from us."

I sensed my skepticism rising. Were they imagining that I didn't know how long Waller had also worked for *them* – for the Baptist General Convention of Texas?

But I wanted to stay positive and so I decided to let it slide.

Mostly, Jan and Sonny seemed to say the right sorts of things. And they sounded sincere.

Nabors didn't say much at all. But at least he wasn't saying anything hostile. He just nodded his head vigorously when Waller started talking about what a good guy the music minister Jim Moore was.

"He tried to do what he thought was right at the time, and you can't fault him for that," said Waller.

"But what about *now*?" I asked. "Where is he? Why isn't he doing something *now*? Maybe he made a mistake back then, but why isn't he helping me *now*?"

Jan Daehnert spoke up then and told me that the Baptist General Convention of Texas had put Eddie Dunagan's name in its file of clergy sex abusers. I knew Jan was in charge of the office that kept that file, and so this was important news.

"I assume this means that he either confessed to it or you all decided there was substantial evidence. Is that what happened?"

"Yes."

I had read their policy, and I knew what it took for a minister's name to go in that file.[31] It also meant that *a church* had asked for Dunagan's name to go in that file. The policy was very clear that a minister's name could get placed in that file only if *a church* reported him. The Baptist General Convention of Texas wouldn't do anything based on a mere victim's report.

I breathed a sigh of relief. If Dunagan's name was in their file, Dunagan wouldn't be able to get a job working at any other church in the future . . . or at least that's what I thought at the time.

I sat silent for a while, absorbed in the news that Dunagan's name was in the file. Craig continued talking and pressing for my other requests. They seemed so simple: a written apology, a symbolic gesture, counseling costs.

"Look, the church needs to own this," Craig was saying. "It happened on their watch, and they can't just pretend it didn't."

"But it's too negative," countered Waller, the church's lawyer. He was complaining about my suggestion for a small millstone sculpture. I had seen one online and thought it would be a suitable symbol for a church to show that it understood the horror of clergy abuse. I thought it would reflect the words of Jesus, saying that, for anyone who would hurt a "little one," it would be "better for him that a millstone were hanged about his neck and he cast into the sea." The sculpture would have cost around $5,000.00.

"This isn't even the same church anymore," argued Waller. "These aren't the same people, and so why should they have to see such a negative reminder all the time? Why should they have to see something that would bring up such unpleasant thoughts every time they go to church?"

---

31. Christian Life Commission of the Baptist General Convention of Texas, *Broken Trust* at p. 37 ("A case is put into the file only when a minister confesses to the abuse or sexual misconduct; there is a legal conviction; or there is substantial evidence that the abuse took place. The issue of whether substantial evidence is present is always reviewed by Convention attorneys."); Marv Knox, "Churches must act to prevent clergy sexual abuse," *Baptist Standard*, April 22, 2002 ("An accused minister's name may be submitted for inclusion on the list by a duly elected church leader. A case is placed in the file only when a minister (a) confesses to the abuse . . . (b) the minister is legally convicted . . . or (c) 'substantial evidence' points to the minister's guilt. Convention attorneys always review the issue of whether evidence . . . is 'substantial'.") More recently, the website of the Baptist General Convention of Texas indicates that it is allowing churches to put "confirmed" cases of clergy abuse in the file, but it still does not consider abuse reports from victims.

"Negative? They don't want something negative? Well, what happened to me was pretty awfully negative, and that's the way it is. Besides, a millstone is downright biblical." I heard my tone of voice and knew I needed to ease back a little.

"Christa, this isn't personal, you know."

Waller's words slammed into me.

"Not personal? Not personal?" My voice rose and my mind started racing. I was flooded with thoughts. Flooded with images. Flooded with questions. What sort of fool says "it's not personal" when you're talking about something like this? How does it get more personal?

But Waller didn't seem to perceive it as being any big deal. His voice, his expression, his words, his hostility, his letter threatening to sue me – all of it made apparent that he didn't perceive what was done to me as a kid to be a matter of much consequence.

Of course, Waller would probably say that he was just doing his job as a lawyer. And perhaps he was.[32] But that thought only made his actions seem all the more hateful. Why didn't the religious leaders at the Baptist General Convention of Texas put a leash on this snarling dog?

As I felt my adrenaline pumping, I realized I'd better shift gears and so I reminded Waller that the church had a historical marker out front. First Baptist Church of Farmers Branch was one of the first churches in Dallas County.

"These aren't the same people who founded that church back in 1870 either," I pointed out. "But I bet they're still plenty proud of having that historical marker."

Waller was just staring at me blankly. So I continued.

"A church is an enduring body. It's not just a bunch of people. They need to own up to this thing that happened in their church. They need to deal with it. Besides, some of the same people ARE still there. For starters, Jim Moore is still the music minister."

"Christa, you're taking this too personally."

He was repeating himself, and I wanted to scream at his condescension. But instead, I found myself quietly wondering how many times he had said that before. How many other people had sat in a room with

---

32. Lawyers often disagree on where the boundaries of "zealous advocacy" are. Personally, I thought it was beyond the bounds for Phil Waller to threaten "recourse" against a person reporting clergy child molestation, particularly since he was representing another minister who knew about the abuse when I was a kid and who had substantiated it. But I expect some other lawyers might think otherwise.

him and told their stories of childhood molestation and rape, only to hear him say, "It's not personal"?

While I pondered that, I wound up doing my own blank stare, and so Craig took over the talking. No telling what I might have said if I had kept going.

Craig started telling them about our second proposal for a symbolic gesture. It didn't carry any biblical weight, but it also didn't carry any "negative" weight.

"How about a labyrinth in a small contemplation garden?" Craig asked.

Jan and Sonny looked up. They seemed interested. I pulled out my photos. This is what I really wanted anyway.

I told them about a Catholic abuse survivor who listened to me talk about how much I loved to go into great gothic cathedrals and just sit there. With the expansive naves, soaring ceilings, stained glass and sculptural ornamentation, the great cathedrals bear so little resemblance to the church of my youth that I feel safe in them. The Catholic survivor told me that, when he's out driving in the country, if he sees a small white wooden church, he'll always stop and try the door and, if it's open, he'll go inside and sit. For him, those are the churches that are different enough for him to feel safe.

"I'd like it to be someplace that's accessible to the public," I say, "so that people who might not set foot inside any church can still have a place like this to go to. And I'd like for there to be just a small plaque set off to the side, saying that it's dedicated in prayer for victims of clergy sex abuse."

They pass back and forth the photos I brought of labyrinths at other churches. They talk. They throw out possible locations.

"It's mostly bricks and plants and landscaping work," I point out. "And volunteers could probably do some of the labor. I'd be thrilled to wield a shovel myself."

"Christa, we can do this," Jan Daehnert finally says. "We just need to find the right place."

My heart soars. Waller is sitting there glaring, but Jan Daehnert and Sonny Spurger seem enthusiastic.

"Well, ideally, it would be on the church's property, but are you telling me that, even if the church won't do it, the BGCT will?"

"Yes. We'll do it."

We talked just a bit more after that. Craig was trying to lay the groundwork for more discussion on counseling costs. Jan and Sonny were going to look into some specific locations for the labyrinth, and they asked me to look at a possible location in Austin. I asked them to update their policy booklet with a reminder to churches that any suspicion of child sex abuse must be reported to child protective services. Their 45-page policy book told churches to report clergy sex abuse to the Baptist General Convention of Texas, but it said not one word about reporting abuse to secular authorities like the law requires. Jan said it was just an oversight and assured me they would post a reminder about it on their website.

Finally, we stood, shook hands and said good-bye. Craig and I walked to the door. But at the last instant, I hesitated. It seemed too easy. I didn't trust what had just taken place.

So with my hand on the door-knob, I turned around.

"Look, I just need to know. If this was nothing but a bunch of talk here today, then I'd rather know it right now. I don't want to walk out that door thinking something's gonna happen if it's not."

Jan Daehnert looked up.

"Are you really going to do this?" I asked. "Are you going to build this labyrinth?"

Jan Daehnert looked me straight in the face, eyeball to eyeball.

"Yes, ma'am."

21

Substantial Evidence of Abuse

The very next day, I went out to scout the location Jan Daehnert had suggested. I walked all around, sized it up, and listened to the surrounding traffic to see how noisy a site it would be. I tried to visualize it.

Though I was still hoping the church would agree to put the labyrinth on its own property, at least I now had Jan Daehnert's word that, if the church wouldn't do it, the Baptist General Convention of Texas would.

"You see Christa," said Craig when he called. "This was just one of those things that needed a face-to-face sit-down. Now it's just a matter of working out the details."

"Yeah, I'm so excited. When it's all said and done, I think I may wind up feeling really good about this."

"I'm glad you did it this way, Christa. It's so much better than just asking for money. A stone labyrinth with a garden and a plaque – this is something that will endure."

For days afterwards, I went around almost whistling as I walked. In my head, I'm already drafting up words to say at the dedication ceremony for the labyrinth. "Clergy abuse can happen anywhere. It happened to me and it happened here. But I am SO proud that THIS church – the church of my childhood – chose to try to do something positive." In my head, I can see the smiling faces as I speak – faces of people in the community who knew me when I was a kid. I can imagine myself shaking their hands and I see my own tears of joy. It's a healing and hopeful scene. But of course, it's just in my head.

I had asked Jan and Sonny if I could email them directly, and they said fine. Then one day, I was surprised to pick up the phone and find Sonny on the line. So the three of us continued to talk with emails and phone calls.[33]

---

33. Multiple email correspondences between December 3, 2004 and April 6, 2005 to Christa Brown from Wm. Jan Daehnert and Sonny Spurger of the Baptist General Convention of Texas.

Jan and Sonny repeatedly confirmed that they were working on my request for a dedicated labyrinth. They said they were making "headway."[34]

I asked for written confirmation that Dunagan's name was indeed in their clergy sex abuser file, and Jan Daehnert provided it.

"We have placed Eddie Dunagan in our file."[35]

There it was in black and white. Over and over, I looked at Jan's words on paper, and every time, I breathed a sigh of relief.

"This file works in an attempt to protect other congregations from being victimized by predators," he wrote.[36]

I breathed yet again.

On the phone, Sonny talked about it some more and explained that attorney Waller himself had reviewed all the information about Dunagan and had determined there was "substantial evidence" the abuse took place. From their policy booklet, I already knew "substantial evidence" was their standard, but it was still nice to hear Sonny say it.

For a few weeks after getting Daehnert's written confirmation that Dunagan was listed in their file of clergy-predators, I actually slept at night.

Then I noticed that music minister Jim Moore's name had been removed from the online registry of Southern Baptist ministers that's kept in Nashville. Why?

In the same letter where the church threatened to sue me, the church's attorney, Phil Waller, had said other obnoxious and contrived stuff. He had insisted that Jim Moore wasn't even an ordained minister as though to suggest that the church couldn't possibly be responsible for him.

At the time, I couldn't figure out why Waller would bother saying such a thing. Lots of Baptist ministers aren't formally ordained. They aren't even required to go to seminary. But they're still ministers and they're still church employees. So it didn't make any sense to me, but I figured it might just be Waller's attempt at a snow-job.

---

34. Email correspondence of April 6, 2005 from Sonny Spurger and Wm. Jan Daehnert of the Baptist General Convention of Texas.
35. Email correspondence of December 16, 2004 from Wm Jan Daehnert of the Baptist General Convention of Texas (with copy shown to David Nabors and Sonny Spurger of the Baptist General Convention of Texas), and included as an exhibit to the Plaintiff's Response to Nonparty's Objection to Subpoena of Documents in Cause No. DV05-05669M, in the 298th Judicial District, Dallas County, Texas, C. Brown v. First Baptist Church of Farmers Branch.
36. Email correspondence of December 16, 2004 from Wm. Jan Daehnert, *supra*.

But now, seeing Moore's name disappear from the registry made me wonder whether Waller was already setting things up to try to make a legal argument that the church couldn't be responsible for Moore because Moore wasn't even a minister. It would be a contrivance, of course, but I didn't imagine that would stop a guy like Waller. Fortunately, before Moore's name disappeared, I had printed out the page on the Southern Baptist registry, listing him as a music minister. So I had proof if I needed it. But I still kept wondering about why his name had disappeared.

I decided to phone up the church. With a 30-second phone call, the church secretary confirmed that Jim Moore was still the music minister. "We're blessed to have him," she said.

So Moore wasn't removed from the registry because he left the ministry. What other reason could there be? Suddenly, it seemed obvious that the registry of ministers was easy to manipulate.

Why was Moore's name taken off the Southern Baptist registry of ministers? The more I turned that question over in my head, the more it led me to wonder again about Dunagan. Could he still be a minister even though his name wasn't on the registry? Could he still be a minister even though Southern Baptist officials in Nashville wrote that they had no record of him?

I decided to start looking for him again.

22

No Help for Counseling

While I was looking for Dunagan, things stalled out with Jan Daehnert and Sonny Spurger at the Baptist General Convention of Texas. There were more emails and more talk, but nothing happened. Finally I wrote to Jan.

"Over six months have passed since I made my original report," I said. "So far, I feel as though I have been further victimized by this process, by the church's response, and by the many requests for delay. . . . It has not been a process conducive to any healing. My impression is that I am merely seeing stall tactics – but at this moment in time, I am still willing to believe that my impression may perhaps be mistaken."

"Can we please get this resolved quickly?" I continued. "My requests were deliberately narrow and very specific in order to facilitate a quick resolution. And it was my hope that it would be a constructive resolution. . . . It is not essential that we immediately have a location for the labyrinth, but it is essential that I have a firm, written commitment consistent with my requests. . . . I need to have some closure, and if I'm not going to get it through this process, then please let me know plainly."[37]

Jan wrote back, politely explaining that things are slow because "we want to get this right."[38]

Sonny called me and tried to smooth things over on the phone. But he's a talker, and seems like the kind of guy who probably has a habit of putting his foot in his mouth. The more he talked, the less smooth things got.

"Christa, I've been thinking about you and about the kind of effect this might have on your family. What about your daughter? Have you thought about the impact it might have on her to know this about her mother, particularly since she's a teenager herself now?"

---

37. Email correspondence of February 2, 2005 from Christa Brown to Wm. Jan Daehnert of the Baptist General Convention of Texas.
38. Email correspondence of February 2, 2005 from Wm. Jan Daehnert to Christa Brown.

I caught my breath in my throat. I felt my skin crawl. I sensed the hair rising at the nape of my neck. I knew I wasn't going to talk with Sonny Spurger about my daughter, and I resented the fact that he would even mention her.

I cursed myself. I never should have revealed anything personal to these people. I never, ever should have told them I had a daughter.

I thought about the mistake I had made in telling them about how Dunagan's abuse began after the incident when the police were called to our house. I told them that because I thought it would help them understand how clergy-predators operate – how they move in on kids whose families are having trouble. But Phil Waller had seized on it as something to use against me. He twisted that bit of personal information to suggest that my home-life was what had caused my psychological distress[39] – as though I was damaged goods anyway and no greater harm could have been done by the minister who molested and raped me. It was a response that offended me beyond all words.

Now here I was, with Sonny Spurger suggesting that, if I talked about this, it might cause problems for my daughter. Perhaps Sonny would say his intentions were good, but to me, it felt as though he was trying to use my own daughter against me. All I could think was "How dare he?"

The truth was that I worried constantly about Emily and about what effect it might have on her life if she knew this sordid thing about her mother. I also worried about what effect it might have on our relationship. I worried about what she would think of her mother. I worried that she would be so ashamed of me.

I didn't need Sonny to tell me I should worry about my daughter. I was worrying about her plenty enough already.

Worrying about Emily was a huge hurdle. It was a big part of the reason for why I wanted to remain anonymous and never have my name out in the public. I couldn't bear the thought of my daughter knowing this ugly, terrible thing about her mother. And I knew I would never be able to live with myself if I wound up hurting Emily's life by revealing this sordid thing from my own life.

But I wouldn't say any of that to Sonny. Instead, I simply shifted gears and asked him whether they had given any more thought to my request for counseling.

---

39. Letter from attorney on behalf of First Baptist Church of Farmers Branch and music minister James A. Moore, dated August 9, 2004.

"We don't have any money for counseling," he said.

While I made a note of his statement and turned that news over in my head, Sonny just kept talking.

He said the labyrinth was still an "open possibility." I pondered that as well. It sounded very different from the firm "yes, ma'am" response that Jan Daehnert had made at the meeting in Dallas.

Sonny seemed full of evasive hedging and excuses for why the Baptist General Convention of Texas wasn't doing anything. In a follow-up email, he finally stated his view that it was the church that "has some real responsibility here."[40]

I wrote back to both Jan and Sonny. "I would like to go ahead and know," I said, if it's been definitely decided that the BGCT won't make any provision for counseling. "But I will feel hard-pressed to understand how it is that the BGCT can set aside funding to provide counseling services for clergy perpetrators and their spouses but not be able to support counseling for victims."[41]

That only yielded more of Sonny's hedging, and so I wrote back again, trying to be as direct as possible:

> What I know for sure is this – over seven months have now gone by since you all received my report and there has been nothing but talk – and mostly nothing. That's what is real. If you all had the slightest comprehension of what I live with in my head every day – of what haunts my efforts at sleep every night – this would be a very different process and something would have happened by now. At a bare minimum, if the BGCT actually cared about victims, it would want to pro-actively encourage and support the immediate provision of counseling for them. Instead, I'm having to haggle about it.
>
> Jan, in your last email you said that this process was slow because "we want to get this right." From my perspective, I can already tell you that it isn't going to be "right." The time when the process could have been "right" has long

---

40. Email from Sonny Spurger to Christa Brown, February 7, 2005. (Spurger also stated that he didn't feel he had completely "closed the BGCT out" of providing help, but at the same time, he didn't provide any help.)

41. Email correspondence of February 5, 2005 from Christa Brown to Wm. Jan Daehnert and Sonny Spurger of the Baptist General Convention of Texas.

since passed. There is nothing "right" about dragging victims along for this amount of time. . . .

At great pain for myself, I have tried to communicate with you. I don't feel as though my efforts have been useful. Either I'm not effectively communicating, or you just don't get it, or you just don't care, or all of the above. I don't know what to think. I do believe that if you had both understanding and caring, things would be very different.[42]

Things were quiet for awhile after that. They didn't write back.

---

42. Email correspondence of February 8, 2005 from Christa Brown to Sonny Spurger and Wm. Jan Daehnert of the Baptist General Convention of Texas.

23

He's Still a Children's Minister

He wasn't easy to find. "Eddie Dunagan" is a common name. There are a gazillion of them all over the country. I didn't even know what state to start looking in or how to figure out which "Eddie Dunagan" was the right one.

It cost me some money to keep running searches, and I felt guilty about every nickel I spent. I knew I was probably just being compulsive. After all, the letter from Southern Baptist Convention headquarters said that they had no record of him.

I kept looking anyway. But the truth is that I'm not much of an investigator. I don't think I ever would have found him on my own. It was a friend who found him. He was one of the very few people whom I had talked with at that point, and he took it upon himself to do his own looking. I didn't even ask him. But a few weeks after I talked with him, he sent me an email with a link to a church in Florida where Dunagan's photo was shown on the staff directory as the children's minister.

There was no mistaking the photo. It was him.

By then, it had been eight months since I reported Dunagan to church and denominational leaders. And there he was, still working in children's ministry.

Despite the Southern Baptist Convention's letter saying they had no record of him, he had actually been in ministry all along. And the more I kept digging, the more I learned about Dunagan's work history. He had been at very prominent Southern Baptist churches.

The church that showed his online photo was just outside Orlando, the First Baptist Church of Oviedo, Florida.[43] It was the church of recent Florida Baptist Convention president Dwayne Mercer, and it was just up the road from the church of Southern Baptist Convention president Bobby Welch in Daytona Beach. Donna Dean had sent my original abuse report to Welch, and so he had been told about Dunagan. It was

---

43 Lisa Chiaravallo, "Protestors rally in front of local church," *The Oviedo Voice*, April 16, 2006.

hard to imagine that Welch wouldn't have known the ministers on staff at the church of the Florida Baptist Convention president. Yet, everyone in Baptist-land had stayed mum about where Dunagan was.

As I continued my research, I learned that, before he moved to Florida, Dunagan was a children's minister at First Baptist Church of Atlanta.[44] It was a flagship megachurch with 16,000 members and a mighty ministerial staff. The senior pastor was former Southern Baptist Convention president Charles Stanley,[45] a man with a nationwide television ministry and a super-prominent Baptist leader.

Once again, given his high-level connections, it seemed impossible to imagine that no one had known where Dunagan was working. I couldn't believe it.

Despite music minister Jim Moore's confirmation of Dunagan's abuse, and despite the BGCT's determination that there was "substantial evidence," and despite the fact that the BGCT had put Dunagan's name in its file of "known offenders,"[46] no one had done anything to stop Dunagan from working with kids. That realization pretty much unglued me.

His name had been sitting in a file at the Baptist building in Dallas – a file of reported clergy predators for whom there was "substantial evidence" – and yet he was still working in children's ministry in Florida. How many other ministers' names were in that file? How many kids had they hurt? The questions began to haunt me again.

Then I heard Dunagan's voice, recorded in the pulpit of still another Florida church, telling them how blessed he was that they had welcomed him to work with them "in the area of children's ministry." I threw up on the spot.

Months after I reported Dunagan's abuse, months after music

---

44. Bob Allen, "Southern Baptist leaders challenged to get tough on sex abuse by clergy," *EthicsDaily*, September 27, 2006.

45. A couple years later, when I was working with SNAP, four of us tried to pass out flyers to people leaving a Sunday service at First Baptist Church of Atlanta, informing them that one of their prior children's ministers, Eddie Dunagan, was known to have sexually abused a kid in Texas. We were run off the premises. *See* SNAP's letter of February 6, 2007 to Dr. Charles Stanley, Senior Pastor, First Baptist Church of Atlanta, informing him of church officials' rude treatment. [http://www.snapnetwork.org/snap_letters/020607_baptist_atlanta.htm]; see also Bob Allen, "Group asks Southern Baptist leaders to address clergy sex abuse," *EthicsDaily*, February 19, 2007.

46. Christian Life Commission of the Baptist General Convention of Texas, *Broken Trust* at p. 37 (circa 2000).

minister Jim Moore substantiated my report, and months after Baptist leaders in Nashville, Tyler and Dallas all knew about it, Dunagan was standing in the pulpit of still another church and talking about his children's ministry.

His sermon was titled "What's so great about grace?"[47]

I started shaking as I heard his voice talking about how "God wants us to live by faith." I had to stop and listen in small doses.

The part that totally unnerved me was when he talked about how his body was just his "earth-suit."

> And I tell you what, when the junk gets heavy, when the accusations from the world and when the temptations of the flesh, and just all of the junk, begins to pile up on me, I can sit back and remember I'm not here. I'm already with God in the heavenlies. . . . Ladies and gentlemen, what you're looking at today is Eddie's earth-suit. Eddie ejected from this earth-suit when he was a senior in high school and he's been in the heavenlies ever since.

What I heard in it was Dunagan's conjuring of a sick, twisted, religious rationalization for thinking that what he does with his little "earth-suit" isn't of much consequence because, after all, Eddie's "not here." Eddie's already "in the heavenlies" with God.

For Dunagan, it sounded as though "what's so great about grace" is that it gives guys like him a free pass.

I listened to that sermon more often than I should have, as I tried to understand the mind of a predator. It wasn't a healthy thing to do.

Not long after that was when I started seeing fear in my husband's eyes. He was doing everything he could to help me, but the fear was still there. He knew I was getting too close to the edge, and he wasn't sure whether I would hang on or let go. I wasn't sure either.

I couldn't come to grips with what I now knew. Southern Baptist leaders in both Tennessee and Texas had ignored me, misled me, and threatened me, when all the while Dunagan was still working in children's ministry. No one . . . NO ONE . . . thought it mattered enough to do anything about it.

---

47. "What's so great about grace?" sermon of "Eddie Dunagan" delivered on October 3, 2004 to the Cornerstone Community Church of Central Florida.

But even as much as that realization undid me, I still kept thinking that, if I just found the right person, someone might still do something. I couldn't give up.

So Craig and I sent off still more certified letters to leaders at the Florida Baptist Convention, the Greater Orlando Baptist Association, the First Baptist Church of Oviedo, the Georgia Baptist Convention, and the First Baptist Church of Atlanta. We told all of them about my substantiated report of Dunagan's sexual abuse and about the fact that the Baptist General Convention of Texas had placed Dunagan's name into its file of clergy sex abusers.

We also sent another letter to the Southern Baptist Convention in Nashville, telling them the same thing – that we had found Dunagan, that he was still a minister in Florida, and that the Baptist General Convention of Texas had put his name in its file of clergy sex abusers.

The only letter I got back was from the Georgia Baptist Convention.[48] It thanked me for the information.

But Dunagan continued in ministry.

---

48. Letter of April 27, 2005 from J. Robert White of the Georgia Baptist Convention.

24

Starting to Unravel

My friend Elana had the misfortune of calling me on the phone the day after I saw Dunagan's picture on the Florida church's website. She was just wanting to confirm our walk for that week, but what she got from me in return was near-hysteria. Elana worked at trying to talk me down.

Even with Elana, I felt embarrassed. I'm accustomed to being in control. As a lawyer, I've heard people say that, in high-stakes appellate arguments, I'm "cool as a cucumber." I always felt a bit of pride for that. Though in truth I never really lost my nervousness for court arguments, I still liked to at least convey the appearance of calm.

But how cool was I now? This was a Christa that even Elana had never seen before.

Elana was one of the first people to whom I had dared mention that I was sexually abused by a Baptist minister. I tried to segue into it in the middle of some bit of talk about some cover-up connected to local politics. It seemed to fit at the time, but I guess it wasn't as smooth as I thought because Elana came to a stand-still on the trail. She immediately saw the significance of my small statement and of the fact that I had never previously spoken of it.

Through the pink crepe myrtles of summer and the red sumacs of fall, Elana continued to listen as my story unfolded on our weekly walks. While we fended off angry geese, she watched me work at coming to terms with the blasphemous brutality of what a Baptist minister did to me as a kid.

Week by week, she also saw my mental state deteriorate as I struggled with the uncaring, oblivious responses of church and denominational leaders.

Usually, Elana talked more than me on our walks, but lately, she kept refusing to let me shift the conversation. Instead, she kept bringing the topic back to me, wanting to know how I was doing, and what was going on, and whether I had found a counselor yet. Elana wouldn't let up about trying to get me to see a counselor.

Without telling anyone who it was for, Elana started going through her network of people, asking about good counselors. She gave me name after name, and I contacted several. But each time, it was so difficult that I would back off and wouldn't try again for weeks.

I even went to a couple appointments, but each time, I didn't think the counselor had a clue about clergy abuse, and I became even more discouraged.

It felt as though I was cutting myself open and bleeding all over the place just to try to tell someone even the bare gist of why I needed a counselor. I couldn't figure out what to say, or how to say it. My throat would clutch and I couldn't get words out. Even calling for an appointment became an impossible task.

Elana offered to call counselors for me, but I wouldn't let her. So finally, Elana flat-out put the words in my mouth: "Trauma response."

"You need someone with experience in trauma response," she said. "That's what you should ask about."

"Trauma response." I said the words out loud.

This was something I could work with. "Do you have experience in trauma response?" It was something I could ask without having to figure out how to launch into my story. I liked it because it meant I didn't have to start out saying anything at all about religion, sex, church, or ministers. Those were all words that made my throat clamp shut.

By now, even I was beginning to realize that I was unraveling. One night, I was going out to the store for milk, and I managed to back into my own car in my own driveway. The car at the end of the driveway was parked exactly where it was always parked, and yet somehow, I forgot it was there. And when I looked in the rearview mirror (which I swear I did), I somehow didn't see it. I backed the car in the garage straight into that car in the driveway. It was pretty humbling.

My brain just wasn't working right. I couldn't hold all the pieces together. I could hardly hold a coherent thought.

I became even more hypervigilant than usual. My startle reflex had always been strong, but nowadays, it was in overdrive. I pitied any runner who came up too close behind me on the trail. I would jump so wide that runners would wind up stopping just to make sure I was okay. It was never their fault, of course. It was just me.

Several times, I went out for runs and found myself in the middle of the road crying. I couldn't even figure out what had happened or what I was crying about. I would try to think about what triggered it, but I couldn't trace my thoughts backwards. It was as though something alien slammed into me from out of nowhere. I never saw it coming. But suddenly, there I was, in the middle of the road, crying, heaving, and trying to breathe.

I was always scared someone would see me. Then I'd be even more embarrassed. How would I explain it? What would I say?

I started being afraid to run. I was afraid of where my mind might go, without my even knowing it was going there. I was afraid I'd find myself standing in the street, bawling and looking for a place to hide.

After a while, I began to be afraid of even leaving the house. I went out if I really needed to, but every time I opened the front door, I felt a wave of fear, and I hesitated.

Crazily, I was overcome with the sense that the earth was going to crack open beneath me and I would fall straight to the center of the planet. I made light of it and called it my Jules Verne vision. But I think what I was really afraid of is that I would be pulled down straight to hell.

The rational part of me knew this wasn't going to happen, but that was the problem. There wasn't anything rational about it. No amount of knowing it wasn't rational stopped me from feeling the fear.

Dan began to crack jokes about it. "How big is this earthquake gonna be?" he'd ask. "Will it just be a localized sort of thing? If I walk ten paces behind, will I be okay?"

It was his way of trying to help me keep the fear in perspective.

25

Getting Help

"Please, promise me you won't commit me. I can handle this. I'll be fine."

"No. I can't promise that."

Dan is yelling. It's a rare thing. He's scared.

I've seen it in his eyes for weeks. And he's been calling me several times a day lately, just to say hi or talk about the grocery list. I know that what he's really doing is checking on me. He's worried.

I hate seeing that look of fear in Dan's eyes and knowing I put it there. It's a reminder of struggles in the past. Though he hasn't seen me so distraught for more than two decades, it's clear he hasn't forgotten what it was like.

"Look, I can handle this," I say softly. "I'm stronger now than I was back then. And I'm not shadow-boxing this time. I know what I'm up against."

"No. You can't handle it. You aren't handling it. You need help. You've got to start seeing someone."

"Fine, I'll keep looking for a counselor. Just promise me that you won't commit me or anything, okay?"

"No! I won't promise you that. If I think you're drowning, I'm not just gonna stand on the shore and do nothing. I WILL do something. I'm not gonna just stand by and watch you go under."

"Look, I'll be okay. I just need some time."

"No! You aren't okay. You're fooling yourself. Don't you see that?"

I start to open my mouth, but Dan just keeps going.

"Christa, you listen to me and you listen good. I don't know what I'm gonna do. Maybe I'll do the wrong thing. Maybe I'll make a mistake. Maybe you'll hate me forever because of it. But I WILL do something."

He's crying now.

Dan never cries. In the span of half an hour, he looks like he's aged 10 years. He begins to beg.

"Babe, please don't make me have to figure out what to do here. Please. Don't put me in that position. Don't make me have to decide.

Don't. Please. Get help before it comes to that. We've got to get you some help, and you've got to be willing to go."

Dan took off work the next day and spent it trying to find information on therapists who had experience in dealing with clergy sex abuse. All day, I saw the desperation in his face and I knew something had to change. Fortunately, it did.

I started seeing a good therapist. I could tell right away that I wasn't the first clergy sex abuse victim she had ever dealt with. Unfortunately, she wasn't a provider on our health insurance network. That meant the biggest chunk of the cost wouldn't be covered. It would wind up costing a lot of money.

After writing checks for several sessions, I started talking about the money-thing with Elana while we walked around the lake. "Maybe I should try to find someone else – someone who wouldn't cost so much."

"Christa, are you kidding me? You like this counselor, don't you? You should stick with her."

I could see right away that Elana wasn't going to cut me any slack on this.

"Think about it this way, Christa. If you needed brain surgery, and after a bunch of research, you learned that the best person for your kind of surgery was a guy who wasn't on your health plan, would you try to cut costs? Or if you could find a way to pay for it, would you go to him because he was the best surgeon for the job?"

"I'd go to him."

"Well . . . that answers the question, doesn't it? This is serious stuff you're dealing with. You need someone who's been there before and knows what they're doing."

Elana was right. I knew she was. Besides, I just couldn't bear the thought of starting down another list of potential counselors.

Even still, I raised the same question with Dan that night. He didn't take it as well as Elana.

"Christa, why are you even asking me this? Do you really think the money is what I'm most worried about? Is that what you think?"

"Well, if I stick with this, it'll be a lot, and it's not like we have money growing on trees, you know. And what about Emily? Is this fair for her? Every dollar I spend on counseling is money that could be used instead to help her with college."

"Christa. Stop. What are you doing? Emily will get through college. That's not what this is about. Don't use her as an excuse."

"I'm not. I'm just . . ."

"Just what, Christa? Huh? Let me tell you what you're doing. You're looking for reasons not to go to therapy. Why?"

"But I'm not. I'm just worried about the money."

"No. This isn't about money. It's about YOU. Don't you get that?"

Suddenly, I saw the look in Dan's face and realized how much this was hurting him. He was angry. He was scared. He was insulted. He was on the verge of tears. He was all of that all at once.

"Christa, I'm not afraid of not having money. I'm afraid of not having YOU. Why don't you get that? Every day you're more distant. You're being swept away by something I can't even see, and all I want to do is hang onto you. But you won't let me. You're in a world of your own these days. Do you even realize it? You're the same with Emily. It's like you're just gone. Sometimes, we talk to you and it's like you don't even hear us."

"I'm sorry. I've been kind of distracted I guess."

"Kind of? Don't you think that's kind of an understatement? And what about the fact that you hardly ever sleep anymore? How much longer do you think you can keep that up, huh?"

"Sleep's always been a struggle for me. You know that."

"This is different. It's worse. A lot worse."

Dan was right about that. Sleep had become virtually impossible. Even Ambien had little effect. My brain was trapped in an endless loop. I kept trying to make sense of all the thoughts and images that kept swirling in and out, but I just couldn't do it.

It was as though there had been a rending in space – a tear in the very fabric of existence. My waking world had become a tissue-thin veil stretched taut over a much darker world. The veil could no longer hold back the horror, and I was constantly distracted by what I glimpsed through the fabric's tear. My sleeping world was even worse, as some inexorable force would almost invariably pull me through that tear into the dark other-world.

I feared that darkness beyond the tear, but I also wanted desperately to reach into it. I had the sense that there was something just outside my sight. Or perhaps some piece of the puzzle just outside my grasp. If only I could reach through the fabric's tear and find that piece, then perhaps the puzzle would all make sense and I could put it all back into its box, nice and tidy.

Dan was looking at me, and I realized I had been quiet for a while.

"Look. I know I haven't been myself, lately. I'm sorry."

"Where'd you go, Christa?"

"What do you mean?"

"Where'd you go? You weren't here with me. I know that much."

"I'm sorry. I was just . . . thinking about something."

"Christa, I'm not interested in you being sorry. That's what I'm trying to tell you. I want you to be you. That's all. I want you back. I want you well. I want you to be yourself again. That's what I want. That's all I want."

Dan's crying now, and the only thing I want is to try to smooth things over. But he's not going to let me. He's pleading. He's begging. He's not going to let this go.

"Christa, I want you to do whatever it takes for you to be well. I don't know what that is. I don't know how to help you. But if you think this therapist might be someone who can, then please keep going. Please keep trying."

26

Baptist Leaders Cut Off Communication

In the beginning, therapy seemed more backward-going than forward-going. And it was certainly slow-going. But week in and week out, I had the sense that it at least held hope.

I knew I was fortunate to be able to afford therapy, and I found myself worrying about all the people for whom the cost of counseling would be prohibitive. How did they manage to deal with this? Maybe they didn't. Maybe that was part of why there was such a high correlation between suicide and a history of childhood sex abuse.

I thought about how lucky I was to have a mule-headed husband and a strong-willed friend who had worked to find a good therapist for me and who kept after me until I went. If I'd been left on my own, I might have just given up and sunk even further.

The more I thought about what a huge hurdle it had been for me to find a good counselor who actually knew something about clergy abuse, I figured it must be a huge hurdle for other people as well. So I sent off a letter to Jan Daehnert and Sonny Spurger, asking them if the Baptist General Convention of Texas could put together a list of counselors in Texas who had experience with the dynamics of clergy sex abuse.[49] I thought that, if they could give clergy abuse victims a referral list of counselors, it might at least provide people with a starting place for getting help, and it would surely be better than the yellow pages.

A simple referral list wouldn't have even cost them any money. But they wouldn't do it. I might as well have asked for taxis to Mars.

I also asked Jan and Sonny if one of them would read a letter on my behalf at the next business meeting of the First Baptist Church of Farmers Branch. I suspected that the pastor and deacons might be keeping this a secret from the congregation, or at least not telling them the whole story. I guessed that they wouldn't want to embarrass music minister Jim Moore, who had kept quiet for so many years about another

---

49. Letter of April 4, 2005, sent by email and fax, from Christa Brown to Jan Daehnert and Sonny Spurger of the Baptist General Convention of Texas.

minister's abuse of a kid, and who had even allowed the man to go on working with other kids.

Naively, I still thought that, if only people in the pews could hear my story, they would realize how sincere I was and would want to help me. And while I knew that church leaders probably wouldn't be willing to let *me* speak to the congregation, I figured they might be inclined to let one of the top men at the Baptist General Convention of Texas speak.

Jan and Sonny refused my request without any explanation. Worse, they wrote back that I should direct any future requests to their attorney, Phil Waller.[50] So, they cut off the possibility of any further conversations with me. "Don't talk to us anymore – talk to our lawyer." That was the gist of what they were saying.

I knew this meant there would now be little option other than a lawsuit. It made me wonder whether any word Jan and Sonny had ever uttered had ever been sincere. Or had all their talk been nothing more than a calculated stall tactic?

I was heartbroken. I had sat in a room with them. I had listened to their buttery voices saying how much they cared. I had believed them. I had looked eye-to-eye with Jan Daehnert when he said "Yes ma'am" to the building of a labyrinth dedicated to clergy abuse survivors. I had shaken hands with them. And now, there was not even the courtesy of an explanation for why they had changed their mind on the building of the labyrinth.

Their letter also made transparent what I had suspected from the very beginning. Phil Waller was indeed the attorney for both the church and the Baptist General Convention of Texas. Waller was handling it – the guy who threatened to sue me at the very start. This was the kind of guy that the largest statewide Baptist organization in the country sent out to churches to help clean up "the problem" when a clergy sex abuse victim started talking.

---

50. Email letter of April 6, 2005 from Jan Daehnert and Sonny Spurger of the Baptist General Convention of Texas.

27

Getting the Labels Right

"Christa, what you've just described to me is what most people would call oral rape."

I sit quietly for a minute, absorbing what my therapist has just told me.

I started out this session talking about my recurring nightmare. It's the one where I can't move and can't breathe and can't scream. God, how I hate that dream.

Of course, when I'm in it, it doesn't seem like a dream. It's a surreal netherworld and I'm trapped there.

Somehow, I had shifted from talking about that dream to talking about this. I've been going to therapy for months, and this is the first time I've talked about any sort of sexual details.

Most of the time, what I talk about is some version of my "Why don't they do anything?" wail. I'm always trying to figure out what it is that I'm doing wrong and why it is that I can't seem to make them understand. I keep thinking that, if only I could find the key, or find the right words, then I would surely be able to make them see why they can't possibly stand by and let this man continue as a children's minister.

But I keep failing and I don't get it. How can so many Southern Baptist leaders be content to know what they know and to still let Dunagan work in children's ministry? Why have they chosen to threaten me and treat me like trash instead of doing something about him? What part of this haven't I made clear to them? What part of it don't I understand?

These sorts of questions constantly weigh on me and upset me. Since I started down the road of trying to deal with this, everything that everyone in Baptist-land has said and done makes so little sense that I think I must be the one who's crazy. How can so many fine, respectable, upstanding men turn their back on this?

"So am I disposable or am I crazy? Which is it?" These are the questions I ask of my long-listening therapist.

"If all these men are right, then that means I'm the one who's making a big deal out of nothing. If all these men are right, then it means that what happened to me doesn't even matter enough that it's worth the bother of trying to make sure it doesn't happen to someone else. If all these men are right, it means I'm disposable. What happened to me simply doesn't matter and I'm making a big deal out of nothing."

"Christa, you aren't making a big deal out of nothing."

"Well . . . why shouldn't I think that? Why shouldn't I think that I'm the crazy one? I mean, isn't that what a crazy person is? Someone who thinks outside the norm? With all these men who act like it's no big deal – prominent men and pillars of the community – why should I think that all of them are wrong and that I'm the one who's right? That doesn't make sense."

"Which makes more sense?" I demand. "To think that all these upstanding men are outside the norm or to think that *I'm* the one who's outside the norm? Maybe the reality is that normal people think it's no big deal and that *I'm* the one who's weird for thinking it is. Maybe that's what's real and I just can't grasp reality."

I've been round and round with this so many times that it drives me nuts. Whatever part of me wasn't nutty already has become nutty from trying to figure this out. My therapist always assures me that I'm not crazy, but it doesn't stop me from feeling crazy. How could so many grown men be so wrong? I keep thinking there must be something the matter with ME, and I just need to figure out what it is.

I sit on that couch week-in and week-out, and I go through kleenex after kleenex talking about this. But even with all those weeks of soggy kleenex, nothing prepared me for what I feel at this session.

This is horribly uncomfortable. But somehow the dream-talk triggered it.

"He held my head. I couldn't breathe."

But how to go on? How to describe it? Even with my therapist, I'm so extremely uncomfortable that my instinct is to run from the room. I'm almost on my feet. My adrenaline is pumping.

But I myself sense that there's a connection between this cursed dream and what I'm trying to talk about. So I keep my seat with my heart pounding, and I keep trying to talk, stringing together whatever comes out of my mouth.

I see images in my head, but they aren't attached to words. It's not like going on a trip and having a picture of the Grand Canyon and knowing it's "the Grand Canyon." What I've got are just a bunch of jumbled-up snapshots with no sequence to them. And lots of them are distorted, like snapshots taken from odd angles or blown out of proportion. Worst of all, every time I pause over one of those snapshots and try to figure out what it actually is, I feel like I'll throw up.

"I remember being so afraid. I thought I would pass out or something. And then there was the way he always laughed at me and said I would get used to it."

"Christa, the term for what you've described is 'oral rape.' What do you think about that?"

I sat in silence for a long time, pondering the term.

"I never thought of it that way," I finally said. "I just didn't think of it that way."

"I know you didn't."

At the end of the session, I sat there depleted, and I realized she was right. The term matched the description.

"I'm not a stupid person. How come I never saw it that way?"

"Because you didn't know how to label it. And why would you? You were a kid. How could the person you were then have ever thought to stick a rape-label on a minister?"

28

Letter to the Church

Every minute of every day, and most minutes of every night, I worried about the fact that Dunagan was still working in children's ministry. I couldn't believe that no one in Southern Baptist circles would do anything.

Eighteen Southern Baptist leaders in four different states had been told about Dunagan.[51] Leaders in churches where he worked and leaders in state and national offices. Baptist leaders in Texas, Georgia, Florida, and Tennessee now knew about Dunagan, and not one of them would warn people in the pews. And they sure as heck weren't going to do anything to help me.

---

51. The 18 recipients and people informed of my substantiated clergy abuse report, as shown by correspondence and certified mail receipts, were: Wm. Jan Daehnert, Director of the Office of Minister/Church Relations, Baptist General Convention of Texas; Sonny Spurger, Associate Director, Office of Minister/Church Relations, Baptist General Convention of Texas; David Nabors, Chief Financial Officer, Baptist General Convention of Texas; Charles Wade, Executive Director, Baptist General Convention of Texas; Ken Hall, President, Baptist General Convention of Texas; Garry L. Hearon, Director, Dallas Baptist Association; Bobby Welch, President of the Southern Baptist Convention; Robert L. Mounts, Director of Pastor/Church Relations, Florida Baptist Convention; J. Robert White, Executive Director, Georgia Baptist Convention; Kenneth Keene, Office of Minister-Church Relations, Georgia Baptist Convention; Mike Floyd, Chairman of the Deacons, First Baptist Church of Farmers Branch, Texas, Sam Underwood, Pastor, First Baptist Church of Farmers Branch, Texas; James A. Moore, Music Minister, First Baptist Church of Farmers Branch, Texas; Office of Convention Relations, Southern Baptist Convention; Executive Director, Greater Orlando Baptist Association; Chairman of the Board of Deacons, First Baptist Church of Oviedo, Florida; Chairman of the Board of Deacons, First Baptist Church of Tyler, Texas; Chairman of the Board of Deacons, First Baptist Church of Atlanta. (Each of these men might be able to articulate a reason for why it wasn't his problem. But therein lies the problem for Southern Baptists. There is no one who will take responsibility for assuring the conscientious assessment of clergy abuse reports.)

Most had received certified letters. Some had been told more than once. They were on notice. They knew.

I couldn't believe it. Eighteen men, and not a one of them did diddly-squat.

I thought about my own daughter. I thought about how I would feel if she were active in Dunagan's Florida church and I later learned that Dunagan had abused a kid in Texas. I thought about all those other mothers sitting in the pews of that Florida church, and I knew I had to do whatever I could to make Dunagan's deeds known.

But how?

The only remaining possibility I could see was to file a lawsuit and to use the lawsuit to try to get some attention in the press. It wasn't what I wanted. In fact, it was what I dreaded. But what other possibility was there?

Baptists purport to practice "congregational autonomy." At least in theory, that's supposed to mean that church-members make the decisions. I knew that, for most churches, this was more theoretical than actual, and that pastors are the ones who usually run things. But I didn't have any other options left.

So, I decided to put a letter on cars in the parking lot at First Baptist Church of Farmers Branch. I hoped that the actual church members might be different from their leaders and might decide to do the right thing, and I felt like I should give them that chance. I wanted to at least make sure the church members actually knew about this before I filed a lawsuit against them.

Dan and I drove to Farmers Branch on a Sunday morning in May. So much of what I was dealing with was in my own head, and Dan often felt frustrated by how little he could do. He wanted to fix it, but he couldn't. Driving to Farmers Branch gave him a chance to do something tangible, and he was glad to get it.

Months earlier, I had told Dan the gist of things, but I always shared only small bits. Dan struggled with his own unfolding understanding, and he also struggled with a desperate desire to protect me against all that I was dealing with. Dan would have taken on Hades himself to try to save me. But of course, he couldn't.

I grieved for all that I was putting Dan through, and often thought he would be better off without me. But Dan wouldn't hear that sort of talk. He just kept paddling, pouring all his energy into trying to keep our small boat afloat on an endless storm-tossed sea.

Dan knew I had walled a lot off from him, and it irritated him. He thought I was trying to protect *him*. There may have been a small piece of truth in that, but the bigger truth is that I was protecting *myself*.

In Dan's eyes, I saw always and only an image of myself that was far lovelier than what I saw in my own mind's eye. I didn't want Dan to see what I saw, and I didn't want to see it reflected back in his eyes. I clung to the reflected image of the whole and beautiful person in Dan's eyes, and guarded it, as though my life depended on it. There were times when it did.

In Farmers Branch, Dan and I did a few loops through Gussie Field park while we waited for church to start. I looked for my old favorite climbing tree, but couldn't spot it. I figured it had probably been cleared out. The park didn't have the woods that it used to have. Now it was a tidy, manicured sort of park. I wondered if the red-winged blackbirds still nested there.

We parked the car up on the hill by the old cemetery. I sat there looking at the church and sizing it up. It had a big new sanctuary, but the grounds were mostly barren. Even the plantar box around the church sign was empty. It had nothing but dirt.

I thought about how my dad used to plant flowers around the church sign. He would tend to them real early in the morning when no one was around. It was strange how much he cared about those flowers. I don't think anyone even knew that he was the one who planted them.

Dan and I kept sitting in the car and waiting. A few deacons still stood outside the sanctuary doors, smoking their last cigarettes before the sermon started.

As I watched them, I thought about how some things don't change much. When I was a kid, deacon Bill Green always stood outside the sanctuary, puffing away up until the last minute. It really irritated my dad. He thought it set a bad example for the young people in the church. My dad wanted the smokers to light up in back of the church instead of out front. But of course, deacon Green was a church insider. My dad wasn't.

My dad was just a hard-working man, trying to provide for his family, and that often meant working double and triple shifts, including Sundays. That was a sin, of course.

Sometimes Brother Hayden would preach a whole sermon about the sin of working on Sundays, and I would always slump in my seat out of embarrassment, as though my dad's sin somehow rubbed off on all the rest of us. But whenever I asked my dad about it, he just said, "The way I figure it, God expects me to feed my family."

Finally, when we were sure everyone was in the sanctuary, Dan and I got out and started putting the letters on cars. We did the front, back, and sides of the church, and even behind the nursery. Slipping in and out between the cars, we kept watch on the church doors the whole time and made a sort of surreptitious game out of it. We had some fun with it.

To Members of the First Baptist Church of Farmers Branch:

I grew up in your church. I went to morning and evening services, Sunday School, training union, Girls' Auxiliary, prayer meeting and revival services. I marched into your sanctuary to the sound of "Onward Christian Soldiers" during Vacation Bible School, and I paraded down the aisle for G.A. coronation ceremonies every year until the Queen Regent cape was placed on my shoulders. I served as a substitute pianist when the regular pianist was gone, and I sang in the youth choir. I went on countless retreats and trips with the youth group. Two of my sisters were married in your church.

I loved the church. And I loved God with all my heart. I was driven by a sincere desire to try to know God's will and do God's will. I was a true believer.

All of those memories were supplanted by the degradation and defilement of what your former youth and education minister did to me there. I was just a naive 16-year-old church girl who had never been on a single date and never even held hands with anyone. Eddie Dunagan was a married adult, a parent, and a minister. He was also counseling me at the time – counseling that he himself initiated.

I was raised to respect the church ministers and to believe that they were called by God. Nevertheless, when Dunagan pressed himself on me, I still said "no" – at first. But he persisted, and little by little, he convinced me that it was what God wanted from me. "Think of Abraham – think of Noah – think of Moses," he said. "Do you think what

God wanted from them made sense to them?" He told me that I wasn't supposed to try to understand and that I had to be willing to "live by faith." So, that's what I tried to do. And using my own adolescent faith, trust and gullibility against me, your man of God violated me in unspeakable ways – all with words of God and in the name of God. Such despicable blasphemy, and yet God makes for a powerful weapon when used by a predator.

I was so totally conned that I actually felt special and cho- sen. I thought I was following God, but the path ultimately led me to a place of total darkness. After months of abuse, Dunagan started telling me that I was the serpent and Satan's ally. He said that I harbored evil, and he made me kneel in his office while he prayed to God to cast Satan from me. He even made me apologize to his wife for what I had done, and I begged her to forgive me. Through all of this, I became so confused and distraught that I finally broke down crying at my piano lesson one day, and I told my piano teacher – the music minister – about it. I felt so horribly guilty and believed I was going to hell.

Shortly after I told the music minister, Dunagan left to go to a new position at a bigger church in Tyler. He was sent on his way with praise from the pulpit about how blessed we all were to have known such a man of God.

The abuse had a soul-murdering impact on my life, although I wasn't able to understand until recently. I now know that, because of the level of trust involved, many psychologists compare the harm that kids experience from clergy sexual abuse to the harm that is caused by incest. Ordinary, decent people feel revulsion at the mere thought of incest and in- stinctively know how extremely damaging it must surely be for the kids. I hope there will come a time when ordinary, decent people will feel the same way about clergy sexual abuse, and that is why I am writing you this letter.

When my own daughter became 16, it began in my mind a process of resurrecting all the memories of what was done to me at that age. As a mother, I know that my fury would know no bounds if any trusted adult – any coach, teacher or minister – ever did to my daughter what was done to me. Thinking about it as a mother to my own daughter made me finally weep for the young girl that I myself once was. I finally understood that it wasn't a wrong done by me, but rather a horrific wrong that was done against me.

I wish I could say this story had a constructive ending. But so far it doesn't. I sent a detailed report of my abuse to your church and denominational leaders. I thought my report would be met with care and concern, and I hoped something positive could come of it. I assumed that church and denominational leaders would act so as to assure that Dunagan could not hurt anyone else. How naive I was. . . . Your church responded through its lawyer with what seemed to be an attempt to intimidate me. I perceived it as an effort to silence me, and this upset me more than words can say. I cannot help but wonder how many other clergy abuse victims have been intimidated right back into their quiet dark corners of shame by letters such as the one sent by your church's attorney.

With such a response, how can I possibly believe that your church would be able to prevent the same horror from happening all over again to some other young church kid? One thing I know for sure is this: Silence serves only the predators.

It is degrading, humiliating and painful for me to even speak of this. Nevertheless, I flew to Dallas at my own expense last November to meet with three men from the Baptist General Convention of Texas and with one of your deacons. In fact, the meeting was delayed and rescheduled for the sake of allowing one of your deacons to attend. Yet, when I got there, not a single deacon from your church showed up. Only the church's attorney was there. I was deeply disappointed. Even though I agreed to meet in your city, your church did not even do me the courtesy of sending a single deacon to talk with me face-to-face, one human being to another.

I tried to provide an opportunity to make some amends. In response, I feel as though your church chose to essentially spit on me. I sought to reopen this old wound to drain and heal it. And in response, I feel as though your church chose to reach in and savage the wound.

However, I know that a church is more than its deacons, and certainly more than its mere lawyer. So I am making this attempt to reach out to you as the members of the congregation and to inform you. My understanding is that, in a Baptist church, each and every member has a voice and a vote.

I don't believe anyone actually doubts my story. The Baptist General Convention of Texas keeps a file of clergy abusers. By their own written policy, they will add a minister's name to that file only if the sexual abuse is reported by a church and only if there is a confession, a conviction, or "substantial evidence that the abuse took place" as determined by denominational attorneys. I have been informed that the Baptist General Convention of Texas has now added Eddie Dunagan's name to that file.

What I don't understand is why the names in that file are kept confidential. As a parent, if your kids were active in one of Dunagan's other churches, wouldn't you want to know about this?

Over ten months have passed since I made my report, and I stay awake at night worrying about how many others Dunagan may have hurt and may yet hurt. I worry about how little it seems to me that the denomination is doing to protect against Dunagan and others like him. I don't understand why Dunagan has still been able to work in children's ministry. Even if church and denominational leaders are willing to believe that this man will not abuse anyone else, shouldn't parents be informed and allowed to decide for themselves about where they will entrust their kids?

If I could have spoken of this sooner, I would have. However, I know my response to this trauma was normal. For people abused by clergy as teens and preteens, the amount of time before a first report is often several decades. As with me, it often happens when their own children reach the same age. It is the very nature of the harm that victims suppress the darkness and the shame of it.

Because a clergy predator often has multiple victims, I think church leaders should openly inform congregations about reports such as mine so as to reach out to other possible victims and so as to avoid an institutionalized culture of secrecy. . . .

Clergy sexual abuse can happen anywhere. It happened to me and it happened in your church. I have seen no remorse and no one has asked my forgiveness, but even if they had, there is no amount of forgiveness on my part that would serve to make kids today any safer.

What will make kids safer is for church and denominational leaders to treat clergy sexual abuse as the horrific crime that it is. What will make kids safer is for church and denominational leaders to be supportive of victims because when victims come forward, predators are revealed. What will make kids safer is for church and denominational leaders to make protection of kids the very highest priority. What will make kids safer is for church and denominational leaders to act with openness, forthrightness and vigilance in dealing with the hellish reality of trusted clergy who sexually abuse the young and vulnerable.

Looking back on this letter now, I can't imagine what I was thinking. Where in the world did I ever get the notion that church people might voluntarily choose to do something compassionate and decent for a person abused by one of their own clergy? In hindsight, my optimism seems downright delusional.

29

Cult-like Behavior

Back then, I not only still believed in the possibility that the church might do the right thing, I also believed in the possibility that an old friend might want to help.

Wanda grew up in the church with me, but she was a year ahead of me in school. I remembered how she used to be the one Eddie would take home last, before he started taking me home last. She only lived a block from the church, but she would always ride along while he took everyone else home, and then she would be the last one left in the car. And like me, Wanda used to babysit for Eddie's kid.

I remember how I used to feel a little jealous of all the attention Eddie heaped on Wanda. At the time, I thought it was because she came from such a poor and troubled family. Once Eddie took me with him to Wanda's ramshackle little house and I watched while he handed Wanda's mom a stuffed envelope. He said it was money to help them out.

I thought about how Wanda had gone off to Dallas Baptist College. Even at the time, I wondered how she could possibly afford a private college like that, but Wanda said the church was helping her.

Putting together the pieces, I decided that, if Eddie had abused another kid in the church, Wanda would have been the most likely one. So I tracked her down and wrote to her. I knew her last name because she married a boy in the church. He became a Southern Baptist preacher.

As gently as I could, I told Wanda the gist of what happened to me in the church we both grew up in, and about how I had reported it to church and denominational leaders. I had heard that Wanda had kids, and so I tried to relate to her as a mother and told her about my own daughter.

> She is far better grounded, not half so gullible, and far more self-assured than I ever was. But she is still just a young girl, and I see her natural vulnerabilities, her trusting nature, her impressionability and her idealism. As her mother, I know that my fury would know no bounds if

any trusted adult – any teacher or any coach – ever did to her what Eddie Dunagan did to me. Somehow, thinking of it in this manner . . . I began to finally understand that what Eddie Dunagan did to me was predatory, abusive and profoundly wrong. . . .

"I cannot help but wonder whether Dunagan had other victims," I continued. "Studies have shown that teen victims of clergy predators are typically the most devout of kids. . . . So I am wondering whether there is any chance that you may have had some sexual contact with Dunagan as an adolescent? I hate asking such an intrusive question, but if you were also one of his victims, then perhaps we could help each other."

I wondered what Wanda would think, and what her preacher-husband would think. There was no getting around the fact that it was an intrusive question. But once upon a time, Wanda and I were good friends, and I hoped she would respond on the basis of past friendship. In any event, I figured it was best to put the question out in the open without hedging.

"My goals in this process are healing – for myself and others – and prevention," I concluded. "I am trying to find a way to make something positive come out of this experience."

I gave Wanda all my contact information and hoped she would call me, but she didn't.

Her husband signed for the certified letter, and within a matter of weeks, it was in the hands of the church's lawyer.

Phil Waller wasn't happy. He fired off a letter to Craig, complaining about the letter on the cars and also about my letter to Wanda. He said it was inappropriate because Wanda was the daughter of a church member and he considered the members of the church to be his clients.

I pondered that and knew it made no sense. He surely didn't represent every single member of the church individually.

I also wondered about the truth of his letter. Wanda's mom didn't go to church when we were growing up. She was always "sick." So, though I didn't doubt that Wanda's mom might have been kept on the church roll all these years, I doubted that she was actually an active member.

But it didn't matter. Even if Wanda's mom was perfectly well and sitting in a pew every Sunday, it was still ludicrous to imagine that I couldn't write to an old friend just because her mom happened to be a church member. It made about as little sense as Waller's earlier complaint about how we had erroneously referred to Jim Moore as a "minister" even though Moore wasn't "ordained." Plenty of Baptist ministers aren't formally "ordained," and besides, Moore had been listed on the Southern Baptist Convention's own website as a "minister of music."

Waller was full of gamesmanship and bluff. As a lawyer myself, I could see that. But I also knew that, most of the time, that sort of bullying bravado would be enough to give a lot of clergy abuse survivors second-thoughts about reporting the preacher-predators. It's not as if sexual abuse victims *like* to talk about it. So when they finally do reach the point of trying to tentatively talk about it – usually many years after the abuse – it doesn't take much to shove them back into silence.

A couple months later, I was digging through old photos and came across a picture of Connie Griswell giving Eddie a head and neck massage. It was taken in a booth at a roadside diner when we were on a trip with the church youth group. Connie was probably about 28 or so at the time. She went on a lot of our church trips with us.

I remembered how Eddie used to talk about what great legs Connie had. Then I remembered how I would sometimes see Connie leaving Eddie's office when I was at the church for piano lessons. One time, she was crying and looked all disheveled when she came out the door. Her mascara was running and her hair was a mess.

Back then, Connie had one of those Texas-style big-hair bouffants that was always ratted up high and lacquered in place with a fog of spray. So, since her hair always looked exactly the same and with every hair immovable, it wasn't hard to tell that something was amiss.

After she breezed past me, I asked Eddie if Connie was okay. He chuckled a bit and then said she was having marital problems and that he was counseling her. What I remember is how his chuckle seemed so out of place, but I knew better than to ask any more questions.

With those memories on my mind, I decided Connie might possibly know something, and so I looked her up in the Farmers Branch phone book. She was still listed at the same house she lived at when I was a kid. Of course, I had no way of knowing whether she was still a member of the First Baptist Church or not, and I decided to write her a letter.

I gave Connie the gist of my story and told her that I had been sexually abused by minister Eddie Dunagan. I wasn't quite as direct as in my letter to Wanda, but there was still no mistaking what it was that I was asking.

I think it's possible that Dunagan may have had other victims, either among girls in the youth group or among young women he may have been counseling. Whether as a minister or as a counselor, sexual exploitation and abuse is a dreadful crime that causes great harm. If you know anything at all that might be helpful to me, I'd greatly appreciate it if you would contact me.

Finally, I told Connie about the other churches where I now knew Dunagan had worked.

I think it's wrong that this man should still be allowed to stand in a pulpit and carry the authority and credibility of being a Baptist minister, and I'm trying to get the church and denomination to do something about it. So far, I have not been successful. If I were a parent in one of Dunagan's other churches and realized that the denomination knew about Dunagan's conduct and kept it a secret, I would be furious. What I want is to know that teenage girls in Baptist churches today are a lot safer than I was. So far, I haven't seen anything that allows me to believe that.

I sent the letter off by certified mail and hoped Connie would contact me. She didn't.

Just three days later, Phil Waller faxed a letter to Craig complaining about what I had done.

Three days: that's all it took for my letter to get from me to Connie to the church's lawyer. I couldn't believe it. And once again, Waller insisted that the members of the church were his client . . . as if I could possibly know who all the members of the church were . . . and as if he was representing them as individuals instead of as a church entity. It was silly.

When I told my therapist that, this time, it took just three days for my letter to get into the hands of the church's attorney, she nearly spewed her Diet Frostie.

"What is this, some kind of cult?" she asked.

I turned the word over in my head for a moment. It did seem pretty strange that neither Wanda nor Connie would even pick up the phone to call me. They couldn't even muster it up to drop me a note and tell me for themselves that they didn't want to help me. Instead they just went straight to church officials.

"Well, of course, they would never call themselves a cult," I said. "They're Baptists. But it sure seems like cult-like behavior, doesn't it?"

Then I wondered whether there would be any church anywhere that would call itself a "cult." Doesn't *every* church think of itself as a church and not a cult? I thought about how over-controlled and cult-like my own behavior had been when I was growing up in that church.

Whatever label anyone wanted to stick on it – church or cult – one thing was for sure: I drank the Kool-Aid.

30

Church Leaders Brag

My letters didn't get any response from Wanda or Connie or any church members, but they got a response from the church leaders. The church's attorney got on the phone with Craig and asked if the church leaders could schedule an "in person" meeting with me. Finally.

I had wanted to meet with the church leaders from the very beginning, but they couldn't be bothered. Now, I guess they were hoping that, if they agreed to meet with me, I might stop writing letters.

In between my letters to Wanda and Connie, I had also put a lawsuit on file.[52] So that might have also been what nudged them. I couldn't help but think how sad it was that it took filing a lawsuit to get the church leaders to even sit down and meet with me.

By now, over a year had passed since I reported Dunagan's abuse. I desperately wanted something to happen. And naively, I still thought that, if the church leaders would just talk with me, they would understand and would see the need to do something.

It turned out to be a profoundly painful meeting.

As soon as I saw the pastor walk in the room, I cringed. He was the man that Donna Dean had reported several years earlier, alleging sexual abuse of her as an adult congregant.[53] I had specifically requested that he NOT be one of the church's representatives for the meeting. Whatever his version of the story might be, I just didn't want to have to think about it while I was dealing with my own trauma. I didn't want to feel as though this man, who himself had been accused of sexual abuse,

---

52. No. DV05-05669-M in the 298th Judicial District, Dallas County, Texas; and No. 05-06465 in the 192nd Judicial District, Dallas County, Texas, C. Brown v. First Baptist Church of Farmers Branch and James A. Moore (with both eventually consolidated into the 298th Judicial District).

53. Affidavit of D. Dail, Cause No. DV05-05669M in the 298th Judicial District, Dallas County, Texas, C. Brown v. First Baptist Church of Farmers Branch and James A. Moore; *see also* Dee Ann Miller, "The Collusion Act of the Southern Baptist Convention and Clergy Sex Abuse," *TakeCourage.org* [http://www.takecourage.org/updatesbc.htm]; Tara Dooley, "When clergy prey, women pray to be heard," *Fort Worth Star-Telegram*, November 8, 1998.

might be sitting there leering at me. I had hoped that, as a pastor, he might simply have the decency to respect my wishes and the sensitivity of the situation. He didn't.

But when I saw the music minister walk in the room, my heart lifted. I immediately recognized him. It was music minister Jim Moore, my old piano teacher. Seeing his face yanked me back to that docile girl who, once upon a time, followed Moore's every instruction and sought only to please.

I went straight to Jim Moore and shook his hand. I was so glad to see him that I started crying. I felt certain that he was there to try to help me.

I was wrong.

When we all sat down, he started right in. "Here's what I remember," he said, and he proceeded to lay out his memories by number. "One – two – three." His spiel was cold and calculated. There was nothing remorseful in his words. And there wasn't any concern for me.

I wished I could have such a clinical attitude toward my own memories. If I could just number them and put them in order, maybe I could make sense of them. And if they were just numbers, maybe they wouldn't hurt so much.

Moore sat at the far end of that big conference table, and when he got to "number 3," I peered down the table. He was talking about how Dunagan had come to him one day and told him how afraid he was that someone in the congregation had seen him "in a compromising position" with me.[54]

I listened in stunned silence. Moore was talking about a point in time *before* that piano lesson when I myself broke down crying and told him about it. This meant that Moore had known about the abuse even earlier.

He could have stopped the abuse sooner. But he didn't.

I turned that new information over in my head. I thought about how the abuse had escalated at the end. I thought about how it wouldn't have happened if only Moore had done something when he first learned about the abuse from Dunagan himself.

I looked at this man, the music minister who had also been my piano teacher. He was bragging – BRAGGING – about how he was the person who had eventually convinced Dunagan – my perpetrator – to move

---

54. Affidavit of James A. Moore in Cause No. 05-06465 in the 192nd Judicial District, Dallas County, Texas.

on to another church. He looked all puffed up with pride, seemingly oblivious to the horror of what he had allowed to happen.

He was proud of himself!

I tried to keep my gaze steady. I tried to hold on . . . and I did for a little while. But sometimes the body has a mind of its own. Within minutes, my chest clamped shut. I couldn't breathe. Waves of grief and nausea overtook me. I stood and turned my back to the table, and then I was doubled-over and heaving.

Thank goodness I had enough sense not to eat anything that morning, and so there wasn't anything in my stomach to throw up. But that didn't stop my body from trying.

Craig declared a break and ushered them all out of the room to try to give me some dignity.

When I recovered, they filed back in.

"Look, you've known about this for more than 30 years. Why bring it up now?" The pastor didn't waste any time digging back into me. "And we can't understand why you're upset with Jim here. He's the person who got Dunagan out of the church. I should think you'd be grateful to him."

"Besides, it's not as if you told me any details." Jim Moore jumped in to vindicate himself. "I didn't know any details," he repeated.[55]

I immediately realized that his "I didn't know any details" line was how he lets himself off the hook and how he convinces himself that he didn't do anything wrong. Even though Moore had just admitted knowing that Dunagan had "sexual contact" with me, and even though he had just admitted that Dunagan himself told him he was afraid someone had seen him "in a compromising position" with me, and even though he knew enough about what happened that he told Dunagan to leave the church, and even though he had just bragged about how he was the one who got Dunagan out, Moore still tells himself that since he didn't know "details," he didn't have any obligation to do anything more.

I saw how entrenched they were in their own self-righteous self-image, and I tried to think of what I could possibly say that might help them see a different perspective.

"I know I didn't tell you many details," I finally said quietly. "I can't imagine that many 16-year-olds *would* talk about the details of something like this. Maybe if you had suggested that I talk with a woman in the church, I might have said something more, but you didn't. And I'm

---

55. Affidavit of James A. Moore, *supra.*

not sure I would have talked about details even with a woman. I mean, I don't even think I would have known what words to use back then. I wouldn't have known *how* to talk about it. And I would have been way too embarrassed. I can't imagine."

"To this day," I continued, "there are parts of it that I can hardly bring myself to talk about even with my therapist. And actually some parts that I still haven't. I can't imagine that a 16-year-old girl could have talked about the details with you."

"I'm not sure I even know for myself what all the details are. I'm still trying to sort out all the pieces, and I had hoped that you could help me." I looked straight at Moore then, but he was a wall of stone.

"I feel as though it's a big jigsaw puzzle and it's all just swirling around and I can't see the whole picture. I've got some of the pieces put together, but there's all sorts of other pieces that are flying around. They're there, but I can't quite latch onto them, and even when I manage to grab one, I can't always figure out where it goes. And then there's some holes where I think maybe the pieces are just completely gone and maybe I won't ever find them. It's confusing."

I looked at their faces and saw zero comprehension. Worse, I saw zero caring. Why did I even bother trying to explain?

"Look, I can see that you don't understand," I said. "And maybe we're going to have to find a way to resolve this without understanding one another. So let me just tell you one thing I know for sure. I have felt from the beginning as though you were trying to silence me – you and your attorney here. That is what will NOT work. I will not have any part of your desire for secrecy."

There was a moment of quiet. I looked around the table at them. They looked back at me. The deacon broke the silence.

"Christa, I know we got off to a rocky start with you, but let's try to get back on track and see if we can start fresh."

Then he started in with his tough-guy talk. "Why . . . if I could," he drawled, "I'd like to take a baseball bat and teach that man a lesson." The pastor and another church representative both nodded vigorously.

"Kids are the most precious thing," chimed in the pastor. "In our church, the kids are what we care about the most."

I looked at all of them. I suppose this sort of talk made them feel good about themselves, but I wasn't impressed. It had been over a year since I had given them my report about Dunagan's abuse, and they hadn't done anything to stop him from working with kids in Florida or to warn people in the pews. In fact, rather than trying to stop Dunagan, these church leaders had chosen to threaten ME. So the tough talk about "taking a baseball bat" to Dunagan seemed a bit silly when the actual intimidation tactics had been inflicted on ME for trying to report him.

And despite the deacon's tough talk about "taking a baseball bat," in actuality, he hadn't even shown the courage of sending a simple letter to the church where Dunagan was working. Perhaps his tough-guy talk made the deacon feel better about himself, but it didn't mean anything to me. I didn't want a baseball bat, and I sure wasn't interested in their braggadocio or their self-congratulatory words on how much they cared about kids. It was all-too-obvious that their words were all-too-meaningless.

So I decided to shift gears. I brought up again the possibility of a millstone sculpture or a dedicated labyrinth. But they rejected those ideas outright, without even any possibility of discussion.

"There's no need for such a negative thing," said the pastor. "We believe in God's power to heal, and we want to take this and turn it into something positive."

As he spoke, he reached out his arm and latched onto a handful of air, as though to grab onto whatever that something positive was, I suppose. It was a contrived preacher-in-the-pulpit sort of gesture.

His words were just empty talk. Any fool could see that. But I decided to call him on it anyway.

"That's what I want as well – to turn this into something positive – and I thought my proposal for a dedicated labyrinth WAS something positive. So what sort of positive thing are YOU proposing?"

"Well . . . well . . . we put our trust in God in all things. We know He is the one who can make all things work together for good."

I just looked at him. Clearly, he was the sort of pastor who simply carried around some rote lines in his head and, most of the time, they were probably sufficient. But this wasn't one of those times. Without a script, he didn't seem to have a clue how to relate to someone like me as a real human being.

I sat silent, remembering the countless times when Dunagan himself had used that same Bible verse: "All things work together for good to them that love God." It was a verse I now hated.

I wondered whether I would go to hell for hating Bible verses. But it was a visceral response and there wasn't much I could do about it.

While I sat wondering about that, the deacon decided to pick up the slack. "Well . . . maybe we could put together some sort of special

Sunday School lesson to teach kids how to say no and run away – like a 'stranger danger' program."

"Stranger danger?" I looked at him. I couldn't believe he had said that.

"Stranger danger?" I said it again and heard the edge in my voice this time. I knew I should probably back off, but I kept on.

"What are you talking about? Your minister wasn't a stranger to me. This has nothing to do with 'stranger danger.' "

"Well . . . maybe not in your case, but for others. We could teach kids about 'stranger danger'."

I stared at him, trying to figure out how to get through to these people who clearly didn't have a clue and didn't seem to want to have a clue. But the deacon had an authoritarian air about him, and so he just kept on talking, as though he thought the mere sound of his voice could somehow demonstrate how knowledgeable he was. Yet, with every word he spoke, his ignorance became all the more apparent.

After a while, he began bragging about what a loving church they were. His spiel went sort of like this:

> Why . . . just a few weeks ago, my own step-daughter came parading into the church on Sunday morning. She's 25 and she's been nothing but trouble her whole life. It's just been one thing after another. So there she is, parading into the church, when she hasn't been in ages, and she's pregnant out to here. She's NOT married . . . AND . . . (his voice dropped to a hushed whisper) . . . her boyfriend's a BLACK man. Well . . . she just paraded herself into that church, and made such a spectacle, and I was SO ashamed of her. But I want you to know that those good church ladies just gathered all around her and loved on her. And I KNOW they would have done the same thing for you if you had just come to us with the right attitude.

I sat there dumbfounded, trying to figure out what part of his story could possibly have any relevance to what happened to me.

And "right attitude"? What was that supposed to mean?

I tried to think of what to say, but before I could get words out, the body once again took over. I stood, turned my back, and then doubled-over, heaving.

After they filed back in again, the deacon and preacher continued to talk, but it was nonsense. At that point, I think they were mostly just talking to hear themselves talk. They sure weren't expressing any compassion or concern for me. And my hope that Jim Moore might voice some feeble apology was a hope long-gone. Why had I ever clung to such a silly hope?

In my head, I kept pondering the deacon's story about his step-daughter. I suppose he thought that it was all related to "S-E-X" and so it was all the same. From his perspective, an unmarried 25-year-old getting pregnant by her boyfriend wasn't much different from me being sexually abused as an adolescent church girl by a married minister almost twice my age.

When the meeting ended, the only thing I could think to say was to congratulate him on his upcoming grand-baby.

Then, as we were all standing to leave, I spontaneously asked Jim Moore whether the church still had the same piano that I used to play. He said they still had it, but it had been moved into the recreation building.

"Do you think I could come play that piano again sometime?" I asked. "Would you all be willing to let me do that?"

They all stood quietly, just looking at me. I saw the fear and awkwardness in their faces, and I guessed what they were thinking.

"No, no. I'm not talking about any kind of performance or playing for the church or anything like that. I'm just talking about sitting and playing the piano all by myself."

They laughed a bit. It was obvious they were relieved. And when I saw their relief, I also saw what an idiot I was, and my mind started down its endless "kick me" track.

Whatever had possessed me to ask about the piano? I had just spent hours talking about this terrible thing that happened in that church, and what do I ask for at the end? I ask to play their piano. How brainless is that?

Worst of all, when they all looked mortified at the thought of me playing their precious piano, I rushed to assuage their worries. Why am I the one trying to quell *their* worries instead of them trying to comfort *me*?

If I had any brains, I would have insisted on a full concert performance and let them sweat over what I might pick to play. What an idiot I am.

I guess the old piano was the last connection I had to that church. It was the only memory that still held anything good for me.

31

Butterfly on the Run

The next day, I went for a run, hoping it would get the pain of that meeting out of my system. As I ran down the path under the bridge, a huge butterfly flew a circle around me and then hovered in front of my face. As I ran on, it flew beside me and made two more circles around me. I marveled at the wonder of a butterfly as a running companion.

Then, from out of nowhere, I felt his breath on the back of my neck and heard his voice in my ear. "Don't worry, you'll still be a virgin."

I hurled into the tall grass and wiped the last trail of vomit on my shirt. I stayed bent over, hands on my knees, trying desperately to breathe. My chest was clenched shut. I began to shake.

Memory fragments filled my head. They were all fragments that I had glimpsed before, but they always swirled away. This time, I decided to try to line them up – "one-two-three" – the way the music minister had done with his own memories the day before.

I managed to put my legs in motion again. As I walked, I started trying to put the fragments in order in my head.

One: I'm at the church parsonage in the same bedroom where my two sisters and I slept when my mom stayed at the hospital after my dad's back surgery.

Two: I go in the kitchen with Dunagan, and he takes a couple beers from the refrigerator. "But it's against our religion," I say. He just laughs. He says that's another one of those rules for lesser, weaker believers, and not for people like us.

Three: He puts the can in my hand and insists I drink. I don't want to, but he keeps pushing the can up to my mouth. Finally, I take a sip. It tastes awful. He keeps drinking from his own can, and then starts in on another.

Four: He takes my beer and pours it in a glass. He says it will taste better that way. I take a sip, but it still tastes just as bad. He keeps putting the glass back in my hands, but mostly I only pretend to sip it. He yells at me to get away from the window.

Five: I'm naked on my stomach on the bed. He is on top of me. I am saying "no" and squirming. I hear my own crying. His voice is in my left ear, shushing me. "Don't worry. You'll still be a virgin."

Six: I hear his laugh. "Do you think God made this part of the body for only one purpose? God is a lot more creative than that."

At this point, I smell his breath, as real as if he is with me on the running trail. I stop and vomit into the bushes again.

"God is a lot more creative than that." I keep hearing him. It's an endless loop in my head. His voice is there with me on the trail. His laugh goes on and on.

I keep walking. I know I've got to get home. I've got to get to safe ground. As I walk, my mind continues lining up the memory fragments.

Seven: I am standing naked in the bathroom with a washcloth. He is in the bathroom doorway, telling me to clean myself. I'm trying. He blocks the doorway, telling me to clean myself better. He gives me another washcloth. I am crying. I don't know how I can possibly clean myself any better than I already have. But he just keeps saying that I should clean better. Finally, he makes me stand in the shower. He yells at me not to get my hair wet.

Eight: He tells me to put on my clothes.

Nine: As we're going into the garage, his voice softens and he tells me how special I am. "God loves you, Christa."

Ten: It hurts to walk.

Now I'm doubled over on the trail yet again. I'm shaking. I think about the butterfly I saw minutes earlier and try to focus my thoughts on it. Maybe it was there to comfort me.

The instant I think this, I know I'm a fool.

There she is again, that same little girl wanting to believe in miracles and magic.

But I hold the image of the butterfly in my head anyway, and I begin to breathe.

32

The Unspeakable

"Why can't I remember more?"

That was what I asked when I went to see my therapist the next day. It wasn't the first time I had asked it, but this time, it seemed more urgent.

"Why don't the pieces all fit? Why are there so many holes? Why can't I actually remember exactly what happened there?"

She starts talking about people who have diving injuries and bad car crashes. Sometimes they remember the before and the after, but they don't remember the actual moment of impact. The brain protects them from that because it's too traumatic. She thinks my brain probably did something like that.

But there are other possibilities, she points out. "He might have drugged you."

I had thought of that possibility myself. The whole beer-drinking thing was so weird. And he was so insistent. What if he put something in it when he poured the beer in the glass? Was that why he kept shoving it back in my hands? Maybe if I had drunk more of that beer instead of just pretending, I would remember even less.

As it is, I have enough memory pieces that I can deduce what happened. But the truth is that, to this day, I don't actually remember it. For some reason, that makes the memory gap seem all the more ominous.

About a year after that trail run with the butterfly, and after I had begun working to bring attention to the problem of Baptist sex abuse, I found myself sitting at a Starbucks being interviewed by a magazine reporter. By then, I had made a lot of progress in therapy and I thought I was plenty strong enough that nothing could throw me. Everything was going along smoothly, and I was telling her the whole history of my efforts to get church and denominational leaders to address the problem. I thought I was doing just fine.

Then she asked, "Well so, what exactly did he do to you?"

I fell silent and tried to figure out how to answer her.

"Did he rape you?"

I couldn't figure out what to say. The word didn't carry the content of the reality.

I turned the letters over in my head: "r-a-p-e." Four of them. Would those four letters communicate what was done to me? Four little letters. How could they be enough?

If I said "yes," would that be the right answer? Would it be truthful? Would it tell her what happened? Would it convey the experience? I knew it wouldn't.

But what if I said "no"? Would *that* be the correct answer? I weighed it in my head and knew it wouldn't. I was raped.

But how could I explain it? Somehow a simple "yes" didn't seem like it would really answer the question either. She would think I meant one thing when I meant another. After all, I had technically stayed a virgin. The word was ambiguous. And it also wasn't nearly enough to convey the whole of what he did to me.

But I didn't want to try to parse "rape." Even thinking about it took my breath away.

Oral rape, anal rape, vaginal rape, spiritual rape, statutory rape, repeated rape, aggravated rape, and on and on. I ran through my head all the possible meanings the word "rape" could have, and I knew I didn't want to go into it.

So there I was, a grown adult woman – a woman who had already spent a lot of time in therapy – and I still couldn't manage to answer a simple question: "What exactly did he do to you?" It seemed literally unspeakable.[56]

The reporter was just looking at me.

I knew I had been out in the ozone, but I wasn't sure for how long.

"He did whatever he wanted," I finally answered.

At first I said it so quietly that I wasn't even sure I had actually spoken. So I said it again.

"He did whatever he wanted."

She just kept looking at me blankly, and I knew my answer wasn't good enough. She wanted something more. But it was all I could say that day.

And it was the simple truth: He did whatever he wanted.

---

56. "Certain violations of the social compact are too terrible to utter aloud; this is the meaning of the word *unspeakable*." Judith Herman, *Trauma and Recovery*, at p. 1 (Basic Books 1997).

33

Getting Him Out of Ministry

After our meeting, the church followed up by having their attorney send me a secrecy agreement. They had said they would put together a proposal with what they were willing to do, but when I saw the keep-it-quiet clause, I knew that all they really wanted was for me to sign a contract saying that I wouldn't speak to anyone else about my abuse.

Some would call it a "hush money" agreement. Some would call it a confidentiality clause or a secrecy contract. Whatever it was called, I knew the effect was the same. The church wanted to toss a few coins my way, and in exchange, they wanted my agreement that I wouldn't speak of this to anyone else. That's what they wanted me to sign.

As soon as I saw it, I knew the pain of that meeting had served no purpose. They were still totally oblivious.

I had told them straight to their faces, "I will not have any part of your desire for secrecy" and yet they still didn't get it. What part of those words didn't they understand?

I didn't sign their stupid, immoral secrecy agreement.

Instead, I fired off an email to reporter Mark Pinsky in Orlando. I saw that Mark Pinsky had written a prior story about priest abuse, and so he seemed like the right reporter to contact since Dunagan was still a minister at an Orlando church.

Pinsky went to work. I didn't realize it at the time, but he was actually a pretty extraordinary religion writer and journalist. I was lucky in that respect. Pinksy was willing to stay on the story and to push on getting it out.

When Pinsky started phoning around and asking questions, Dunagan's attorney threatened to sue the *Orlando Sentinel*. At least, that's what I heard. Thank God the *Orlando Sentinel* didn't back down.

Dunagan had one of those tall-building sorts of lawyers who probably charged about $400 per hour. I wondered how in the world a children's minister could afford a lawyer like that. And how did he find a lawyer so fast? Even though Dunagan was in Orlando, he had this Dallas lawyer on board within just a few days after I filed the lawsuit.

I figured there had to be others in Southern Baptist circles who were helping Dunagan.

Perhaps because of the threat, the article that finally made print in the *Orlando Sentinel* was a bare-bones piece.[57] But it named Rev. Eddie Dunagan as being charged in a Texas lawsuit with sexual abuse of a teen girl. And it pointed out that the Farmers Branch music minister had made a sworn affidavit saying he told Dunagan that, if he didn't leave, he would take the matter before the whole church. It was the same court-filed affidavit in which minister Jim Moore admitted that Dunagan had told him how afraid he was that a congregant had seen him "in a compromising position" with me.[58]

It was enough. Or at least I thought so at the time.

I felt like the weight of the world had been lifted from my shoulders. Parents in those Florida churches would see the *Orlando Sentinel* article and be warned. And Dunagan had finally resigned.

But I was also afraid. If Dunagan's lawyer was the kind of lawyer who would threaten a baseless lawsuit against the *Orlando Sentinel*, I figured he wouldn't hesitate to try to sue me as well, particularly since he could just file a counterclaim in my own suit that was already on file.

It would have been so much easier if only music minister Jim Moore, knowing the truth of my allegations, had joined forces with me in trying to expose Dunagan. And perhaps I wouldn't feel so paranoid if only the Farmers Branch church hadn't started out by threatening to sue me, even though their own music minister knew the truth of what I was saying. And perhaps I wouldn't be so fearful if only the Baptist General Convention of Texas had stepped up to the plate to help me instead of sending their rabid-dog lawyer to assist the church in trying to silence me.

I could go down those "if only" rabbit trails all day long. How I wished that someone in Baptist circles would have voluntarily chosen to help me. But there was no longer any point in trying to imagine how things might have been different. I had given them every opportunity to help me and they never chose to. That was what was real.

So, I knew I was out on a limb all alone against Dunagan. Not only was I afraid he would file a baseless countersuit against me, and possibly have behind-the-scenes help from high Southern Baptist leaders with

---

57. Mark I. Pinsky, "Lawsuit charges sexual abuse of teen by minister," *Orlando Sentinel*, October 22, 2005, B3.
58. Affidavit of James A. Moore in Cause No. 05-06465 in the 192nd Judicial District, Dallas County, Texas.

financing it, but I also figured his attorney would do everything possible to inflict as much punishment on me as he could in a deposition.

By then, I had put a criminal complaint on file, and Dunagan knew it. Because too much time had gone by, there was not the slightest possibility for criminal prosecution, but his lawyer still said that Dunagan would take the Fifth on any questions we might ask him in my civil suit. In other words, he would simply refuse to answer on the ground that it might incriminate him.

So, Craig wouldn't be able to put Dunagan under a microscope, or to put him at risk of perjury. Dunagan would just take the Fifth on everything. The only way around it would be to spend still more money going to court to try to compel him to answer.

I wondered whether I had done the right thing in making a criminal complaint. Maybe things would have been easier for me if I hadn't.

Meanwhile, Dunagan's attorney was pressing Craig to schedule my own deposition. And Craig was concerned.

At the meeting with the church leaders, he had caught a glimpse of how much this thing was affecting me. He had seen me so reflexively overwrought that I was overcome with dry heaves. Though I liked to pride myself on keeping my emotions under control, my body had betrayed the truth, and Craig had seen it. This thing was tearing me up.

Now, Craig was afraid of how much more it might affect me if I had to relive the whole nightmare in a hostile deposition with Dunagan's lawyer, and possibly with Dunagan himself sitting there glaring at me.

Craig was trying to set things up so that Dunagan would watch the deposition on a video-monitor in a different room. Though that sort of arrangement was common in cases of sexual assault, it wasn't a done deal, and we might have to go to court just to get an order that Dunagan couldn't sit in the same room during my deposition.

More cost. More money.

And it didn't seem fair that they would be able to grill me all day long, but we couldn't do the same to him. But it was easy enough to see that this was how it would be.

On top of all that, I needed to find an expert witness to try to explain to the judge the psychological reasons for why sex abuse victims wait so long to talk about the abuse. That would cost at least $6,000.00, and probably more. The money was starting to add up.

And for what? I figured we had only about a 10 percent chance that a judge would even let the case go to trial. Most other lawyers would probably say it was more like 5 percent. The low odds had nothing to do with truth or justice. It was about nothing more than the short statute of limitations, and the fact that Texas courts don't allow much wiggle-room on time limitations. The law hasn't yet caught up to the science of human psychology.

So, Dunagan's lawyer would get to beat up on me in a deposition, and I'd spend a lot of money on an expert and on other court hearings, and at the end of the day, I would probably still get thrown out of court because too much time had passed. I wouldn't even get to tell my story in an open courtroom to an impartial panel of jurors. That was the most likely scenario for how things would play out, and I knew it.

It was times like this that I wished I wasn't a lawyer. It would have been easier not to know how little hope my case had. And it would have been easier not to have both parts of my brain on overdrive at once – the lawyer part and the wounded part.

But of course, I probably couldn't have stopped thinking about it even if I had tried. Over the course of a lot of years, a lot of trial lawyers had asked for my opinion on the odds for winning with different sorts of lawsuits, and on the odds of just being able to get a case to trial. Thinking about that sort of thing was part of what I did for a living. How could I not think about it in my own case?

For my sake, Craig just wants this to be over. He thinks that's what I need. He thinks it's what would be best. Maybe he's right. But I still can't walk away from it.

Once upon a time, I thought I knew what I needed: a sincere apology and a recognition of the wrong. I thought if music minister Jim Moore would just apologize, everything would be fine. I thought if the church would just own up to what happened, everything would be fine. I thought if the Baptist General Convention of Texas would just make some small symbolic gesture of care, everything would be fine.

Now I don't know what I need anymore. Whatever it is, I know better than to believe that anyone who carries the name "Baptist" is going to help me.

Finally, Craig and I decide to drop the suit against Dunagan, but I retain the right to sue him again later if I want. And perhaps I will if the Texas Legislature ever passes laws similar to those in California and Delaware. They're laws that make it easier for child molestation victims to at least have a shot at exposing their perpetrators in civil suits. They're laws that at least let child molestation victims get in the courthouse doors and get before a jury. But that day isn't here yet in Texas.

I continue on with the suit against First Baptist Church of Farmers

Branch. At least this way, I'll only have to fight one lawyer, not two. And I want the church to have to own up to this thing. It happened on their watch. It happened in their church. It happened with their minister. And it happened with other ministers knowing about it.

And then, even all these years later, that church had the arrogant gall to threaten to sue me when I reported it.

34

The Creature on the Couch

At my therapist's office, I always sit in exactly the same place at the far right end of the couch, pressed up against the arm bolster. I often catch myself looking to my left, as though I can almost see my 16-year-old self there on that couch with me. But she's a pathetic, sniveling, naked creature sprawled out on her belly there as though she were nothing more than an animal.

"He treated me like a dog."

My eyes turn to the left again. I can almost hear that creature whimpering. "No. It was worse than that," I whisper. "Most people wouldn't treat their dogs the way he treated me."

How I loathe that pathetic, throw-away creature who is so often there on the couch with me. I cannot bear the dehumanized horror of her presence in my consciousness. I don't want her to be any part of me. I don't want to see her.

When Emily graduated from high school, I was still in the thick of this. I watched every kid who crossed the floor at her graduation ceremony, and I looked at their faces as they were blown up on a screen in the events center. Some of them I had known since they were in kindergarten and others I didn't know at all. But I looked at every single kid and couldn't see a single one that I could ever think might deserve to have done to them what was done to me.

Most of these kids were 18, a couple years older than I was when I was abused. But it didn't make any difference. Even at 18, none of them could possibly ever deserve what was done to me. I knew that.

Some of the kids who crossed the stage had lots of tattoos and piercings. A few of them had been in various sorts of trouble. I knew that about them. But nothing about their appearances or anything that I knew made even the tiniest difference in how I felt.

I looked at every single kid who crossed that stage, and I couldn't see a single one who could possibly ever be deserving of what was done to me at the First Baptist Church of Farmers Branch.

"So why do you imagine that you were somehow different?" asked my therapist at my next session. "Why do you imagine that you were somehow a bad kid who may have deserved it when you can't imagine a single other kid who would ever deserve such a thing? What is it about that 16-year-old Christa Brown that makes her so unworthy of your compassion? Why do you keep blaming her?"

"I don't know."

That's how it is with most of the questions my therapist asks me.

"What I see is an incredibly courageous kid," she says. "She's a kid who had something terrible done to her. But it was something that was done *to* her. It wasn't something *she* did. That's the kid you need to see, too."

This is a frequently recurring theme in my therapy sessions. Not only do we talk about the revulsion I feel toward that 16-year-old girl but also about the way I never cut myself any slack in the here and now.

I sat at a SNAP meeting one time and listened to Catherine talk about how she felt as though her priest's abuse had deprived her of the ability to have more kids. She had one son, and with him she had learned how much she loved being a mother. But she had previously been so terrified of motherhood that she waited until she was older to have her first. Then by the time she realized how great it was to be a mom, she couldn't get pregnant again. She had gotten too old.

I sat and wept for Catherine. I knew exactly how she felt. I had thought the same thing – that Dunagan's abuse had deprived me of more children. But every time I thought it, I felt like a whiner. How could I blame his abuse for my inability to have more kids?

Was it his fault that I waited so long to have my first? Maybe it was. I went years thinking that I wasn't psychologically stable enough to have kids. It seemed irresponsible. Then, when I felt like my head was on straight enough, and had my first kid, I realized how much I loved being a mom. And I was a good mom. I saw that about myself. But by then, though we tried and tried, I wasn't able to get pregnant again. My ovaries were too old.

No amount of throwing money at the problem changed anything. And no amount of willingness to undergo invasive procedures changed anything. I couldn't have more kids. It was a huge and long-lasting heartbreak.

So why do I view myself as a whiner whenever I go down that path of thinking the abuse limited my ability to have kids, and yet for Catherine, my heart splits open and my compassion pours forth? Why do I feel for Catherine what I can't seem to feel for myself?

In other ways as well, I often wind up wondering what my life might have been if I hadn't spent so much of my younger years' energy in struggling with psychological instability. I try to reach back into the past for that girl who might have been – that girl who was *not* molested and raped by a trusted minister – that girl who grew up free of the debilitating self-doubt and self-loathing that such trauma induces. What might *her* life have been?

But she's gone, bludgeoned into oblivion. That identity and whatever life it would have led to was annihilated. I can never retrieve her.

Perhaps the only good to come from her vanishing is that my own daughter was raised without the tiniest shred of Baptist thinking in her brain. Though I often read Bible stories to her, she grew up without one bit of indoctrination in that man-made, pseudo-religious, female submissiveness, authoritarian culture of conformity that so plagues so many Baptists. She is stronger and healthier because of it.

About the time of Emily's graduation, my mom came to visit. She sat at my kitchen table and started regaling me with her story about the voice in the air conditioner.

Mom had taken to sleeping in the middle bedroom a couple years ago, after my dad died. So she was lying there in the room I used to have as a kid, and she started hearing a voice coming through the air conditioner. She couldn't make out what it was actually saying, but it was definitely a human voice.

She heard it the next night and the next. She couldn't figure it out. Then she remembered that I had once told her about a voice in the air conditioner.

Finally, the voice bothered her so much that she asked my oldest sister, Sarah, to come over and sleep with her. Sarah did.

Together they finally figured out that the voice was the announcer at the Little League field a block away. Somehow the sound waves were hitting the metal of the air conditioning unit and were being distorted to the inside of the bedroom.

I sat there with my jaw open, pondering my mom's story.

My mom laughed and laughed. To her, it was just a funny story. But for me, it called forth the feelings of that traumatized girl who was told she harbored Satan. Then when the air conditioner took on a voice, and with no one to help her figure it out, that girl convinced herself it might actually BE Satan, and that he was coming into her room.

Believing she was crazy or evil or both, she became all the more terrified. Terrified of what lurked outside the window. Terrified of what was creeping into her room. Terrified of what might dwell within her own head.

But who could she have talked to? Who would have listened? Who would have cared?

She was alone. It was up to her to figure it out on her own.

35

At His Florida Church

The day after I dropped the lawsuit against Dunagan, Mark Pinsky forwarded me an email he had gotten from a woman who saw his article in the *Orlando Sentinel*. She had been a secretary at the First Baptist Church of Oviedo, where Dunagan worked in Florida, and she had been treated terribly.

Kaye said she knew without a moment's hesitation that I was telling the truth about Dunagan. I was glad to hear from her, but sad as well. She had been through a lot.

Kaye was the granddaughter of a Southern Baptist preacher. She was raised in a Southern Baptist church and she had raised her own children in a Southern Baptist church. She had spent her whole life working and volunteering in Southern Baptist churches.

All of that was yanked out from under her when she reported sexual harassment and sexual abuse by ministerial staff at the Oviedo mega-church.

Week after week, Kaye had watched while Dunagan brought new young mothers into his office to "counsel" them with the blinds shut, the door locked, and instructions that he was not to be disturbed. She felt uncomfortable but didn't know what to do.

As time went on, Kaye found that she herself was subjected to lewd jokes and lewd conduct.

The lurid details that she spilled forth described a church office with a sick environment. One of the two ministers involved was Eddie Dunagan.

Kaye tried to talk about it, but others simply ignored her or laughed at her.

Eventually, Kaye recounted that the sexual harassment escalated to sexual groping by the other minister. She was shocked and confused that he would put his hands on her. But there was no mistaking what he had done.

That's when Kaye overcame the fear of losing her job and directly reported the conduct to other ministers in the church. She expected them to say it was wrong and wouldn't be tolerated. She thought they might offer counseling for the minister who groped her so that he would grow to understand how wrong his conduct was.

But that isn't what happened. Kaye was effectively put on trial and forced to sit at a table and lay out her grievances with her abuser and other ministers.[59] She was the only woman in the room.

The abusive minister said nothing ever happened. Kaye was asked to give two weeks' notice, and she was told not to repeat her accusations to anyone else.

Later Kaye's husband was asked how many times his wife had lied. And he was told not to talk about it either. Kaye was called "divisive," and they fired her before the two weeks were even up.

The minister she reported for abuse stayed on the church's staff. And Eddie Dunagan stayed too.

Kaye and her husband left the congregation where they had been members for more than 12 years.

She went to a lawyer who talked about what a powerful church it was and said they would "crucify" her if she tried to do anything.

Kaye went home and closed her blinds. She couldn't bear to see people. Mostly, she just stayed inside her home for a long time after that.

59. Bob Allen, "SBC president questions motives of SNAP, says sex abuse everywhere," *EthicsDaily*, May 2, 2007.

36

The Court-ordered Mediation

I had requested that the pastor *not* attend the court-ordered mediation as one of the church's representatives. But there he was again, this man who himself had been reported for sexual abuse.

I had requested that music minister Jim Moore be present for the mediation, because I still had some questions I wanted to ask him. But Moore was *not* there.

As soon as I walked into the room, I felt as though the church had told me all I needed to know about how little it cared. The person I wanted to be there wasn't, and the person I didn't want to be there was. Why had their attorney even bothered to ask about my preferences?

Involuntarily, my hand moved to my chest where I felt the cross necklace beneath my blouse. I suppose it amounted to little more than an amulet for me, but I had thought of it that morning and decided to dig it out and put it on. It was a necklace I hadn't worn in more than 30 years.

We started out all sitting in the same room together, and I told them flat-out that I wouldn't let go of this until they gave me a written apology. I knew it seemed silly, and I told them so. But it was what I had wanted from the beginning and it was what they should have done from the beginning, and I intended to make them do it.

By that time, it was nothing more than the principle of the thing.

"Any apology you make can no longer hold any meaning for me," I told them. "But I'm insisting on it anyway because I hope that it may somehow hold meaning for others."

I looked at their faces. I tried to speak slowly. I tried to see if any tiny bit of anything registered with them. Did they care? Or did they just want to be rid of me?

The answer was obvious. It had always been obvious. I just hadn't wanted to see it. The church of my childhood didn't give a shit. They just wanted me to shut up and go away.

Nineteen months had passed since I gave the church my written report about Dunagan's abuse. And I had tried to get help from music minister Jim Moore several months before that. Almost two years had gone by. I wasn't the same person anymore.

I had drafted several different apology letters. It started with the one my therapist asked me to draft. She knew how badly I wanted an apology from the church, and so she asked me to write down what I thought church leaders should say.

What I wrote was pretty simple. It was what you might imagine ordinary, decent people would say. My therapist read it back to me out loud. I cried and cried.

They were words I wanted so badly to hear. "We're so very sorry, Christa, for what our prior minister did to you when you were a church girl here."

Feeling how much it affected me to hear the words out loud only made me realize how much I wanted them. But of course, I wanted them from the right source.

I drafted several other versions of an apology, and even sent a couple off to the church's attorney, hoping he would relay them to the church leaders as an option. I would have preferred that they take the initiative on their own to make an apology. But since they couldn't seem to figure out how to do that, I thought I'd try to nudge them and show them in print the words they needed to say. Of course, they wouldn't. Looking back, I can't imagine how I ever held such optimism.

The church offered some abstract, non-specific language. It wasn't what any normal person would call an apology. And it certainly didn't have any ring of authenticity. They ended by urging that I should find it within myself "to forgive those within the congregation whom you feel did not measure up. . . ."

I wasn't willing to accept that. So here we were, at a formal, court-ordered mediation session, haggling over the words of an apology. We haggled for hours, with the mediator going back and forth between our separate rooms, carrying proposals and revisions.

I was determined to fight for every word. I didn't care about their money. I wanted signed words on paper.

Finally, at the end of the day, the mediator brought in an apology letter that had some decent language in it.[60]

---

60. Apology letter of First Baptist Church of Farmers Branch, dated January 18, 2006, attached as exhibit to Plaintiff's Motion to Dismiss in Cause No. DV05-05669-M in the 298th Judicial District, Dallas County, Texas, C. Brown v. First Baptist Church of Farmers Branch.

I express to you this church's most profound regret for the very serious sexual abuse that . . . our prior youth and education minister, Eddie Dunagan, inflicted on you when you were a girl in the church youth group. We are very sorry for the harm and suffering that this caused in your life. We know this apology cannot even begin to undo that harm or give back all that was stolen from you. . . .

We are sorry for the fact that, though informed, in a general way, of Dunagan's conduct, a church leader in 1969 did not realize the seriousness of what had occurred or its effects on you. . . .

A church leader who was also here during Dunagan's tenure was able to substantiate that sexual contact with Brown as a minor occurred in 1969. Our response, while probably not unusual among churches, was inadequate and less than compassionate. . . .

We know that your road to healing has been made more difficult because you yourself, as the victim, had to take on the burden of trying to educate us. We hope that by providing you this apology, some other church may wind up being better educated, with the result that some other victim may be spared some of the anguish that you have gone through. . . . We wish we had responded better. . . . We hope denominational leaders will consider the need for a means by which autonomous congregations may responsibly share information about clergy predators. We also pray that you may find peace and comfort from the sincerity of our efforts.

For those typed and signed words of apology – words that should have been said long ago – I agreed to settle my lawsuit. The official, court-filed settlement agreement required that the church send certified copies of the apology letter to the other churches where Dunagan worked and that it pay me some money for counseling.[61] I also insisted on an express provision making clear that there was no restriction on my ability to speak about all that had happened.[62]

At that point, I didn't have any plans of ever speaking publicly. In fact, I was still actively trying to guard my privacy by insisting that every court document refer to me only as "C. Brown." But the one thing I knew for sure was that I wanted to be in control of whatever I might choose to do and that I wasn't going to let that church intimidate me into silence ever again.

In addition to the church's admissions in the apology letter, the settlement agreement itself included as a material term the church's express acknowledgment that, during the time I was a kid in the church youth group, the music minister had obtained "general knowledge about Dunagan's sexual contact with Brown as a minor."[63]

Of course, the church leaders were the ones who insisted on saying that the music minister had only "general" knowledge, and I couldn't help but marvel at their ongoing self-delusional ignorance. They seemed to think the word "general" was exculpatory. I thought the very fact that they insisted on it showed their continuing complicit blindness.

On the one hand, they acknowledged that a church leader knew about Dunagan's "sexual contact" with me as a kid. On the other hand, they repeatedly insisted that he only knew about it "in a general way" and that he "did not realize the seriousness" of it.

It was lunacy. How could someone not realize "the seriousness" of a grown, adult minister's "sexual contact" with a kid? By its very nature, it's a serious thing. It's impossible for it not to be. Yet, even the current church leaders *still* seemed to think that knowledge of a minister's

---

61. Compromise settlement agreement, attached as exhibit to Plaintiff's Motion to Dismiss in Cause No. DV05-05669-M in the 298th Judicial District, Dallas County, Texas, C. Brown v. First Baptist Church of Farmers Branch. Under the terms of the agreement, the church did *not* deny wrongdoing but merely denied "legal liability" for the harm.
62. Compromise settlement agreement, *supra*, at ¶ 10.
63. Compromise settlement agreement, *supra*, at ¶ 16.

"sexual contact" with a kid could be minimized by describing it as mere "general" knowledge.[64]

I wondered exactly what sort of "sexual contact" they were imagining might be okay for an adult minister to engage in with an underage church girl. Exactly what sort of "sexual contact" did they imagine might *not* be something serious?

They were obviously stuck on their same old self-serving "we didn't know details" excuse, as if knowledge of a minister's sexual contact with a kid should require "details" – and as if not knowing the "details" could somehow excuse their do-nothing complacency.

The music minister knew enough. He knew enough all those years ago when I was a kid; and he knew enough in the here and now. There was no legitimate excuse for his blind-eyed do-nothingness. Yet, even now, the church was still trying to contrive an excuse rather than fully owning up to the horror of their music minister's mistake.

The church's signed apology letter was handed off from their attorney to mine, and then filed with the court. Neither Jim Moore nor any other church leader ever even had the decency to look me in the face and say "We're so sorry."

---

64. Months later, despite having signed the settlement agreement saying the church's music minister had knowledge of Dunagan's "sexual contact with Brown as a minor," the church's attorney (who was also attorney for the Baptist General Convention of Texas) downplayed that knowledge by publicly stating that the minister had only "limited information." *Spiritual Samurai blog*, May 26, 2007, comment posted June 1, 2007 at 2:03 p.m. Perhaps it's not surprising that Baptist churches handle clergy sex abuse reports so abysmally when the long-time attorney for the largest statewide Baptist organization in the country so minimizes knowledge about a minister's "sexual contact" with a minor as to call it mere "limited information."

Part Four

An Activist

Throw away the lights, the definitions,
And say of what you see in the dark . . .

That it is this or that it is that,
But do not use the rotted names.

WALLACE STEVENS,
"The Man with the Blue Guitar"

37

The Curse of Knowledge

Perhaps I should have felt victorious, but I felt cursed.

I had made the church leaders do what they didn't want to do. I had made them apologize. But so what?

I had made them own up to the fact that their music minister knew about Dunagan's abuse of me as a kid. But so what?

I had made them send a certified copy of the apology letter to every church where Dunagan worked. But so what?

Would people in the pews ever find out? I figured the answer to that question was "No."

First Baptist Church of Farmers Branch would send a copy of the apology letter to the chairman of the deacons at each church where Dunagan worked. And at each church, the chairman of the deacons would probably sit on it. It would stay a secret. Parents in the pews wouldn't find out, and so they wouldn't be able to talk to their kids about Dunagan.

I felt sick. So much effort and so little gained.

When I thought of all that it had taken to get the church that knew about the abuse to even send a letter to other churches, I knew that most of the time, it would never happen. There was no way that most abuse survivors could possibly put themselves through so much for the simple sake of trying to get one Baptist church to inform other Baptist churches about a clergy-predator.

Most survivors wouldn't be able to jump through so many hoops. They wouldn't be able to afford it. They wouldn't be able to sustain the emotional energy. They wouldn't be able to psychologically bear up. They wouldn't be able to take so much time away from their jobs. They wouldn't be able to take so much time away from their families.

It was a system that virtually assured that most clergy abuse survivors would NOT be able to successfully inform people about their perpetrators. It was a system that made Baptist churches a perfect paradise for predators.

Over and over again, I read the final words of the church's apology letter:

> We hope denominational leaders will consider the need for a means by which autonomous congregations may responsibly share information about clergy predators. We also pray that you may find peace and comfort from the sincerity of our efforts.

The first sentence was one I had drafted. I wanted the church on record as recognizing that denominational leaders needed to help churches with sharing information about clergy predators. The second sentence was one the church threw in. I suppose it made them feel good to say that they would pray for me. I saw it as just more phony baloney.

After all, what "efforts" were they actually going to undertake? Were they going to take on the burden of pushing denominational leaders to do something about clergy predators?

No. Those were just words on paper, and I knew it.

They just wanted to say they were praying for me because that's what good church people say. But even if they prayed from now to kingdom come, how should I find peace from the "sincerity" of their "efforts" if their "efforts" are non-existent?

The reality was that the church leaders would go right back to their comfortable little status quo. I knew that. There would be no "efforts" on their part. If any "efforts" were going to be made, they would have to be my own efforts. The church wasn't going to do diddly-squat.

The more I thought about it, the more depressed I got. If the church had really felt any remorse, it would have taken upon its own shoulders the task of working for change within the denomination. But that wasn't going to happen. The weight was still on my own shoulders.

Not long after that, an old friend called to congratulate me. She had seen the TV news coverage about the settlement of my lawsuit. Looking up at her TV, she had seen the photo of my 16-year-old self along with the photo of Dunagan.

"Christa, you educated them. You taught them. They won't make the same mistake again, that's for sure."

Her words were like a knife in my chest. Hearing them spoken out loud was physically painful. They made a dull, hollow thud of a sound, and the dissonance of it resonated throughout my whole body. It hurt.

"No, I didn't educate them," I said quietly. "They'll do the exact same thing to the next person. Nothing has changed."

I hated hearing myself say it. This was something I hadn't wanted to admit. I wanted to believe I had accomplished something. I wanted to put all of this back in its box and be done with it. But now, here I was saying out loud what I knew to be true – nothing had changed.

We continued to talk for a while, and she insisted I was wrong.

"You can't allow yourself to think that way," she told me. "These people made a terrible mistake, but they just didn't know any better. You've shown them their mistake. And now you've got to let it go."

I listened politely but ended the conversation as soon as I could. It hurt too much. I curled up on my bed and cried.

I hadn't educated anyone, and I couldn't engage enough denial to let myself believe that I had. It wouldn't be true.

If I could have, I would have lobotomized that part of my brain. So desperately did I want to be done with all this that I would have done almost anything to not know what I knew.

I cursed God. I cursed myself. But I couldn't alter reality.

Now that I had heard my own voice say the words out loud, I couldn't fool myself. Nothing had changed. Baptist leaders would treat the next person just the same as they had treated me.

Their hardline do-nothing tactics had always worked for them. They had kept clergy sex abuse and cover-ups under the radar. I was just a tiny little glitch.

38

Reliving It with Debbie

I am embarrassed to admit how impatient I often felt with Debbie. I tried hard not to show it.

Debbie couldn't let go of believing that the Baptist General Convention of Texas would want to help her. She tried and tried to communicate with people there, but they wouldn't listen. She tried and tried to tell them about her perpetrator who was still in the pulpit, but they wouldn't do anything.

Debbie kept thinking that, if she just tried harder, or if she just reached the right person, or if she just spoke more clearly, they would understand and they would do something. She kept blaming herself for not finding the right words and for not being able to explain things to them. It drove me nuts. I saw too much of my own former self in Debbie.

Watching how things unfolded with Debbie was like watching my own history re-enacted. The Baptist General Convention of Texas was just as big on talk and short on action as it had always been. People there weren't any better educated than before, and they still wouldn't do anything to help someone like Debbie. They were still more focused on protecting themselves than protecting kids. Nothing had changed.

As a teen church girl, Debbie was abused by Richard "Dickie" Arnold, who was nearly twice her age.[65] When she became pregnant with his child, Debbie was made to go before the church and ask the congregation's forgiveness for being a pregnant, unwed teen. But she was instructed not to tell who the father was.[66] "It would hurt the church," they said.

---

65. Hannah Elliott, "Sex-abuse victims speak up to help others & find healing themselves," *Associated Baptist Press*, June 8, 2007.

66. Rose French (Associated Press), "Baptists asked to crack down on abusers," *New York Times*, February 21, 2007 (also available at http://www.msnbc.msn.com/id/17265721/); Elizabeth Ulrich, "What would Jesus say?" *Nashville Scene*, February 14, 2008; Marci A. Hamilton, *Justice Denied*, at pp. 70–71 (Cambridge University Press 2008); Hannah Elliott, "Sex-abuse victims speak up to help others & find healing themselves," *Associated Baptist Press*, June 8, 2007.

So Debbie did as she was instructed. She kept quiet. And Arnold went to pastor a church in Arizona. Several years later, he moved back to Texas, where he became pastor of a Southern Baptist church in Denton County.

Debbie was a single mom who struggled to support her daughter. Though she desperately needed help, Arnold didn't provide for the child until Debbie finally got a paternity judgment against him.[67] Her daughter was eight by then.

Years later, in 2003, Arnold started telling Debbie about his "friend-ships" with some high school girls who talked about "sexual exploits."[68] It was then that Debbie began worrying that Arnold might be abusing other girls. Suddenly Debbie realized that she might not be the only one.

She went to the police, but they couldn't do anything.[69] The statute of limitations had run, they said. They set Debbie up with a tape recorder and encouraged her to talk to Arnold and to try to get the name of one of the girls he had recently bragged about.

Debbie did that, and in the recorded conversation, Arnold talked about how one of the girls was "in love with him." Debbie expressed concern and said she wanted to talk to the girl to put her mind at ease. Arnold denied any sort of involvement, and he wouldn't give Debbie the girl's name.

Then he said something that made Debbie all the more uneasy: "If something happens between me and these kids, I doubt she would be telling anybody."[70]

Debbie couldn't live with that. She was haunted by Arnold's words and by her fear that he was abusing some other girl. With the weight of worry, fear and memories closing in on her, Debbie became suicidal.[71]

She talked to a Southern Baptist minister at her current church. But he told her to "leave it in God's hands."[72]

---

67. Cause No. 324-104507 in the 324th Judicial District, Tarrant County, Texas, Default Judgment Establishing Paternity, November 4, 1987; *see also* Bob Allen, Baptist clergy sex-abuse case settled out of court, *EthicsDaily*, June 10, 2008.

68. Elizabeth Ulrich, "What would Jesus say?" *Nashville Scene*, February 14, 2008.

69. Donna Fielder, "Pastor, accuser settle out of court," *Denton Record-Chronicle*, June 8, 2008.

70. Elizabeth Ulrich, "What would Jesus say?" *Nashville Scene*, February 14, 2008.

71. Elizabeth Ulrich, "What would Jesus say?" *supra*.

72. *See also* Elizabeth Ulrich, "What would Jesus say?" *supra*.

She talked to another Baptist minister, and he told her "to let the past be in the past."

"But it's not in the past," thought Debbie. "How can it be in the past when he's still in the pulpit and could still hurt others?"

About that time was when Debbie saw the TV news coverage about the settlement of my lawsuit and about the fact that the name of my perpetrator was in a confidential file at the Baptist General Convention of Texas.[73] It was the first time Debbie had ever heard about such a file, and suddenly she thought that the Texas Baptist convention's file might be a way to warn people about Arnold.

Seeing the news coverage on my case made Debbie decide to try talking to people at the Baptist General Convention of Texas.[74] She would tell them about the paternity judgment and the tape recording and surely they would do something, she thought. They would want to make sure others were protected. "How could they not?" she thought.

So Debbie wrote to the Baptist General Convention of Texas, telling them about pastor Dickie Arnold and what he had done to her. She also told them how worried she was that Arnold might hurt someone else.

In response to her pain and concern, Debbie got back a perfunctory note from Sonny Spurger, telling her that "every Baptist church is an autonomous body."[75]

Debbie couldn't believe that he wouldn't actually do anything. She thought that maybe he hadn't understood. So she wrote to Sonny Spurger a second time.[76] This time, Debbie didn't even hear back from Spurger. That really hurt her.

Debbie didn't know what else to do. With enormous reluctance, and after weighing it back and forth for a couple months, she finally contacted a lawyer. Then, after waiting still longer, she finally asked her attorney to file a lawsuit against the church and pastor Dickie Arnold.

73. FOX 4 News at Nine, KDFW-TV Channel 4, Dallas, February 20, 2006 ("The Baptist General Convention of Texas acknowledges it keeps a confidential file of preachers reported for sexual abuse."); WFAA-TV News 8 Midday (ABC) Dallas, February 20, 2006; KTVT-TV Channel 11 (CBS) Dallas, 4 PM, February 20, 2006; John Hall, "Victims urge BGCT to release list," *Baptist Standard*, March 3, 2006.
74. Eileen Flynn, "Austin lawyer pushes Baptist churches to confront sexual abuse," *Austin American-Statesman*, June 9, 2008.
75. Email correspondence from Sonny Spurger, Associate Director, Baptist General Convention of Texas, to Debbie, dated February 24, 2006.
76. Email correspondence from Debbie to Sonny Spurger, dated February 24, 2006.

She didn't want to, and she resisted the very idea of it. But finally, a lawsuit seemed like the only way to get anyone to pay attention.

In his deposition, pastor Arnold admitted to having sex with Debbie between 20 to 40 times. "I hated it that it happened," said Arnold. "I told her many times that I never meant to hurt her, and if I did, I'm sorry."[77]

But then Arnold made this assertion: "I didn't have sex with her when she was 16 or under."[78]

When Debbie was a kid, the age of consent in Texas had been dropped from 18 to 17. So Arnold was defending himself by claiming that Debbie was at the age of consent.[79]

Arnold's deposition testimony was stomach-churning. It seemed as though, in his mind, it didn't matter that he was a minister. It was as though he knew that, if he just claimed to have waited till her 17th birthday for intercourse, then he could simply thumb his nose. There would be no consequences.

And Arnold was right. He faced no consequences.

Of course, I didn't believe Arnold for one second. In Debbie's sworn deposition, she said that the abuse began when she was 14 and that Arnold first raped her when she was 15.

Debbie's deposition wasn't something that any sexual abuse survivor should have to go through. Under hostile questioning, she agonizingly relived the trauma, piece by piece, recounting the details to a room of strangers.[80] Debbie went through it because she kept telling herself that it might be a way to make other girls safer. She kept telling herself that, when it was all put into sworn testimony, and when the people at the Baptist General Convention of Texas saw the things Arnold said, they would surely do something. After all, Arnold had admitted to having sex with her and she had a paternity judgment against him. Court records also showed that Arnold had an earlier conviction for giving alcohol to a minor.[81]

---

77. Donna Fielder, "Suits allege clergy misconduct: Two Baptist ministers apologize after women bring forth accusations," *Denton Record-Chronicle*, December 17, 2006.
78. Donna Fielder, "Suits allege clergy misconduct," *supra*.
79. *See* Bob Allen, Baptist clergy sex-abuse case settled out of court, *EthicsDaily*, June 10, 2008.
80. Elizabeth Ulrich, "What would Jesus say?" *Nashville Scene*, February 14, 2008.
81. Hannah Elliott, "Sex-abuse victims speak up to help others & find healing themselves," *Associated Baptist Press*, June 8, 2007.

Debbie's thought process was reasonable. Most of the other major faith groups in this country now have review boards to assess the credibility of clergy abuse accusations.[82] They've realized what law enforcement professionals also know – that most child molestation cases can never be criminally prosecuted because of short statutes of limitation and because the nature of the psychological damage keeps the victims quiet for so long.[83] So Debbie thought that Baptists would surely come around to doing what other major faith groups do if only she showed them enough evidence.

Debbie was wrong about that. But she just couldn't let go of her basic belief in Baptist leaders.

Sixteen months after she had first written to Sonny Spurger, she wrote to the Baptist General Convention of Texas yet again. "I was raped by a Baptist minister," she began. Then she proceeded to tell them how hurt she was that no one had helped her the first time she contacted them. But she begged them, once again, to help her with trying to protect other kids. He's "still a minister at a Baptist church," she pointed out. "Please, more needs to be done."[84]

This time, Baptist official Emily Prevost wrote a note back, explaining to Debbie that the Baptist General Convention of Texas receives clergy abuse reports only from churches and not directly from victims. Prevost suggested that Debbie take her information to the church.[85]

Debbie couldn't believe it. She sounded nearly hysterical when she called me.

"How can they imagine that I could just take this to the church? He's their pastor! They trust him! That's the whole point! Someone else has to look at it. Why don't they get that? Why don't they understand?"

There's nothing I can say that will comfort Debbie. I've seen this coming from the get-go.

---

82. Heather Hahn, "Southern Baptists rule out sex-offender list," *Arkansas Democrat-Gazette*, June 11, 2008; Greg Warner, "Betrayed trust: the recycle of abuse continues at Baptist churches," *Associated Baptist Press*, June 11, 2007.

83. Marci A. Hamilton, *Justice Denied*, at pp. 2–3, 18–19 (Cambridge University Press 2008); "National District Attorneys Association endorses statute of limitations reform in childhood sexual abuse cases," National Association to Prevent Sexual Abuse of Children, August 2, 2007 (NDAA resolution adopted July 29, 2007).

84. Email letter of June 6, 2007 from Debbie to Emily Prevost of the Baptist General Convention of Texas.

85. Email letter of June 7, 2007 from Emily Prevost of the Baptist General Convention of Texas to Debbie.

Despite all their nice words, the Baptist General Convention of Texas won't do diddly-squat. Their nice words are just a front. I know that by now, but despite everything she's been through, Debbie's still struggling to come to grips with it.

"How can they not be worried after all that I've told them? Don't they care? What good does it do for Emily Prevost to tell me she's sorry I've suffered if she won't do anything to prevent someone else from suffering?"

This is how it is with Debbie. She worries endlessly about the suffering of others. But as I keep listening to her, what makes me the angriest is that Debbie herself has suffered so much. She can't afford to pay for good professional counseling, and no one in Baptist circles is going to provide her with any. Debbie loves her church and loves her faith. She can quote Bible verses with the best of them. But where is her faith community now?

This is the thing that drives me the nuttiest. As far back as 1990, the Baptist General Convention of Texas began providing a "two-year restoration program" of counseling for ministers who committed sexual abuse.[86] It was designed to "restore" them to volunteer ministry within six months and to paid ministry within one year. It even provided counseling for the ministers' spouses. In about mid-2007, they quit calling it a "restoration" program,[87] but they still provide the ministers with a counseling referral network and financial assistance to pay for the counseling.[88]

None of this makes sense to me. Why is there so much readily available help for the abusive ministers, but so little of nothing for the abuse survivors? Maybe Baptist leaders are afraid that, if clergy abuse survivors get therapy, they'll become more inclined to talk. Maybe it's just one more way for Baptist leaders to try to keep things quiet about clergy sex abuse.

If that was what they thought, Debbie proved to be an exception. Even without therapy, she wouldn't keep quiet. She not only wrote to

---

86. Ken Camp, "Stepping over the line: Should sexually straying clergy be restored to ministry? *The Baptist Standard*, June 18, 2007; Christian Life Commission of the Baptist General Convention of Texas, *Broken Trust: Confronting Clergy Sexual Misconduct,* at p. 36 (circa 2000).

87. Ken Camp, "Stepping over the line: Should sexually straying clergy be restored to ministry?" *The Baptist Standard*, June 18, 2007.

88. John Hall, "BGCT offers psychological services," Baptist General Convention of Texas news release 8/13/08; [http://www.bgct.org/texasbaptists/Page.aspx?pid=5391&srcid=178].

Baptist officials in Texas, but also to Baptist officials at national headquarters in Nashville. But despite her many letters, no one ever offered to help her, to counsel her, or to refer her to a therapist.[89]

Ultimately, Debbie settled her lawsuit for $22,500.00.[90] Most of the money went to her attorney and court costs. Debbie herself got a total of $9,659.38. It was typical.

For that small amount of money, Debbie was dragged through two-years of hell in her effort to expose pastor Dickie Arnold and protect others. And in reality, Debbie was luckier than lots of other Baptist clergy abuse survivors. At least she was able to get a lawyer.

Lots of Baptist abuse survivors tell me they can't even find a lawyer who will take their case. It's because there's more to bringing a lawsuit than having a claim. A lawyer needs to be able to size up the case on the front end and believe it will be cost-efficient. That's often hard to do in a Baptist clergy abuse case.

In most states, by the time child sex abuse victims grow up and become psychologically able to talk about it, the time period for filing even a civil lawsuit has already passed.[91] Many victims *never* disclose their abuse, and when they do, it is often decades later.[92] This time lag, caused by the psychological damage of the abuse itself, creates an often insurmountable legal hurdle at the very start.[93]

Lawyers considering Baptist abuse cases face still more hurdles. They confront the Southern Baptist Convention's "Teflon tendency" in court.[94] It's because, in the autonomous system of Baptist churches, the buck

89. Elizabeth Ulrich, "What would Jesus say?" *Nashville Scene*, February 14, 2008.

90. Donna Fielder, "Pastor, accuser settle out of court," *Denton Record-Chronicle*, June 8, 2008.

91. Marci A. Hamilton, *Justice Denied*, at pp. 2–3, 18–19 (Cambridge University Press 2008); "National District Attorneys Association endorses statute of limitations reform in childhood sexual abuse cases," National Association to Prevent Sexual Abuse of Children, August 2, 2007 (NDAA resolution adopted July 29, 2007).

92. One expert reports that the average age of a sexual abuse victim is 12 and the average age at the time of disclosure is 42. Mark Sauer, "Waiting decades to break the silence," *Union Tribune*, June 3, 2007 (citing A.W. Richard Sipe).

93. Marci A. Hamilton, *Justice Denied*, at pp. 2–3, 18 (Cambridge University Press 2008)(Statutes of limitation . . . "are exerting a cruel force throughout our society . . . they are set to favor the child predator and shut out the sexual abuse survivor.").

94. Elizabeth Ulrich, "The Bad Shepherd," *The Nashville Scene*, April 24, 2008.

stops nowhere.[95] By contrast, with Catholic cases, there's a clear line of responsibility allowing for "relative ease of litigation against Catholic dioceses."[96]

One expert has observed that this "ease of litigation" is what has created the public misperception that clergy abuse is "a Catholic problem," when in fact, it's just as big a problem for other faith groups.[97] But because there are more lawsuits and bigger lawsuits against Catholic dioceses, there is also more media exposure.

Not only does the "clear line of responsibility" make Catholic cases easier, but lawyers can also gain cost-efficiencies in Catholic cases when they have groups of victims from the same diocese. With only 194 Catholic dioceses in the country, that sort of clustering happens frequently. By contrast, Southern Baptists have more than 42,000 churches in the country, and so clustering is far less likely. For media purposes, every case winds up looking like an isolated incident.

Baptist cases can face still more hurdles that help to insulate the denomination from scrutiny. While most Catholic dioceses endure virtually forever, Baptist churches have no trouble in dissolving,[98] reorganizing and renaming themselves.[99] In fact, the church in which Debbie was first abused had dissolved. This too can make Baptist cases more difficult. And unlike with other faith groups, there's no Baptist policy of even

---

95. Terry Mattingly, "Sex scandals in free-church pews," *GetReligion.org*, May 18, 2008 [http://www.getreligion.org/?p=3512].

96. Philip Jenkins, *Pedophiles and Priests*, at p. 51 (Oxford University Press 1996).

97. Philip Jenkins, *supra* at p. 51–52.

98. During the time-period when Debbie was abused as a child, minister "Richard 'Dickie' Arnold" was at Calvary Baptist, a now-defunct church in Lewisville, Texas. *See* Elizabeth Ulrich, "What would Jesus say?" *Nashville Scene*, February 14, 2008.

99. For example, Walnut Grove Baptist Church in Cordova, Tennessee, renamed itself to Gracepoint Baptist after its long-time pastor was indicted on charges of child molestation and child pornography. Splashed in the news was also the fact that the same pastor had been accused of molesting another boy a decade earlier, and although 30 families left the church at that time, the pastor remained. Lindsay Melvin, "Gracepoint Baptist's pastor sparks church's revival," *Memphis Commercial Appeal*, May 19, 2008; Lawrence Buser, "Federal grand jury indicts former pastor on child pornography charges," *Memphis Commercial Appeal*, October 16, 2007; Lawrence Buser, "Young victim: former pastor said sex was 'a test of faith'," *Memphis Commercial Appeal*, August 30, 2007; Bob Allen, "Alleged victim says former pastor told him sex was test of faith," *EthicsDaily*, September 20, 2007; Jason Miles, "Former church member speaks out about accused pastor," *WMC-TV Memphis*, July 20, 2007.

providing a bare-bones counseling stipend for clergy abuse victims.[100] With all of these realities in mind, many lawyers reject Baptist abuse cases because they can't justify the financial cost to themselves or the emotional cost to the client.

Debbie never had any negotiating power in her lawsuit, because of the difficulty with a Baptist line of responsibility and because the Texas statute of limitations is too short.[101] But her lawsuit at least provided a vehicle for getting some media attention, and often, it's the media attention that will finally nudge a church to let go of an abusive pastor. Unfortunately, in Debbie's case, even the media attention didn't wind up making much difference.

Pastor Dickie Arnold remained a Southern Baptist minister.[102] He has not faced any sanction, and the Southern Baptist Convention is "seemingly content to sit on the knowledge that . . . a minister who admitted to having sex with a teenager is prepping next week's sermon."[103]

---

100. Greg Warner, "Betrayed trust: the recycle of abuse continues at Baptist churches," *Associated Baptist Press*, June 11, 2007 (stating policy of Catholic dioceses to provide care for the victims).

101. Elizabeth Ulrich, "What would Jesus say?" *Nashville Scene*, February 14, 2008 (stating that Debbie's lawsuit was "over because of the statute of limitations").

102. As recently as the 2008 SBC Annual, which was released late in the year, "Dickie Arnold" (under his real name) was listed as a "Senior Pastor." He is also listed in the online directories of the Baptist General Convention of Texas and the Denton Baptist Association. (Sites were last accessed on November 7, 2008.). *See also* Donna Fielder, "Pastor, accuser settle out of court," *Denton Record-Chronicle*, June 8, 2008 (stating that he "continues to be paid as a pastor"); Elizabeth Ulrich, "The Bad Shepherd," *Nashville Scene*, April 24, 2008 (stating that he "remains in the pulpit").

103. Elizabeth Ulrich, "Save yourselves," *Nashville Scene*, June 19, 2008.

39

Seeking Clergy Accountability

The temperature was in the mid-90s. The humidity was high. A block from the Alamo, ten of us were handing out flyers on the plaza at the San Antonio Convention Center during the 2007 annual meeting of the Southern Baptist Convention. We were inviting the "messengers" – delegates from all over the country – to a prayer vigil for clergy abuse victims. We were also urging them to support a motion for studying the creation of a denominational database of ministers who had been credibly accused of sexual abuse.

I was drenched and dripping. Another SNAP member was already sitting under a tree, depleted by the sun.

Those trees in the plaza were precious that day. As we tried to extend a flyer to everyone who passed, we also tried to stay in the shade as much as we could.

Two street cops had passed by and said "no problem" to us being on the plaza, but before long, a non-uniformed guy showed up. He told us we had to get off the plaza and move to the sidewalk.

There was no shade on the sidewalk.

One of the men from the San Antonio SNAP group insisted on seeing the guy's badge. He had one. I asked him why we couldn't stand in what was clearly a wide-open public-access area, and he explained that the Southern Baptist Convention had rented the entire convention center and that included the entrance plaza area. So they were entitled to have us removed from the premises, he said.

I couldn't believe it. It seemed so small-minded and mean-spirited.

You might imagine that good Christians would have been sending out water bottles to a group of childhood molestation victims who were leafletting about a prayer vigil. But no . . . . Southern Baptist officials chose to push us from the shade into the sun. And it was a very, very hot day.

A TV camera crew saw what was happening and stuck around. I was grateful. Three men in suits stood about 30 yards away, watching us from the shade of the convention center's awning. I recognized one of them, and I couldn't help but wonder whether those Southern Baptist men would have had us handcuffed and hauled away in a paddy wagon if the camera crew hadn't been there.

Sensing the measure of safety that the camera crew provided, our compliance was half-hearted. Though we moved further toward the sidewalk, and even spent a bit of time actually on the sidewalk, we also continued to move in and out of the plaza's shady patches as much as we could. The men in suits watched, but they weren't foolish enough to have us arrested in front of cameras. They went back into the air-conditioning.

We handed out over 2000 flyers. I was so proud of our effort, and I thought about all the steps that had brought us to that place.

My own coming-out was in a guest column for the *Dallas Morning News* in April 2006.[104] That was the first time I publicly identified myself as a Baptist clergy abuse survivor. My column was about the confidential file of clergy predators that's kept at the Baptist General Convention of Texas. They've repeatedly admitted that their file includes ministers reported by churches for child molestation, but they don't tell people in the pews who those men are.[105] That's how Dunagan was able to go right on working in Florida even though his name sat in that file in Texas.

When I wrote the column, there was a part of me that thought it would close the door on all this. So I was thrilled when the newspaper told me they were going to run it. I imagined that, if I could just say what I wanted to say, and get it published in the newspaper, I might be able to put all this behind me. I thought I might be able to shove all the ugly stuff back into its box, nice and tidy, and then I would hoist it back up to that dark corner in my brain. And I wouldn't have to think about any of it anymore.

Things didn't turn out that way. At the bottom of my column, the *Dallas Morning News* printed my StopBaptistPredators email address. Within days, I had heard from others with stories much like my own. They had been sexually abused by Baptist ministers. They had tried to report it to the Baptist General Convention of Texas and to others. They were stonewalled. They got no help. No one would do anything.

Now I knew that what I had suspected was indeed true. My story

---

104. Christa Brown, "No more church secrets about sex abuse," *Dallas Morning News*, 23A, April 28, 2006.

105. John Hall, "Victims urge BGCT to release list," *Baptist Standard*, March 3, 2006; Donna Fielder, "Victims' group calls for Baptist convention's list of offenders," *Dallas Morning News*, December 17, 2006.

wasn't anything unusual. Lots of other people had similar stories, and no one in the denomination was listening to them.

Not long after that, the Southern Baptist Convention elected a new president, Frank Page. He was widely praised as being a less fundamentalist Baptist leader and a man of irenic temperament. So I decided to get SNAP's leadership on board with sending him a letter.

In drafting the letter, I thought long and hard about how Southern Baptists might be able to systematically address clergy sex abuse. I had a pretty good notion about what they would claim they *couldn't* do, and so I tried to focus on what they *could* do.

I knew, for example, that denominational leaders would say they had no power to hire and fire ministers. But I figured that, no matter what, denominational leadership could at least provide churches with expertise and information. After all, Southern Baptist churches may be autonomous, but on Sunday morning, all those autonomous churches all across the nation are all autonomously teaching the exact same Sunday School lesson sent to them from national headquarters in Nashville.[106] So I figured that, if churches could get Sunday School lessons from Nashville, they ought to also be able to get information about credibly-accused clergy child molesters.

Other faith groups now have review boards to assess clergy abuse reports. In fact, that's how most clergy wind up being removed from ministry. They lose their jobs, not because they're criminally convicted of abuse, but because a denominational review process concludes that they should no longer be allowed to work in a position of high trust as a minister.

Southern Baptists don't have such a review process. They don't have an oversight system for their ministers.[107] So I figured that was what they needed most. Even if Southern Baptist leaders couldn't actually fire ministers, like leaders in other faith groups, I figured they could at least provide professional assessments of abuse reports and relay that information to people in the pews.

---

106. Susan M. Shaw, *God Speaks to Us, Too*, at p. 26 (University of Kentucky Press 2008).

107. One writer listed these "factors that make Baptist churches a breeding ground for clergy sex abuse: a trusted ministerial position, a winsome authority figure, an inadequate background check, church members who want to believe the best, a church's fear of embarrassment and liability, a tradition of autonomy, no denominational certification or safeguard, and no clearinghouse to identify repeat abusers." Greg Warner, "Betrayed trust: The recycle of abuse continues at Baptist churches," *Associated Baptist Press*, June 11, 2007.

I also knew for sure that it was something clergy abuse survivors needed. More of them would speak up if the denomination provided a trained review panel to whom they could safely report abuse. It was flat-out cruel the way Baptist leaders kept telling clergy abuse survivors that they should report it to the cronies and colleagues of the perpetrator. It was like telling bloody sheep to go back to the den of the wolf who savaged them.

After much thought, I finally put SNAP's letter onto paper. I began by congratulating Dr. Page on his election and urged him to give special attention to the problem of clergy sex abuse. "We want to help," said the letter.[108]

"No faith group is immune from this crime. . . . Your own Southern Baptist scholars have reported that clergy sex abuse is as prevalent among Protestants as among Catholics. Yet they point out that . . . abuse is 'routinely covered up,' and that 'church officials largely have not been responsive.' "[109]

The letter then pointed out to Dr. Page that the accuracy of the scholars' statements was reflected in my own actual, documented experience. "The horror," I said, "rests not only in the crime of what a Southern Baptist minister did" to me as a kid, but also "in the hostile, hurtful, and inadequate responses that were made in the present day" when I reported the abuse. "When 18 church and denominational leaders can be informed of a substantiated report involving a minister's sexual abuse of a minor . . . and the man remains in ministry . . . then this, the largest Protestant denomination in the country, has a serious problem."

We asked Dr. Page to launch an immediate investigation into the denominational mishandling of my abuse report and to use it "as a launchpad for change."

We asked him "to institute a centralized location for receiving and recording reports of clergy abuse," and "to establish an independent

<hr />

108. Letter from SNAP to Dr. Frank Page, president of the Southern Baptist Convention, dated August 2, 2006.
109. *See* Joe E. Trull & James E. Carter, *Ministerial Ethics*, at p. 162 (Baker Academic, 2d ed. 2004).

denominational review board for investigating and considering reports of clergy abuse."[110]

"Whether or not the Southern Baptist Convention is capable of removing an abusive minister from ministry," we pointed out, "it is at least capable of informing and warning." We asked that a procedure be established for notifying people in the pews when a report of abuse is made about a minister who worked in their congregation.

Finally, we asked Dr. Page to meet with us in person at Southern Baptist headquarters in Nashville. We wanted to "sit down together and see what can be done to make Southern Baptist churches safer."

Dr. Page wrote back to tell us what a "disturbing and frightening example" our letter provided of "what happens when those in spiritual places of authority misuse that authority."[111]

"I know that this has happened on multiple occasions," he affirmed.

But despite his admitted knowledge of "multiple occasions," Dr. Page proceeded to simply "remind" us of the "structure of the Southern Baptist Convention." Each church is "autonomous and separate," he explained, and if abuse is covered up, then it's the responsibility of that particular church.

In other words, it was the standard "not my problem" excuse. It was the same excuse that had allowed 18 Southern Baptist leaders to turn a blind eye to my own substantiated report of abuse, while leaving the molester in ministry.[112]

To this day, I will never understand how Baptist leaders can fling out that "autonomy" excuse in the face of information about clergy child molestation. I can't even pretend to understand. They chant "autonomy"

---

110. "The idea was simple: By creating a database that would shine light on abusers, most of whom are never criminally charged and convicted, church officials across the country could run a pastor's name through the computer to see if he were flagged for sexual impropriety before hiring him. Victims' advocates proposed establishing an independent panel to investigate claims of abuse, especially those that can no longer be taken to court. In some cases, pastors have copped to detailed allegations of misconduct, which would make it rather easy to add their names to a database." Elizabeth Ulrich, "Save Yourselves," *Nashville Scene*, June 19, 2008 (describing the database suggestion that was made to the Southern Baptist Convention).

111. Letter from Dr. Frank S. Page, president of the Southern Baptist Convention, to SNAP, dated August 15, 2006.

112. One reporter wrote: "She contacted 18 influential Baptist leaders in four states between July 2004 and May 2005, warning there might be a sexual predator among their ranks. Not one offered to help." Bob Allen, "SBC to consider national clergy sex-offender database," *EthicsDaily*, June 11, 2007.

as though it were a magical incantation to relieve them of moral obligation. It's a radicalized version of church "autonomy" that is "so loose" even "a criminal conviction does not necessarily end the career of a Southern Baptist preacher."[113]

This is a denomination that boasts 16.2 million members and that is widely credited with helping to elect a United States president.[114] The Southern Baptist Convention's national offices take in $200 million annually, and the state Baptist organizations take in an additional $300 million. A total of $10.3 *billion* is collected each year in Southern Baptist church offering plates across the country.[115] Yet, the powerful men who run this mega-monied tentacular organization claim to be utterly *without* power when it comes to ridding their ranks of clergy who prey on kids.[116]

We decided to write to Dr. Page again and to direct this second letter to two additional Southern Baptist officials: Morris Chapman, president of the Executive Committee, and Richard Land, president of the Ethics & Religious Liberty Commission. This time, we also decided that we would hand-deliver the letter to Southern Baptist headquarters in Nashville and would schedule a press conference in front of the building.[117]

---

113. Jim Haug, "Pastor scandals erode trust in pulpit," *Daytona Beach News Journal*, June 24, 2007 (paraphrasing Clyde Fant, professor of religion at Stetson University, who also pointed out that, unlike in many other faith groups, "no credentials, not even a seminary degree, are required for Baptist preachers"). *See also* Michael Leathers, "Illinois church knowingly placed convicted sex offender in pulpit," *Associated Baptist Press*, August 22, 2007; Susan Hogan-Albach, "Sex offender back in pulpit," *Chicago Sun-Times*, August 20, 2007.

114. Christine Wicker, *The Fall of the Evangelical Nation*, at p. xii and 24 (HarperOne 2008) (Though Wicker acknowledges the Southern Baptist brag of 16 million members, Wicker suggests that 4 million may be a more correct number.).

115. Bob Allen, "Moderate Baptist leader says SBC is neglecting the hungry," *EthicsDaily*, October 19, 2007.

116. One scholar explained the Baptist system of unaccountability this way: "There is no Baptist clearing house for this information – anywhere. There is no one keeper of the files, nobody out there who has the power to intervene when something goes wrong and people start pointing fingers. There is no there, out there." Timothy Weber, dean of Northern Baptist Theological Seminary, as quoted by Terry Mattingly, "Where does the Baptist buck stop?" *On Religion*, June 19, 2002 (reprinted in the *Knoxville News-Sentinel*, June 22, 2002).

117 Bob Allen, "Group asks Southern Baptist leaders to address clergy sex abuse," *EthicsDaily*, February 19, 2007.

I knew we had to get outside the insular Baptist system and start bringing the Baptist clergy abuse problem into the public eye. There was no other way. Baptist officials had made it plain that, without outside pressure, they weren't going to step outside the safety of their institutionalized do-nothing status quo, not even for the sake of protecting kids against predators.

Nashville is like the Vatican of Southern Baptists, and I had to battle demons to get myself to go there. I scheduled it. I recruited a couple other SNAP people to help. I wrote the letter. I set up the StopBaptistPredators website. I wrote the media advisory. I put together press packets. I bought an airplane ticket. Then my brain started doing weird stuff on me.

I felt as though I was going straight into the heart of darkness, and my mind kept racing through all sorts of bizarre possibilities. I conjured both the vengeance of men and the vengeance of God. My Jules Verne vision returned full-force, and I could see the sidewalk in front of Southern Baptist headquarters splitting open and swallowing me whole. I feared that I would be struck dead by a freak bolt of lightning. And I even imagined that God might be so filled with rage for all the trouble I was causing that He would make the plane crash.

My fears were totally irrational, of course, but my brain fixated on them anyway. I knew from my therapist that what my brain was doing was pretty common. Raw fear can be completely paralyzing for many clergy sex abuse survivors – fear of the perpetrator, fear of church people, and fear of God. The fear becomes like God's own almighty vice-grip around your throat.

Dan drove me to the airport, cracking jokes the whole way. "I think you have an obligation to warn the other passengers," he deadpanned. "You can go to the gate and just shout it out: 'Warning! This flight is at risk of God's wrath.' "

I just looked at him.

"No, I'm serious. You have to tell them. They're entitled to know that they're getting on a plane with a passenger who's pissed off the Almighty, don't ya think?"

I glared at Dan and rolled my eyes. He grinned.

That smirky grin and those mischievous blue eyes kept me from freaking out and got me onto the plane. I settled into my seat, clenched my fists the whole way, and kept reciting the 23rd Psalm in my head.

"Yea, though I walk through the valley of the shadow of death, I will fear no evil. . . ."[118]

If there was ever a place that felt like "the shadow of death," it was surely Nashville. But in September 2006, I went there anyway. Fortunately, a couple other SNAP leaders picked me up at the airport. So I didn't have to manage my anxiety and drive at the same time.

We delivered our letter to Southern Baptist headquarters and did a sidewalk press conference in front of the building.[119] Miguel, who's a Catholic abuse survivor himself, told the press that, although Catholics had certainly handled things poorly, in his contacts with Baptist abuse survivors, "they said almost to a person that they wished their denomination was doing as much as Roman Catholics."[120]

I knew the sad truth of what Miguel was saying. By then, I myself had talked with enough Baptist survivors to know that this was how many of them felt. They would read news articles about Catholic abuse survivors who reported their priest-perpetrators to Catholic review boards, and they wanted to be able to do the same thing. They would read about how Catholic dioceses were providing counseling for Catholic abuse survivors, and they wanted to know what Baptist official they could go to for help with the cost of *their* counseling. But there was never anyone in Baptist circles who would help them.

While we stood there on the sidewalk outside Southern Baptist headquarters, I kept looking at the sky, half-waiting for a lightning bolt out of the blue. But it never happened. The ground didn't split open either. I wasn't swallowed away to the center of the earth to live with Satan. It was just an ordinary day. But it was also a day that set something in motion.

In our letter,[121] we again asked for "a dialogue" on making Southern Baptist churches safer, and while acknowledging the concern about local church autonomy, we pointed out that Baptists "have shown themselves capable of all manner of cooperative endeavors when they choose." After

118. Psalm 23:4 (KJV).

119. Anita Wadhwani, "Group asks Baptists to form board to track clergy linked to abuse," *The Tennessean*, September 27, 2006; Bob Allen, "Southern Baptist leaders challenged to get tough on sex abuse by clergy," *EthicsDaily*, September 27, 2006; Hannah Elliott, "Victims of Baptist clergy abuse urge SBC leaders to take action," *Associated Baptist Press*, September 27, 2006.

120. Bob Allen, "Southern Baptist leaders challenged to get tough on sex abuse by clergy," *EthicsDaily*, September 27, 2006.

121. SNAP's letter of September 26, 2006 to Southern Baptist officials Morris Chapman, Richard Land, and Frank Page.

all, they make a cooperative effort for international mission work, for providing ministers with retirement services, and for maintaining an archive of Baptist historical records.

"Given that congregational autonomy does not preclude a cooperative denomination-wide effort for these other endeavors, why should it preclude a denomination-wide effort at protecting kids against clergy-predators?" we asked.

Again we pointed out my own case in which "18 Southern Baptist leaders in four different states were all put on notice of a substantiated report involving a minister's sexual abuse of a minor" and yet the minister continued in the pulpit. "This reveals all too clearly the institutionalized nature of the problem," we said. "Despite the documented awareness of so many, there was apparently no one in leadership who considered it their responsibility to take action so as to assure the safety of others."

We asked Southern Baptist officials to do what other faith groups have done and to establish an independent review board "to receive and investigate reports of clergy abuse and to arrive at a determination of whether the report should be deemed credible."[122] And we asked them to keep a centralized archive for records about ministers reported for sexual abuse – i.e., a database.[123]

We didn't ask them to punish credibly-accused clergy sex abusers, rescind their ordinations, or remove them from ministry. We simply asked that they implement a system to provide churches with objective information. As one reporter observed, the reform measures that we requested didn't go nearly as far as what Catholics were already doing.[124] We were asking for *less*.

"We look forward to your further response, and we hope to work with you in the future," we concluded.

Southern Baptist high-honcho Augie Boto responded with a terse

---

122. Bob Allen, "Former Southern Baptist pastor pleads guilty to sexual abuse," *Associated Baptist Press*, April 30, 2009 (recounting prior history on request for review board); Gary Soulsman, "Keeping doors open," *Delaware News-Journal*, March 3, 2007.

123. Constitutional law professor Marci Hamilton later described this database suggestion as "visionary" because it provides a way for Baptist churches to coordinate together on a national strategy in favor of protecting children. Marci Hamilton, "The Southern Baptist Convention's unconvincing claims as to why it cannot effectively report or prevent clergy child abuse," *FindLaw.com*, June 12, 2008. [http://writ.news.findlaw.com/hamilton/20080612.html].

124. Greg Warner, "Betrayed trust: The recycle of abuse continues at Baptist churches," *Associated Baptist Press*, June 11, 2007.

brush-off letter saying "continued discourse between us will not be positive or fruitful."[125]

Boto's letter went to SNAP's Chicago office, miles away, and I didn't find out about it for months. But given the tone of the letter, it hardly mattered. It wasn't as if anyone in Southern Baptist circles wanted to talk to us.

So there was nothing to do but keep working. Together with other SNAP people and other Baptist abuse survivors, I continued to try to bring attention to the problem and to gather momentum for reform. I was just a volunteer, and SNAP is an organization run on a shoestring. We had no money for travel, public relations work, or media consultants. But we chugged on as best we could.

At the Nashville press conference, one of the reporters was a guy named Bob Allen. When he first introduced himself, he said he was from the Baptist Center for Ethics. The instant I heard the word "Baptist," I felt myself flinch. But I shook his hand and tried not to let the flinch show.

As it turned out, my flinch-reflex was faulty. Bob Allen wound up being the journalist who covered more Baptist clergy sex abuse stories than any other journalist in the country.[126] He was the managing editor for *EthicsDaily*, an online publication of the Baptist Center for Ethics,[127] which is an organization affiliated with smaller Baptist groups but not directly with the Southern Baptist Convention. Over the next 18 months, Bob Allen put into print more than 80 articles and columns about Baptist clergy sex abuse and about our repeated calls for a system of accountability.[128] Other reporters, newspapers and media outlets all over the country covered particular stories, but it was Bob Allen's work that first gave our efforts some traction. I never would have predicted that one.

125. Letter of D. August Boto, vice-president of convention policy for the Southern Baptist Convention, dated September 29, 2006.
126. Currently, Bob Allen is writing for the *Associated Baptist Press*, which describes itself as "the only independent daily news agency that reports on and for Baptists." *See* Robert Marus, "Veteran journalist Bob Allen tapped as ABP senior writer," *Associated Baptist Press*, September 29, 2008.
127. The Baptist Center for Ethics is not connected to the Southern Baptist Convention. According to its website, the Baptist Center for Ethics receives funding and support from *other* Baptist groups and from some Baptist churches.
128. Bob Allen, "SBC seminary president labels clergy sex-abuse victims' group 'evil-doers'," *EthicsDaily*, February 15, 2008 (showing list of many of Bob Allen's articles on Baptist clergy sex abuse).

As we continued to call attention to Baptist clergy sex abuse and cover-ups, our efforts gained wider notice when the Associated Press picked up on the story in February 2007. The Associated Press article went out in the *New York Times* and in over 170 other media outlets.[129] All across the country, people were reading about our repeated attempts to get Baptist leaders to do what other faith groups have done and establish a review board for assessing reports about clergy child molestation.

"They don't want to see this problem," I told the press. "That's tragic because they're imitating the same mistakes made by Catholic bishops."[130]

Not long after that, the Reverend Thomas Doyle himself wrote to Southern Baptist officials, saying much the same thing.[131] Doyle, a former Vatican canon lawyer, is the whistleblower priest who, in the mid-1980s, first warned Catholic bishops of the "looming clergy sex abuse nightmare."[132] His warning went largely unheeded until 2002 when the United States Conference of Catholic Bishops finally established the Office of Child and Youth Protection and began implementing review board processes.[133] By then, countless more kids had been hurt, and the truth of Doyle's prophetic warning had become tragically apparent.

Now Doyle was issuing a similar warning to Southern Baptist officials, telling them of his fear that the largest Protestant denomination was demonstrating a similar pattern.

"Clergy sex abuse is a scourge that knows no bounds of theology, denomination or institutional structure," wrote Doyle. "To effectively address this scourge requires a strong cooperative effort. Yet . . . I have seen that Southern Baptist leaders disclaim that possibility on the ground that the Southern Baptist Convention has 'no authority' over autonomous churches."

---

129. Rose French (Associated Press), "Baptists asked to crack down on abusers," *The New York Times*, February 21, 2007; see also "Southern Baptists urged to root out molesters," *MSNBC* (AP), February 21, 2007 [http://www.msnbc. msn.com/id/17265721/]; Rose French (AP), "Baptists asked to crack down on sex abusers, *The Christian Post*, February 21, 2007.

130. Rose French, "Baptists asked to crack down on abusers," *supra.*

131. Letter of Rev. Thomas Doyle to Dr. Frank Page, president of the Southern Baptist Convention, and Dr. Morris Chapman, president of the Southern Baptist Convention Executive Committee, dated March 30, 2007.

132. Audrey Barrick, "Southern Baptist abuse cases garnering more attention," *Christian Post*, April 15, 2007; Anita Wadhwani, "Sex abuse victims turn focus to Baptists," *The Tennessean*, April 29, 2007.

133. Audrey Barrick, "Southern Baptist abuse cases garnering more attention," *supra.*

156 — Christa Brown

While acknowledging Baptists' congregationalist structure, Doyle nevertheless pointed out that Baptist leaders' "no authority" argument was actually quite similar to what Catholic bishops were espousing prior to 2002.[134] Doyle explained that, to a large degree, Catholic bishops consider themselves to have dominion over their own diocese and "as essentially being autonomous." For this reason, it was an "extraordinary and unprecedented" step when the U.S. Conference of Catholic Bishops created an Office of Child and Youth Protection.

Though many people misunderstand the structure of the Catholic Church, said Doyle, in fact the U.S. Conference of Catholic Bishops has "no direct authority" over any bishop.[135] Each diocese is independent, he explained. This lack of "traditional oversight mechanisms" meant that clergy accountability had to be established "in a new way."

Doyle went on to explain that it wasn't the structure of the Catholic Church that allowed for the creation of an oversight mechanism. Rather, "it was the desperate need for a system of accountability that drove the creation of an oversight mechanism, and that mechanism was created *outside* the usual structure."[136]

"If children in Southern Baptist churches are to be made safer," he urged, "accountability for Southern Baptist clergy may also need to be established 'in a new way.'"

It was an obviously sincere letter, expressing grave concern. But Southern Baptist president Frank Page responded to Doyle with dismissiveness. After thanking Doyle for writing, Page wrote that "while Catholic bishops did claim to have 'no authority,' Southern Baptist leaders truly have no authority. . . ."[137]

In later comments to the press, Doyle said he wasn't surprised by Page's response because "such reactions are standard for people in church leadership positions, who tend to place the needs of the institution be-

---

134. Bob Allen, "*20/20* airs report on predator preachers," *EthicsDaily*, April 13, 2007; Anita Wadhwani, "Sex abuse victims turn focus to Baptists," *The Tennessean*, April 29, 2007.

135. Audrey Barrick, "Southern Baptist abuse cases garnering more attention," by Audrey Barrick, *Christian Post*, April 15, 2007

136. Audrey Barrick, "Southern Baptist abuse cases garnering more attention," *supra.*

137. Letter of Frank S. Page, president of the Southern Baptist Convention, to Rev. Thomas P. Doyle, April 4, 2007; see also Elizabeth Ulrich, "What would Jesus say," *Nashville Scene*, February 14, 2007 (quoting Page's letter); Bob Allen, "*20/20* airs report on predator preachers," *EthicsDaily*, April 13, 2007 (quoting Page's letter).

fore their Christian obligations."[138] Doyle again expressed his concern that Baptist officials had responded, similar to the Catholic church, "by worrying more about the image and the system."

I thought Doyle's remarks were well-tempered and mild. For myself, I couldn't help but ponder the level of condescending arrogance it took for Frank Page to think he could tell a Vatican canon lawyer that Catholic bishops were merely *claiming* to have "no authority." And Page's insistence that Baptist leaders "*truly*" had no authority seemed ridiculous. Either way, whether it was Catholic leaders claiming "no authority" or Baptist leaders claiming "*truly* no authority," it was an excuse that left innocent church kids at risk of being molested and raped by clergy-predators.

Not long after that, ABC News aired a *20/20* program called "Preacher Predators."[139] It was the culmination of a six-month investigation, and I had talked extensively with the producer during the process. The program showed numerous Southern Baptist preachers who had been convicted or charged with child sex abuse, including some who were still listed as ministers on the Southern Baptist Convention's own website.[140]

My on-camera interview was filmed at a little chapel on the campus of Texas Women's University in Denton. I had spontaneously suggested the location when the producer told me how her scouting crew couldn't seem to find a suitable place. I knew that two of the churches *20/20* would be filming were in Denton, and so I told her about the little chapel there. Her crew went out and took pictures, and she said it was "perfect."

It was perfect for me as well. The little chapel had been a special place for me when I was younger.

During my childhood, my family used to drive up from Dallas to visit relatives in Denton. Sometimes, my mom would stop off at this little chapel in the woods. Back then, the chapel was completely hidden away because the woods around it were so dense.

You could see that there had once been gardens, stepping stones, sitting areas, and walking paths around the chapel. But everything was

138. Elizabeth Ulrich, "What would Jesus say," *Nashville Scene*, February 14, 2007.

139. Jim Avila, Bonnie Van Gilder and Matt Lopez, "Preachers accused of sins and crimes," *ABC 20/20*, April 13, 2007 [http://abcnews.go.com/2020/story?id=3034040&page=1](news article that accompanied the TV show).

140. Bob Allen, "*20/20* airs report on preacher predators," *EthicsDaily*, April 13, 2007.

overgrown and untended. As a kid, that unkempt wildness only made the place seem all the more magical. It was like a secret garden that no one else seemed to know about. And there was never anyone else around. Mom would spend a little time in the chapel and my sisters and I would play hide-and-seek in the woods.

Years later, when I went to college in Denton, I would sometimes ride my bike across town to the little chapel in the woods. Just as when I was younger, there was never anyone else there. But the doors were always unlocked, and I liked to sit in the chapel's quiet stillness.

That was when I noticed how beautiful the chapel itself was. It had a perfectly proportioned small nave and spectacular stained glass windows. Most remarkable of all, every window depicted women. There was the glorious "motherhood" window behind the altar, and other windows showed women engaged in all manner of work – nurses, teachers, musicians, artists, and more.

For me, the little chapel was a place of great peace and beauty. The windows alone would take your breath away. It was a place I had once loved, and so I was thrilled that it would be the place for my *20/20* interview.

In the days leading up to that interview, my head was flooded with a single thought. It was my first thought on awakening and my last thought before sleeping. It was such a constant presence in my head that I could scarcely escape it: "Let the words of my mouth, and the meditation of my heart, be acceptable in thy sight, O Lord, my strength, and my redeemer."[141]

It annoyed me that my brain locked in on such a rote thing. Yet there it was, an incessant loop of this prayer in my head, if indeed a prayer is what it was.

I worried constantly about whether I was doing the right thing by doing an interview for national television. I worried about whether my words would serve a good purpose. I worried about whether I would speak well or poorly. I worried about whether my words would help others or hurt them. I worried about whether I might start shaking on camera. I worried that I might hyperventilate and find myself unable to breathe.

I worried so much that I made myself sick. At the hotel the evening before the interview, I suddenly starting coughing and couldn't stop. Then I stayed up all night blowing my nose. I was hacking something

141. Psalm 19:14 (KJV).

awful and my head felt huge. First thing in the morning, Dan went out to find me some Robitussin and Benadryl, and I downed as much as I thought I could get away with. I was scared the Benadryl would make me spacey, but I was even more scared of having a perpetually runny nose in front of the camera. It was one more thing to worry about.

I worried nonstop about all of it until just as I arrived at the interview site. As soon as I opened the car door, I heard them. I looked to the sky, and the cedar waxwings were everywhere. They filled the treetops. They filled the air. They were flitting back and forth. They surrounded me.

I smiled and let the wave of relief wash over me. Tears rolled down my cheeks and I said a quiet "thank you." I knew that all was well.

The cedar waxwings have long been a sort of good harbinger for me. So their presence there at that precise moment seemed nothing short of magical.

The *20/20* show didn't change anything, but it was an eye-opener for a lot of people. And what they saw didn't make Baptists look very good. There they were on national television with case after case of preacher-predators and no one was doing much of anything to prevent their hopping from one church to another. The *20/20* newscaster summed up the problem when she said that what had surprised *20/20* in its investigation was "how little is being done to stop it."

Southern Baptist president Frank Page made the usual remarks about how Baptist churches are all independent and how it's up to the local churches to do background checks. But then he had a deer-in-the-headlights look when Jim Avila, the *20/20* correspondent, told Page that, even at national headquarters, there were convicted sex offenders still shown as "preachers in good standing" on the Southern Baptist Convention's ministerial registry.

"So you're telling me that there are convicted predators on that list?" asked Page. "Yes," answered Avila.

That exchange took place weeks before the *20/20* show actually aired on television. Yet, even though Frank Page was told face-to-face about convicted child molesters on the Southern Baptist ministerial registry, those names were still on the list when the show aired.

An ordinary person might have imagined that a high-level religious leader like Frank Page would have left that *20/20* interview and gone straight to Nashville headquarters and instructed someone to get the convicted child molesters off the list. But that didn't happen. Decent people might have even imagined that Page would have publicly apologized to families whose kids were molested and who then endured the salt in the wound of seeing the perpetrators continue to be held forth publicly as Southern Baptist ministers. But that didn't happen either.

Instead, after the *20/20* show aired, Southern Baptist official Augie Boto used the *Baptist Press* to publicly justify KEEPING the names of convicted child molesters on the Southern Baptist Convention's ministerial registry.[142] It was Orwellian. He insisted that the registry was really a "list of *serving* ministers" rather than "*available* ministers" as *20/20* had described it.[143] For the life of me, I never could see how Boto's bizarre fixation on whether the ministers were "serving" or "available" could possibly make a difference. To me, it was just one more example of the nonsensical rationalizations that Baptist leaders were conjuring to defend the indefensible.[144]

Ultimately, the child molesters revealed by *20/20* were finally removed from Baptists' ministerial registry, but it took even *more* media exposure. After the *20/20* show, *EthicsDaily* printed the names of the convicted child molesters that *20/20* had uncovered.[145] But Southern Baptist officials still did nothing. So SNAP did a widely dispersed press release

---

142. Bob Allen, "SBC officials criticize 'Predator Preacher' report on *20/20*", *EthicsDaily*, April 18, 2007.

143. D. August Boto, "Response to ABC *20/20* segment on sexual predators in ministry," *Baptist Press*, April 16, 2007.

144. Southern Baptist president Frank Page took the prize for double-talk defense of the indefensible when, in talking to the *Louisville Courier-Journal*, he voiced this reason for not creating a denominational database of clergy sex abusers: "What we know happens with true abusers, they just switch to another denomination that doesn't access a denominational database." As I told *EthicsDaily*, this sounded a lot more like an argument for why there *should* be a denominational database: "If perpetrators switch to denominations that don't have a database, and if Southern Baptists persist in not having a database, then perpetrators will gravitate there." Peter Smith, "SBC president responds to 'discontent,'" *Louisville Courier-Journal Faith & Works blog*, November 16, 2007; Bob Allen, "State convention resolution indicate increased awareness of Baptist clergy sexual abuse," *EthicsDaily*, November 26, 2007.

145. Bob Allen, "SBC president says denomination looking into sex offender registry," *EthicsDaily*, April 16, 2007. For one of the convicted sex offenders listed in the article, it was actually the *third* time that *EthicsDaily* had printed his name and pointed out that he was still on the Southern Baptist Convention's ministerial registry. *See* Bob Allen, "Clergy sex abuse activist awaits response from SBC," *EthicsDaily*, October 11, 2006; Bob Allen, "Baptist minister, volunteer track coach charged with rape," *EthicsDaily*, March 28, 2007.

listing the names of the child molesters uncovered by *20/20*.[146] Only then, *after* national media exposure on *20/20*, *after* another *EthicsDaily* article, and *after* a SNAP press release, did Southern Baptist officials finally remove the names of those men from their ministerial registry.[147]

When the *20/20* show aired, Emily was away at college, living in a dorm. I had already told her the gist of my story when she was not quite 19. It was something I had to finally force myself to do because I didn't want to risk the chance that Emily might see some news article without having heard the news from me first.

I was scared of what her reaction might be, but I didn't need to be. Emily showed only wisdom, understanding, and compassion.

Just before the *20/20* show, I called and told her not to worry if she didn't want to watch it on the TV in the dorm, with other people around. "We'll tape it," I said, "and you can watch it the next time you're home."

"Are you kidding me, Mom? My friends are all going to sit and watch it with me. We're gonna have piles of popcorn. This is big stuff!"

I laughed and laughed. Once again, I had underestimated my own daughter. I was still blinded by my shame. But she felt none of that. She was showing me off. She was proud of me.

A couple months after the *20/20* show aired, the Southern Baptist Convention had its annual meeting in San Antonio. Oklahoma pastor Wade Burleson put forward a motion to direct the Southern Baptist Executive Committee to study the feasibility of creating a denominational database of ministers who had been credibly accused of sexual abuse or who had confessed to abuse or been legally convicted.[148] It was a big part of what we in SNAP had been asking for,[149] and so we were there in the humid heat of San Antonio, handing out flyers to urge support for Burleson's motion.

---

146. "Six pedophile preachers still listed on national Southern Baptist website," SNAP press release, April 18, 2007 [http://www.snapnetwork.org/snap_press_releases/2007_press_releases/041807_six_baptist_preachers.htm].

147. Adelle Banks, "Southern Baptists confront their own sexual abuse scandal," *Religion News Service (Chicago Tribune)*, April 19, 2007.

148. Peter Smith, "Baptists eye sex-offender database," *Louisville Courier-Journal*, June 13, 2007; Audrey Barrick, "Resolution passed to prevent clergy sex abuse in SBC churches," *Christian Post*, June 13, 2007.

149. "Resolution passed to prevent clergy sex abuse in SBC churches," *supra* (recognizing that the database proposal was a recommendation of Christa Brown and SNAP).

When the motion passed by a near-unanimous vote of the 8600 messengers,[150] it felt like there was reason for hope that Southern Baptists might finally step up to the plate and start working to pro-actively address clergy sex abuse in the ways that other major faith groups do.

---

150. Peter Smith, "Baptists eye sex-offender database," *Louisville Courier-Journal*, June 13, 2007; Sam Hodges, "Southern Baptists' vote may be reformists' victory," *Dallas Morning News*, June 13, 2007.

40

A Tsunami of Survivors

Until the passage of Wade Burleson's motion, Southern Baptist officials were putting on a public face of pretending that clergy sex abuse wasn't a serious problem for them. In fact, just a month before that June 2007 convention, Southern Baptists' vice-president for news services, Will Hall, told the press that the relatively low number of Baptist abuse cases proved that the way Baptists deal with the problem was working.[151] He suggested that there had been only 40 "incidents" of Baptist clergy sex abuse in the past 15 years.[152]

Forty in 15 years. I was outraged. This was a high-level, paid, professional Southern Baptist spokesperson. He should have known better and he probably did know better.

One Baptist pastor alone had admitted to molesting more than 40 boys as he moved from church to church.[153] No telling how many "incidents" there were. And in less than a year, I had compiled scores upon scores of publicly reported cases on my StopBaptistPredators website. Many involved multiple victims and multiple incidents. And of course, publicly reported cases were the bare tip of the iceberg. Many more Baptist abuse survivors had contacted me personally. There had been

---

151. Bob Allen, "SBC official says relative 'low' number of cases proves system working against sexual predators," *EthicsDaily*, May 14, 2007; Bob Allen, "EthicsDaily.com tracks clergy sex abuse in the Southern Baptist Convention," *EthicsDaily*, December 31, 2007; Jamey Tucker, "Sexual abuse of children in Southern Baptists targeted by watchdog group," *WKRN-TV-Nashville*, May 11, 2007.

152. Bob Allen, "SBC official says relative 'low' number of cases proves system working against sexual predators," *supra*; Bob Allen, "EthicsDaily.com tracks clergy sex abuse in the Southern Baptist Convention," *supra*; Jamey Tucker, "Sexual abuse of children in Southern Baptists targeted by watchdog group," *supra*.

153. Jim Avila, Bonnie Van Gilder and Matt Lopez, "Preachers accused of sins and crimes," *ABC 20/20*, April 13, 2007; Brooks Egerton and Holly Becka, "Man who admits years of molestations gets prison," *Dallas Morning News*, July 14, 1999; Audrey Barrick, "Southern Baptist abuse cases garnering more attention," *Christian Post*, April 15, 2007.

40 of those in just the first six months after my September 2006 trip to Nashville.[154] Some specifically told me that they had also contacted denominational officials. This amounted to a whole lot of people that Baptist leaders should have known about, and it was way more than 40 in 15 years.

I wondered exactly which child molestation victims Will Hall wasn't counting. Which kids who were raped, molested and sodomized just didn't matter enough to even count? To Will Hall, it was apparently a whole heckuva lot of them. I vowed then and there that I would keep posting the publicly reported cases on the StopBaptistPredators website for as long I could bear it, if for no other reason than so that Southern Baptist officials could never again get away with pitching such a grotesque minimization of the problem.[155]

EthicsDaily pointed out that Hall "got his facts wrong" and publicly called on the Southern Baptist Convention to issue a correction.[156] But of course that never happened.

The truth was that I was flat-out overwhelmed by the number of people who were contacting me. After the Associated Press article in February 2007, it took me a full month to clear out my email inbox. I got initial responses out to that batch barely in time to handle the tsunami of survivors who contacted me after the *20/20* show in April.

They were from all over the country. Lots of them had already tried to get Baptist officials to do something about their perpetrators, but no one would. From California to Oklahoma to Missouri to Georgia to Florida – things were no better in any of the other state Baptist

---

154. Rose French (AP), "Baptists asked to crack down on abusers," *New York Times*, February 21, 2007; Bob Allen, "SBC official says relative 'low' number of cases proves system working against sexual predators," *EthicsDaily*, May 14, 2007.

155. [www.StopBaptistPredators.org].

156. Bob Allen, "SBC official says relative 'low' number of cases proves system working against sexual predators," *EthicsDaily*, May 14, 2007; Bob Allen, "EthicsDaily.com tracks clergy sex abuse in the Southern Baptist Convention," *EthicsDaily*, December 31, 2007.

conventions than they were in Texas. In big churches[157] and small churches, city churches and rural churches, abuse and cover-ups were rampant.[158] No one was helping the victims when they tried to report abusive ministers. No one was keeping records of their reports.[159] No one was removing the men from ministry. No one was even warning people in the pews. It was as though Baptist clergy sex abuse survivors were simply rendered invisible.

Meanwhile, Southern Baptist officials were still telling people that it wasn't a widespread problem.[160] Southern Baptist president Frank

---

157. Even at a Southern Baptist flagship megachurch, Bellevue Baptist in Memphis, the senior pastor, Steve Gaines, kept quiet about another minister's admitted sexual abuse of his son. Gaines minimized it as "moral failure" and accepted the perpetrator's word that "the activity had not reoccurred." When the abuse and cover-up finally came to light, it was revealed as the minister's "egregious, perverse sexual activity with his adolescent son over a period of 12 to 18 months." In addition to Gaines, other church leaders also knew about the abuse, but an investigation concluded that there seemed to be "no serious consideration given by anyone to the health and safety of the Bellevue family." The admitted child molester was even allowed, as part of his ministerial duties, to interview volunteer child-care workers who indicated on an application that they had been past victims of sexual abuse. Those people said they felt violated by "inappropriate questions" and by the realization that their pastor had allowed an admitted child molester to be in a position to ask such questions. Nevertheless, despite Gaines' blind-eyed approach to clergy child molestation, the Bellevue congregation kept him as their pastor. *See* Bob Allen, "Bellevue report faults handling of minister's sexual abuse," *EthicsDaily*, January 29, 2007; Hannah Elliott, "Bellevue report: Assistant pastor guilty of sex abuse against son," *Associated Baptist Press*, January 30, 2007; Bob Allen, "Victims' advocates criticize Bellevue response to minister's sexual abuse," *EthicsDaily*, January 30, 2007; Bob Allen, "Bellevue investigates minister for 'moral failure'," *EthicsDaily*, December 20, 2006.
158. See news stories linked at [www.StopBaptistPredators.org/news.html].
159. Southern Baptist officials have readily acknowledged that they don't keep records on ministers who have been convicted or accused of abuse. Augie Boto, vice-president for convention policy, said: "There is no Southern Baptist Convention office which collects and provides any qualifying information, including information about sex abuse convictions or accusations, with regard to any local church employees, including ministers." *See* Adelle M. Banks, "Southern Baptists not immune to scandals involving sex abuse," *The Oklahoman*, May 5, 2007.
160. Bob Allen, "SBC president says sexual abuse by clergy not 'systemic'," *EthicsDaily*, April 4, 2007.

Page would acknowledge only that there had been "several reported cases."[161]

Of course, there were way more than "several" even if you counted only the publicly reported cases.[162] If Southern Baptist officials didn't see the extent of the problem, it was only because they chose to put on blinders.[163]

The Associated Press gathered data showing that the number of kids being abused in Protestant churches may actually be larger than the number being abused in Catholic churches.[164] It looked at two decades' worth of data from the major insurance companies that insure Protestant churches, and the data showed an average of 260 cases per year being reported to the insurance companies about kids under 18 being sexually

---

161. Bob Allen, "SBC president labels sexual abuse critics 'opportunists'," *EthicsDaily*, April 20, 2007.

162. Peter Smith, "Kentucky Baptists act to prevent sex abuse in churches," *The Courier-Journal*, November 15, 2007 ("News reports and court cases also have revealed numerous instances of a cover-up of abuse among Baptist . . . denominations.").

163. There were indications that Southern Baptist leaders actually had some awareness about the extent of the problem. For example, in 2002, when the Catholic sex abuse crisis was at a peak, former Southern Baptist president Bobby Welch said this to the messengers at that year's convention: "We shouldn't enjoy this Catholic mess too much. We're waiting for the other shoe to drop, and when it does, don't be surprised if there is more and more within our own ranks." Bob Allen, "Former SBC president defends denomination's record against clergy sex abuse," *EthicsDaily*, March 2, 2007. A 2000 report to the Baptist General Convention of Texas stated that "the incidence of sexual abuse by clergy has reached horrific proportions." Terry Mattingly, "Where does the Baptist buck stop," *On Religion*, June 19, 2002 (reprinted in the *Knoxville News-Sentinel*, June 22, 2002). And an associate director at the Baptist General Convention of Texas stated that "Baptists' disconnected system for securing ministers indirectly shields perpetrators." Marv Knox, "Churches must act to prevent clergy sexual abuse," *Baptist Standard*, April 22, 2002 (paraphrasing Sonny Spurger).

164. Rose French (Associated Press), "3 insurers shed light on Protestant church sex abuse," *Houston Chronicle*, June 14, 2007. The fact that Protestant clergy sex abuse may be even more pervasive than Catholic clergy sex abuse was also the determination of Pennsylvania State University professor Philip Jenkins over a decade ago. Philip Jenkins, *Pedophiles and Priests*, at pp. 50, 81 (Oxford University Press 1996).

abused by Protestant clergy and church staff.[165] The biggest portion of those reports were from Baptist churches.[166]

That 260 number for Protestants compared with the average of 228 "credible accusations" per year in Catholic churches around the country.[167] I couldn't help but wonder whether the 260 number would be even bigger if the largest Protestant denomination in the land – Southern Baptists – would bother to assess and keep track of "credible accusations" in the same way Catholics do.[168]

In any event, based on the number of people who were contacting me, I knew for sure that it was a much bigger problem than what Baptist leaders were admitting to.

One day, two middle-aged men contacted me within hours of each other, and both of them named the same Southern Baptist church in Louisiana as the place where they were molested as kids. They were men who now lived on opposite sides of the globe, and they hadn't talked to each other since childhood. Yet, somehow, they had both found my website and had chosen to email me on the same day.

It was a day when I was ready to throw in the towel. The enormity of this problem and the pain of the people who contact me weighs too heavy sometimes. And I feel too inadequate. But when those two men contacted me, my first thought was that it was a sign from God that I should continue with the work.

Of course, I knew it was really just a coincidence. My initial instinct of thinking it was a sign from God was a holdover from my evangelical upbringing. I knew that, too. The habits of evangelical thinking die hard. But even realizing it was a mere coincidence didn't change the reality of

---

165. Rose French (AP), "3 insurers shed light on Protestant church sex abuse," *supra.*

166. Associated Press, "A look at abuse data in Protestant churches," *Seattle Post-Intelligencer,* June 14, 2007.

167. Bob Allen, "Insurance companies shed light on extent of sex abuse in Protestant churches," *EthicsDaily,* July 6, 2007.

168. A FOX news commentator pondered this same question from the opposite perspective. He pointed out that the 228 per year number for Catholics "includes all credible accusations, not just those that have involved insurance companies, and still is *less* than the number of cases in Protestant churches. . . ." Jonathan Morris, "Sexual abuse of minors in Protestant churches," *FOXNews. com,* June 24, 2007 [http://www.foxnews.com/story/0,2933,286153,00.html]; *see also* Bob Allen, "Insurance companies shed light on extent of abuse in Protestant churches," *EthicsDaily,* July 7, 2007.

what I was encountering. Coincidences like that tend to happen only in the midst of large numbers.

The saddest thing about those two men's stories was that they had tried to report that church leader to state and national denominational officials. They had also reported him to the senior pastor of the church. But they were given the cold shoulder. No one would help them, and no one would do anything about the perpetrator.

After Wade Burleson's motion passed at the convention, other Baptist abuse survivors and their families wrote to the committee members who were tasked with conducting the study on clergy abuse. Some of them told about the abuse they suffered from Baptist ministers. But they got no help.

A few of them forwarded me the emails they got back from Southern Baptist officials. In response to painful stories of childhood trauma, officials sermonized the victims on forgiveness, quoted Bible verses, and talked about how powerless they were to do anything.[169] Almost always, they included some version of their self-serving mantra: "Baptist churches are autonomous."

By now, I've heard that line so often that it rings like a curse. It's coded language. What they're really saying is: "Not my problem." It's the ready rationalization of religious powerbrokers who choose to leave kids in harms' way rather than take action to expose their colleagues who prey on them.[170]

How I wish that I could tell the story of every kid who was ever abused in a Baptist church. And I wish I could tell the additional stories that so many of them have of how other Baptist leaders shamed, shunned and ignored them when they tried to report the abuse. Every single one of them deserves to be heard.

---

169. Sometimes, Southern Baptist officials made the "we're powerless" claim publicly. Even "if we knew anything about it, we *could not* have provided any relief or prevention," said a Southern Baptist spokesperson in response to a clergy abuse report. Elizabeth Ulrich, "The Bad Shepherd," *The Nashville Scene*, April 24, 2008; Andrew C. Martel, "Pastor 'groomed' teen for sex, suit claims," *The Morning Call*, March 11, 2008.

170. The Southern Baptist Convention's order of priorities was made express in the words of Southern Baptist vice-president Roger Oldham, who explained that Baptists officials were looking at "how we can best, *first of all*, protect autonomy of the local church, and *second*, protect the children, too." Lillian Kwon, "Southern Baptists consider denomination-wide response to clergy sex abuse," *Christian Post*, September 24, 2007.

Nowadays, I sometimes I have a new dream. All the Baptist abuse survivors who have ever contacted me are in it. So are some of their family members and some of the people who participate on the StopBaptistPredators blog. We're all standing on risers and singing in a great choir. There are several hundred of us.

Even the director of the choir is a Baptist clergy abuse survivor. I think he's the one who probably first triggered this dream. He's a guy who, in real life, once directed a choir at Lincoln Center.

In my dream, we're singing "This Little Light." That was my favorite Sunday School song when I was a kid.

> This little light of mine
> I'm gonna let it shine.[171]

We had hand motions that went with the song. We would hold up our index finger like a candle – our "little light." Then we went through all the places where we were going to shine it. "Shine all over Farmers Branch, I'm gonna let it shine . . . Shine all over Texas, I'm gonna let it shine . . . Shine all over the U.S.A., I'm gonna let it shine . . . Shine all over the whole wide world, I'm gonna let it shine." When we did the "whole wide world" part, we would make a big circle with our "little light." I always liked that part.

But my favorite part was when we sang "Hide it under a bushel, Oh No! I'm gonna let it shine." We would cup our left hand over our "little light" to hide it, and then fling our left-hand-bushel away when we sang "Oh No!" I was one of those over-exuberant kids who always shouted out a little too loud on the "Oh No!" part.

It's such a happy dream. We're all standing there on those risers singing this song that we all learned as children. Our voices fill the air. Our voices are pure and clear.

---

171. Harry Dixon Loes, "This Little Light of Mine," (circa 1920)(gospel children's song inspired by Matthew 5:16).

41

Baptist Blogs

At the last minute before heading off on that first trip to Nashville in September 2006, I decided to send SNAP's media advisory to some Baptist bloggers. I was hoping there might be a few of the blogging Baptist pastors who would be sympathetic to our cause and would write about it. I even imagined there might be some of them who would want to help.

For months after that, I thought I must surely have been delusional to have ever held such a hope. But I continued to insert comments on Baptist blogs and to engage Baptist bloggers in discussion. Other Baptist abuse survivors joined in the effort.

It seemed like a huge waste of time, and I worried about how it might be affecting some of the other survivors. Some of them shared painful stuff in the hope of educating the ministers and gaining grass-roots support for our effort. But they didn't get much of any compassion in return. Worse, some of the pastors seemed intent on perpetually slamming us, and they said amazingly ignorant things. It hurt.

When I saw how a couple of them attacked Stephanie,[172] I wanted to jump through cyberspace and punch them. Stephanie's son was sexually abused by a Baptist minister in East Texas. As is typical, by the time her son grew up and was able to talk about it, 15 years had passed, and it was too late to try to seek justice for what was done to her own son. The statute of limitations had passed.

The minister had moved on to other churches, but Stephanie found where he was. She went out into the community, talking to mothers, and she wound up finding a more recent victim who was still *within* the statute of limitations. The minister was able to be prosecuted on that

---

172. [BaptistLife.com], "Protect Baptist Children" thread, comments beginning October 28, 2006.

more recent crime and he served time for that one. But he admitted to having molested at least 40 other young boys.[173]

Stephanie wrote onto one of the Baptist blogs to tell her story and to urge that the Baptist General Convention of Texas needed to step up and start protecting children rather than protecting itself. She said she wanted them to start listening to the victims and helping them rather than "continually doing nothing."

In response, a rather well-known Baptist pastor on the blog accused Stephanie of "trying to reek vengeance." Then he complained of "sheer boredom" and said that she needed to get her thoughts "better organized." Basically, in the face of a mother's story about the sexual molestation of her son in a Baptist church, this Baptist pastor responded by complaining about her writing style. The hateful pettiness of it was bone-chilling.

Another blog comment then proceeded to lecture Stephanie on how "parents are ultimately responsible when molestation happens within a church" because the parents shouldn't "use a church as a glorified baby-sitting agency." Another suggested that Stephanie was a "public-ity-seeker" and a "whiner."

It was sickening. Baptists should have been *thanking* Stephanie. It was *her* effort that stopped a serial predator and prevented him from continuing to go church to church as a minister, preying on children. It wasn't church leaders who took action to protect kids; in fact, it was alleged that church leaders knew about the minister's "improper behavior" and did nothing.[174] And it sure wasn't officials at the Baptist General Convention of Texas who stopped the minister or protected kids. Instead, it was an extraordinary mother bear named Stephanie who took the task onto her own shoulders and worked to protect *other* people's kids. And then a bunch of petty, do-nothing Baptist drones chose to slam her for it.

It was the endless streams of such asinine stuff that made me con-stantly question my sanity for spending so much time in trying to reach out to Baptist ministers on the blogs. I was also getting an avalanche of

---

173. Jim Avila, Bonnie Van Gilder and Matt Lopez, "Preachers accused of sins and crimes," *ABC 20/20*, April 13, 2007 (The former minister, with a child molestation conviction on his record, voluntarily spoke with *20/20* in an effort to educate people on how easy it is for predatory ministers to move from church to church in the porous Baptist system, as his own history dem-onstrated.); *see also* Brooks Egerton and Holly Becka, "Man who admits years of molestations gets prison," *Dallas Morning News*, July 14, 1999.

174. Brooks Egerton and Holly Becka, "Man who admits years of molestations gets prison," *supra*.

vitriol by email. Of course, there were some exceptions, but they were like lovely small snowflakes in the midst of the avalanche.

Yet, ultimately, there were at least two good things to come from the effort on the Baptist ministers' blogs. Of course, there could have been other good things that I didn't fully see – seeds that were planted, thoughts that were slightly shifted, hearts that were quietly opened – but these were the two things I knew about.

I learned something more about my own past. On one of the blogs, a woman named "Cathy" commented that my story hit "close to home" for her.[175] She talked about how she grew up as the daughter of a Baptist preacher at one of the three Baptist churches in my hometown, and she thought we must have even had friends in common. I knew she had to be talking about Valwood Baptist, First Baptist of Farmers Branch, and Carrollton Baptist. Those were the three Baptist churches in town when I was growing up. I went to First Baptist of Farmers Branch, and so her dad must have been the pastor at either Valwood or Carrollton.

She said that, during that time period, she remembered hearing talk that "this sort of thing had happened at one of the other churches."

This was a preacher's daughter, and so I figured she had probably overheard her parents talking about it. That meant that my own pastor, Glenn Hayden, had probably talked about it with Cathy's dad, who was apparently the pastor at Valwood or Carrollton. So that meant there were still more people in the Farmers Branch community who had known about what happened to me. Yet everyone had stayed quiet.

That set me to thinking again about some of the deacons in my childhood church. They were my friends' dads. I felt certain they must have also known.

I remembered how my friend Stanley and I were going to ride bikes together that summer, but then he told me that his dad didn't want him to hang out with me anymore. Stanley didn't know why. He said his dad thought I might be "a bad influence." I had known Stanley since I was 10 years old, but suddenly that summer after Dunagan left, Stanley's dad decided I might be "a bad influence." Stanley's dad was a deacon at the church.

Then I thought about Brenda, my best friend whom I had told about Eddie when we were at the Girls' Auxiliary convention. Brenda never was any good at keeping secrets. She would have busted if she

---

175. Comment of "Cathy" on [BaptistLife.com] forums, "Denominational solutions to sexual abuse in SBC" thread, October 29, 2006 at 8:19 a.m.

hadn't told someone. So she probably told her parents. Her dad was also a deacon.

Suddenly I saw that, in the place I grew up, there was a whole community of people who were quietly complicit in covering up for clergy child molestation. It wasn't just the music minister and the pastor who knew. Others also knew. Yet no one helped me. No one tried to talk to me. No one even asked if I was okay.

I felt as though the whole town and everything connected to it had imploded in my head. Everything I ever knew as a kid had become scorched earth.

It hurt to realize that even more people must have known about Dunagan's abuse of me, but I was glad for Cathy's blog comment. It gave me one more puzzle piece of the truth about what happened all those years ago in Farmers Branch, Texas.

The other good thing to come from the effort on Baptist blogs was that Oklahoma pastor Wade Burleson eventually seemed to take an interest. I first encountered Wade in a discussion on the BaptistLife forums, and we exchanged a few emails.[176] Then, Burleson did a posting about the clergy abuse issue on his own widely read blog.[177] After that, other clergy abuse survivors contacted him, sharing pieces of their painful stories.[178]

When, just at the time of the *20/20* show, news broke that pastor Wade Burleson was going to put forward a motion at the June 2007 convention, I heard a lot of skepticism.

> "It's just a ruse to buy time until the *20/20* media glare wanes."
> "He's just asking for a study – it guarantees nothing."
> "Because of all the media attention, Baptists HAVE to do something."

I understood the skepticism, and I myself felt some of it. Yet, I couldn't help but hope that perhaps Wade Burleson had indeed been genuinely

---

176. Carla Hinton, "Pastor urges predator database," *The Oklahoman*, June 13, 2007.

177. Wade Burleson, "Preventing child abuse is a calling for us all," *Grace and Truth to You*, June 8, 2007 [http://kerussocharis.blogspot.com/2007/06/preventing-child-abuse-is-calling-for_08.html]

178. Carla Hinton, "Pastor urges predator database," *The Oklahoman*, June 13, 2007.

affected by some of the survivors who contacted him. The pain of abuse survivors' stories is palpable to anyone who is capable of opening their heart to hear it.

In any event, I mostly just figured it didn't matter. Whatever the reason for Wade Burleson's motion, I could see only that it presented an opportunity. It was an opportunity to continue to shine light on the issue and an opportunity for greater media exposure of the problem.

42

Kicking the Messengers

In February 2007, after my second trip to Southern Baptist headquarters, I was almost back at the Nashville airport when reporter Bob Allen called to tell me that SNAP's requests for action were on the agenda for the next day's meeting of the bylaws workgroup of the Southern Baptist Convention's executive committee.[179] I decided to stay over and try to attend. I hoped that they might allow me to speak, and that I might be able to help them see the need for attention to the problem.

That night, I went to the opening session of the full executive committee and picked a seat in the auditorium's upstairs gallery. I got there early, hoping to introduce myself to a few people because I thought they might be less inclined to demonize me if they could meet me in person. But of course, even that requires at least a willingness to meet the person.

Richard Land wasn't willing. As president of the Southern Baptist Ethics and Religious Liberty Commission, Land is the top ethicist for Baptists. He was one of the people to whom we had sent SNAP's September 2006 letter. I recognized Land as I walked up the aisle, and I immediately stepped forward and extended my hand.

"Dr. Land, I'm Christa Brown. I work with SNAP and . . ."

Before I could even finish my sentence, he had turned away. He wouldn't even shake my hand. A reporter was following me up the aisle and saw it. There was no mistaking the incivility of it.

Back at the hotel, I stayed up almost all that night, hoping and praying that I might somehow find words that would awaken the hearts of the committee members. When I left home, I hadn't planned on speaking to the committee, and I wasn't prepared. I hadn't even brought a change of clothes. But I felt it was an opportunity I couldn't let pass. I searched my mind for ways to reach them. How could I help them to understand how desperately they needed to implement accountability measures like

---

179. Bob Allen, "SBC Executive Committee to discuss SNAP requests," *EthicsDaily*, February 20, 2007; Bob Allen, "Group asks Southern Baptist leaders to address clergy sex abuse," *EthicsDaily*, February 19, 2007.

what other faith groups were doing? How could I help them to see the danger and hurtfulness of their do-nothingness?

The next morning, I went back over to that block-long Baptist compound to the meeting of the bylaws workgroup. Once again, I got there early to introduce myself. Then I seated myself in the room's two-row gallery. They debated a bit about whether to even let me stay in the room, but ultimately they chose to let me stay, and they allowed me to speak.[180] It was a room of all men, except for one woman sitting in the back corner, apparently taking notes.

As an appellate attorney, I have sometimes given arguments before judicial panels that were not at all sympathetic. But this was unquestionably the most hostile room in which I have ever spoken. If there had been a pile of stones handy, they might have been throwing them. Such was the mood of that room.

Nevertheless, I felt grateful for the chance to address them, and I gave a short statement, talking about the clergy abuse problem in generic terms and seeking to appeal to them on our common ground as parents who care about kids.

In response, they were "long on criticism" and "short on specifics" about how they might address the problem.[181] They were angry that I had brought media attention to their doorstep. But I bluntly refused to apologize for that.[182] Then I tried to explain to them why I had become convinced that media attention was necessary in order to get *their* attention.

I told them about how I had been raped by a Southern Baptist minister as an adolescent girl, and about how I had tried to report it as an adult, only to find that, among 18 Southern Baptist leaders, there was not a single one who would do anything. I pointed out that the man was forced out of ministry only *after* I contacted the media.

It was a painful story to share, and to do so before such a hostile audience was horrible. One man in the gallery seemed to literally chortle as I spoke. Perhaps he would say that he was just clearing his throat, but as I

---

180. Bob Allen, "SBC leaders deny charge of unresponsiveness about clergy sex abuse," *EthicsDaily*, February 21, 2007.

181. Bob Allen, "SBC leaders deny charge of unresponsiveness about clergy sex abuse," *supra*.

182. Bob Allen, "SBC leaders deny charge of unresponsiveness about clergy sex abuse," *supra*.

spoke of being molested by a Baptist minister, his chortling-sound made such an impression on me that his is now a face I will never forget.[183]

The committee members were seated at a large U-shaped table. I stood just inside the opening of the "U" as I began to speak. A committee member sitting on the left wing of the "U" turned his back to me. He literally turned around in his chair.

I could hardly believe what I was seeing, and so as I continued to speak, I deliberately moved myself forward a bit further into the middle of the "U" to place myself in his peripheral vision to see what he would do. Each time I stepped forward, he repeatedly turned himself even more in his seat so as to physically maintain his back to me.

We did a bit of a dance there. I would step forward and he would turn further. I would step backward and his shoulder would relax. It was downright cartoonish.[184]

---

183. Months later, I again saw the chortling man in TV news coverage about a financial scandal at the prominent Two Rivers Baptist Church in Nashville. Two Rivers is the home church for many of the denominational officials who do the day-to-day decision-making of the Southern Baptist Convention. When the many members of the church's finance committee appeared in news coverage of the scandal, I immediately recognized the chortling man among them. The gist of the scandal was this: A group of church-members sought access to Two Rivers' financial records, but they were accused of "causing disharmony." Church leadership insisted, "There has to be submission and authority." Eventually, a group of 71 members sued the church. Meanwhile, thousands of church financial records were found in a garbage bag behind the church. During that same time period, the Associated Press also reported on allegations that a Two Rivers minister had pornography on his church computer and had an affair with a church staff member – allegations that the church denied. *See* Rose French (Associated Press), "Baptist pastor under scrutiny," *Washington Post*, August 14, 2007; Jennifer Johnson, "Church members fight to view records," *WSMV-Nashville*, April 24, 2008; [http://www.wsmv.com/news/15984282/detail.html]; Anne Marshall, "Second suit filed against prominent pastor," *WSMV-Nashville*, January 17, 2008 (video report) [http://www.wsmv.com/news/15078307/detail.html]; *WSMV-Nashville*, April 3, 2008 [available at http://www.tworiversinfo.org/WSMV-TRBC-040308.mov].

184 Southern Baptists are generally well-known for their dogma on female submissiveness. Citing 1 Timothy 2:11–14 and 1 Corinthians 14:34, Baptists often assert that women should not teach in authority over men, that women cannot be pastors, that women should submit "graciously" to their husbands, and that women should keep silent in church. *See e.g.,* David Waters, "Southern Baptists and their gender double-standard," *The Washington Post*, September 2, 2008. I couldn't help but wonder whether the back-turned committee member would think these *Bible* verses justified his extraordinary rudeness toward a woman speaking before male religious leaders. Or maybe he was trying to send a "get thee behind me" message. Or maybe he was just rude for no reason.

Suffice it to say that there wasn't much compassion in that room. And despite my fervent hopes, I obviously had not found the words to reach them.

They were angry that I had been telling reporters they hadn't responded to SNAP's September 26th letter.[185] They had, and as I sat there, they gave me a copy of their September 29th response. It was the first I had seen of it.

I apologized on the spot. That was my initial instinct, and it's what I did. I also told them that I didn't know whether or not SNAP had actually received their letter, but that I would look into as soon as I got back. And I did.

The next day, after a few phone calls and emails, I learned that SNAP's Chicago office had that letter sitting in a pile. Apparently, a volunteer there was thinking that SNAP's national director, David Clohessy, was going to be in Chicago, and she was letting a pile of stuff stack up to hand off to him in person. David cancelled on a couple Chicago trips, and so the pile continued to sit there.

Immediately, I contacted the reporters I had spoken to, and told them that I had been mistaken and that Southern Baptist officials had indeed responded to SNAP's letter. None of them seemed to think it mattered much. They wanted to know whether Southern Baptist officials were actually *doing* anything. Besides, once I sent them the actual letter, they could see for themselves that it was just a brush-off.

Nevertheless, SNAP's national director, David Clohessy, and I issued a press release, extending a public apology to Southern Baptist officials for our mistake in saying they hadn't responded to our letter.[186] Much to my surprise, Southern Baptist officials then used their own *Baptist Press* to claim that we had apologized for "making false accusations."[187] It was a diabolical distortion.

Then Florida celebrity pastor and former Southern Baptist president Jerry Vines jumped on board the venomous bandwagon. On a widely dispersed Christian news network, he said we made "false charges" and

185. Bob Allen, "SBC leaders deny charge of unresponsiveness about clergy sex abuse," *EthicsDaily*, February 21, 2007.

186. Bob Allen, "SNAP admits error in saying SBC leaders did not respond to letter," *EthicsDaily*, February 23, 2007. (Southern Baptist officials sent 2 letters to SNAP's Chicago office, but only one of them was in response to SNAP's September 26th letter. That was the brush-off letter.)

187. "SNAP apologizes to SBC leaders, admits charges of 'silence' were 'erroneous'," *Baptist Press*, February 23, 2007.

he accused us of being "not really forthright."[188] That was when I realized that Baptist leaders were trying to discredit *me* so as to restore the reputation of my perpetrator, Eddie Dunagan, who was well-known among Florida Baptists. At least, that's the way it looked to me. Rather than telling people in the pews what they knew about *Dunagan* – i.e., that there was substantial evidence he sexually abused a kid and that another minister had sworn to knowledge of Dunagan's abuse – they were publicly smearing *me*.

It was a blow that knocked the wind out of me. Almost all clergy abuse victims internalize the fear that, if they talk about it, no one will believe them and they will be accused of making false accusations. For many, that fear takes on such a life of its own that it becomes a looming bear in their heads. So, in choosing to tar SNAP and me with "making false accusations," Southern Baptist leaders hit at a very sore spot. I couldn't help but wonder whether it was calculated. Perhaps they did indeed understand enough about clergy abuse victims to know exactly where and how to throw a punch so that it would inflict maximum pain.

I thought about how quick they were to kick me because I didn't know about their silly brush-off letter, and yet they themselves seemed to not know about something as important as a Southern Baptist preacher-predator working with kids in Florida. And while I made an immediate effort to find their letter as soon as I was told about it, they apparently made no effort to find the preacher-predator even after receiving a substantiated report about his sexual abuse of a kid. In fact, the Southern Baptist Convention wrote that they had no record Eddie Dunagan was still in ministry . . . even though he was.

I also thought about how David Clohessy and I had immediately apologized for SNAP's loss of the Baptist brush-off letter even though neither of us had any personal knowledge about the letter.[189] Yet, to this day, no Southern Baptist official has ever apologized for the fact that their organization "lost" a reported clergy child molester and gave out the misleading information that there was no record of him in ministry . . . even though he was.[190] Their mistake was obviously one that carried

188. Allie Martin and Jenni Parker, "Former SBC president encourages local churches to prevent sexual abuse," *OneNewsNow.com*, February 28, 2007. (OneNewsNow is part of the American Family News network.)

189. Bob Allen, "SBC president says denomination looking into sex offender registry," by Bob Allen, *EthicsDaily*, April 16, 2007.

190. Bob Allen, "SBC president says denomination looking into sex offender registry," *supra*.

the potential for far more serious consequences than the loss of a mere brush-off letter. But the difference is that Southern Baptist officials have a "buck-stops-nowhere" organization.[191] No one is held accountable.

Finally, I thought how strange it was that Southern Baptist president Frank Page didn't just pick up the phone and talk to me. I had tried to open a line of communication with him and had emailed him personally, giving him my direct-line phone number.[192] So when he saw that I was saying Southern Baptist officials hadn't responded to SNAP's letter, why didn't he just pick up the phone and say, "Christa, why are you telling the press we haven't responded when in fact we sent you all a letter a few weeks ago?" Maybe it was because he knew their letter was so tacky.

Start to finish, the whole episode showed me something foul about how these guys operate.[193] They were obviously oriented toward low-road tactics.

Not long after that, Southern Baptist president Frank Page dropped even lower when he publicly smeared us in the *Florida Baptist Witness*. He said that groups like us were "nothing more than opportunistic persons who are seeking to raise opportunities for personal gain."[194] That hurt big-time.

Where was the "opportunity," I wondered, in being raped as a kid by a minister. It was surreal that any religious leader would even suggest

---

191. *See* Eileen Flynn, Austin lawyer pushes Baptist churches to confront sexual abuse, *Austin American-Statesman*, June 9, 2008.

192. Email correspondence from Christa Brown to Dr. Frank Page, dated January 15, 2007. Page's return email of January 31, 2007 indicates that he received it.

193. Bob Allen, "SNAP cries foul over Baptist Press reporting," *EthicsDaily*, March 27, 2007.

194. Frank Page, "Point of view: Guarding against sexual abuse in the church," *Florida Baptist Witness*, April 19, 2007; Bob Allen, "SBC president labels sexual abuse critics 'opportunists'," *EthicsDaily*, April 20, 2007. Though Page's remarks were picked up by other publications, they were *first* disseminated in Southern Baptists' Florida publication. This made them appear to me as part of an effort to rehabilitate the reputation of former Florida minister Eddie Dunagan by slurring those who brought his abuse of a child to light. Coincidentally, just a week after Page's Florida remarks, the *Tennessean* published an Associated Press photo showing Southern Baptist president Frank Page sitting next to Dwayne Mercer, the senior pastor of First Baptist Church of Oviedo, a church where Dunagan worked as a children's minister. Anita Wadhwani, "Sex abuse victims turn focus to Baptists," *Tennessean*, April 29, 2007; Bob Allen, "SBC president questions motives of SNAP, says sex abuse everywhere," *EthicsDaily*, May 2, 2007 (identifying Mercer in the AP photo).

such a thing. And I couldn't help but laugh at his notion that there was some "personal gain." I had allowed my law practice to become a shambles. I was so flooded with survivors' emails and with trying to figure out what could be done that I had been turning away almost all legal work and my income had dropped dramatically. I wondered how many of those Baptist officials would even consider taking on a full-time ministry and outreach effort for no income.

A group of ten other ministers – Catholic, Presbyterian, Methodist, Disciples of Christ, and Baptist – wrote to Dr. Page, urging him to re-consider his "harsh rhetoric" toward clergy abuse victims.[195] They told him that he was "misguided and misinformed" and that his harshness was "inappropriate for the leader of a religious body."[196] But of course, there was never any apology from Frank Page.

A few months after Page's harsh remarks, the Pope visited this country and made public apologies for the sexual abuse that Catholic priests had inflicted on children. It was a dramatic contrast in how these two high religious leaders spoke about clergy abuse victims. Even if the Pope's remarks were staged and primarily for public relations – which many people said – I still figured it would have felt better to hear even a hollow apology than to get publicly slammed as an "opportunist."

Of course, Frank Page wasn't the only one slamming us. Former Southern Baptist president Paige Patterson called us "evil-doers," and said we were "just as reprehensible as sex criminals."[197] SNAP's founder and president, Barbara Blaine, pointed out that, over the past 20 years, SNAP leaders had met with "hundreds of denominational authorities in various faith groups," and that "none has ever before called us 'evil' or claimed we were as bad as child predators.' "[198] It took a Southern

---

195. Audrey Barrick, "Clergy rebuke SBC head for 'harsh rhetoric' over sex abuse cases," *Christian Post*, July 20, 2007.

196. One of the letter's signers, Dr. Miguel De La Torre, also told the press how disappointed he was that "Dr. Page dismissed child abuse by questioning the integrity of those bringing the issue to light." Dr. De La Torre is a professor of social ethics and director of the Justice and Peace Institute at the Iliff School of Theology. Audrey Barrick, "Clergy rebuke SBC head for 'harsh rhetoric' over sex abuse cases," *supra*.

197. Bob Allen, "SBC seminary president labels clergy sex-abuse victims' group 'evil-doers'," *EthicsDaily*, February 15, 2008; Elizabeth Ulrich, "What would Jesus say?" *Nashville Scene*, February 14, 2008; Elizabeth Ulrich, "The Bad Shepherd," *Nashville Scene*, April 24, 2008.

198. Bob Allen, "SNAP leaders ask Patterson to apologize for 'evil-doers' remark," *EthicsDaily*, February 22, 2008.

Baptist leader to stoop to such low-level name-calling as that.[199]

When the highest leaders of a powerful religious organization use such hateful rhetoric, it has an insidious trickle-down effect. It deters abuse survivors from speaking up, and it establishes a climate that tells others it's okay to say hurtful things. So, I along with other Baptist abuse survivors wound up having a heap of ugly stuff flung at us – in person, via email, and in blog comments. It was all of these words and more: Jezebel, rage-filled, bitter, little Lolita, unforgiving, divisive, tramp, trash, unChristian, anti-Christian, Christian-hater, church-hater, homo, spawn of Satan, trouble-maker, whiner, attention-seeker.

With every hateful word hurled, I felt faith's falsity and the betrayal in all that I had once believed. I saw a sick savage-the-wounded sort of spirituality among Baptist preachers and leaders. Where were the Good Samaritans among them?[200] As best I could tell, if these men encountered a wounded traveler in the desert, they wouldn't just ride their donkeys past him – they would run their donkeys right over him.

I expect these men would sit with you in the hospital if you were sick. And they'd bring you one of the wife's casseroles if someone died. But if you're unlucky enough to have been molested by one of their clergy-colleagues, then you become a leper and an outcast. They will leave you bleeding in the dirt rather than get down off their high donkeys to help.

Paige Patterson's "evil-doer" comment apparently went over the top even for some Southern Baptist officials. In a sort of cloak-and-dagger style, a member of the executive committee had been communicating with me off and on. Sometimes it seemed to me as though he was just fishing to try to figure out what I might do next. And sometimes it

199. Former Southern Baptist president Paige Patterson is currently the president of Southwestern Baptist Theological Seminary, where the next generation of Southern Baptist preachers learns from his example. *See* Bob Allen, "SNAP leaders ask Patterson to apologize for 'evil-doers' remark," *EthicsDaily*, February 22, 2008. Patterson himself has been accused of turning a blind eye to multiple reports alleging sexual abuse committed by former Baptist pastor Darrell Gilyard while he worked in Texas churches. Gilyard, who was allowed to move on, currently faces charges of child molestation in Florida. Jim Schoettler, "Records list lewd texts, molestings by pastor," *The Florida Times-Union*, August 6, 2008; Lindy Thackston, "Local pastor arrested; national religious leader accused of turning a blind eye," *First Coast News*, January 14, 2008 [http://www.firstcoastnews.com/news/news-article.aspx?storyid=99945]; Rebecca Sherman, "The downfall of a pastor," *Dallas Morning News*, July 14, 1991.

200. *See* Christa Brown, "Good Samaritan holds lesson for treatment of clergy abuse victims," *EthicsDaily*, November 30, 2007.

seemed like he was trying to evangelize me and convince me to join a Baptist church. It seldom seemed productive, but I figured it was worthwhile simply to have a line of communication open, and so I was happy to talk with him. After Patterson's "evil-doer" comment was publicized, this guy called me.

"Christa, I just want you to know that *I* don't think you're evil."

He said it with such earnestness that I broke out laughing. I'm sure my guffaw wasn't the best of all possible responses, and it may have even seemed disrespectful, but I couldn't help it. What am I supposed to say when, with all seriousness, someone pronounces me "not evil"?

After I reined myself in, I said, "Well, I'm glad to know you don't think I'm evil, because I certainly don't think I'm evil."

"But you can't ever tell anyone I said that," he replied. "It would be the end of me."

I promised him that I'd never tell anyone he had talked with me, and I kept my promise. But it didn't stop me from thinking how silly it was. Here this guy was probably patting himself on the back because he's enlightened enough that he knows better than to think I'm evil and because he reaches out to tell me so. But at the same time, he didn't ever want news that HE said such a thing to leak out. The fact that he didn't think I was evil was supposed to be our little secret. Such courage!

Besides, his Mr. Nice-guy routine didn't mean much to me, given that just a few months earlier, he had sat stone-silent in that committee room while one of his fellow committee-members railed against me as "a person of no integrity."[201] Neither he nor any other man in that all-white, all-male room would even call his colleague on the carpet for such uncharitable language. Every single one them stayed quiet while their colleague kicked the messenger – me.

That happened on my third trip to Nashville, and they weren't allowing me to speak that time. So I couldn't even defend myself. David Clohessy, SNAP's national director, was there with me on that trip, and they didn't want to hear anything from him either. I couldn't help but think what a terrible waste of an opportunity that was. David is widely recognized as one of the most knowledgeable people in the country on the subject of clergy sex abuse. An ordinary person might have expected that the committee would want to take advantage of David's expertise and ask some questions. But they weren't interested.

---

201. Bob Allen, "Clergy sex-abuse survivor questions fairness of SBC Executive Committee study," *EthicsDaily*, September 21, 2007.

Baptist leaders not only kicked me and other clergy abuse survivors, but they also kicked the media who were reporting on the issue. After *20/20* aired its "Preacher Predators" program, Southern Baptist president Frank Page called it "yellow journalism"[202] and an "attack piece."[203] He railed about the media's "bias against conservative Christians"[204] and said the *20/20* piece was "an intentional slice-and-dice effort to portray the SBC and its president as uncaring and uninformed."[205] So instead of doing something about the problem, he blamed the media for bringing the problem to light.

I wondered how Frank Page could imagine that he should appear as anything *other* than "uncaring and uninformed." After all, he hadn't known there were convicted child molesters on the Southern Baptist Convention's own ministerial registry, which is maintained right there at national headquarters. So it was obvious he was "uninformed." And when he was told about convicted child molesters on the registry, he was so "uncaring" that he didn't even get the names removed. The convicted child molesters *stayed* on the Southern Baptist Convention's registry.

The problem for men like Frank Page is that he wants the Southern Baptist Convention to have an image that is something other than reality. "Uncaring and uninformed" is the way they look because, when it comes to clergy sex abuse, that's the way they behave.

But here's the thing that really got under my skin. Page publicly whined about how his *20/20* interview had actually been two hours long and only about a minute of it was in the actual 16-minute *20/20* segment that aired.[206] I thought about all the Baptist abuse survivors who had given of their emotional energy to help in the making of that program, and most of them got no air time at all. I knew of two Baptist abuse survivors who had gone through the stress of giving on-camera interviews, and no part at all of their interviews were actually shown.

---

202. Bob Allen, "SBC president labels sexual abuse critics as 'opportunists'," *EthicsDaily*, April 20, 2007; "Page says *20/20* segment one-sided," *Baptist Press*, April 16, 2007.

203. Anita Wadhwani, "Sex abuse victims turn focus to Baptists," *The Tennessean*, April 29, 2007.

204. Anita Wadhwani, "Sex abuse victims turn focus to Baptists," *supra*.

205. "Page says *20/20* segment one-sided," *Baptist Press*, April 16, 2007; Bob Allen, "SBC president labels sexual abuse critics as 'opportunists'," *EthicsDaily*, April 20, 2007.

206. "Page says '*20/20*' segment one-sided," *Baptist Press*, April 16, 2007; Bob Allen, "SBC officials criticize 'Predator Preacher' report on '*20/20*'," *EthicsDaily*, April 18, 2007.

Other Baptist abuse survivors had spoken with the *20/20* producer by phone. All of them had engaged painful conversations and had gone through a difficult process in even considering whether they were capable of speaking on-camera. Some had gone to extra counseling sessions to grapple with it. They got absolutely nothing for their effort and anguish. But even though they wound up without so much as a millisecond of air time, not a one of them ever whined about it. To the contrary, they were grateful for the chance to do what they could to help.

I myself was interviewed for over two hours and was filmed on two separate days, at my childhood church and at the little chapel. All of it was emotionally wrenching, and barely a minute of my interview actually made it into the final program. But it never would have occurred to me to whine about it. I felt only profound gratitude for the opportunity to assist in shining a national spotlight on the problem.

Months later, when the *Nashville Scene* did a series on Baptist clergy sex abuse and the failure of leadership to address it, Southern Baptist officials also accused the *Nashville Scene* of acting "with deliberate deceit to portray SBC officials as uncaring."[207] The *Nashville Scene* publicly responded that every abuse victim the reporter had interviewed said it "all on their own" – that Southern Baptist officials are "uncaring."[208]

---

207. Elizabeth Ulrich, "Baptism by fire," *Nashville Scene*, February 21, 2008.
208. Elizabeth Ulrich, "Baptism by fire," *supra*. In another article, the *Nashville Scene* pointed out that the Southern Baptist Convention had treated many victims "in a manner that's dismissive and uncaring – and at times, downright unconscionable." Elizabeth Ulrich, "The Bad Shepherd," *Nashville Scene*, April 24, 2008.

43

Belief Is Gone

In San Antonio, I was the last of the SNAP people to leave the convention center. I was exhausted. In addition to handing out flyers in the sun, we had done three press events in two days' time, and I had talked one-on-one with at least a dozen reporters.

I was sitting on a bench outside the press room, waiting for news about the vote on Wade Burleson's motion when a man from the Baptist General Convention of Texas came up and extended his hand. He said he recognized me because he had seen my picture on my blog, and he introduced himself as Frank Fulmore, the media person for the Baptist General Convention of Texas.

Frank seemed like a good-hearted extrovert, and I was glad to sit and visit with him. I try not to close the door to anyone, because I figure you never know when you might meet someone who will choose to help. Besides, the Baptist General Convention of Texas likes to position itself as the "moderate" good-guy Baptists compared to the more fundamentalist Baptists at Southern Baptist headquarters in Nashville. I guess I still bought into some of their public relations spin and thought it might mean something. So, I sat down with Frank and we had a nice chat. He told me about his kids.

After a while, he asked if he could introduce me to Charles Wade, the executive director of the Baptist General Convention of Texas. Wade was one of the Baptist officials to whom I had sent my initial report three years earlier, and he hadn't done diddly-squat to help me. But I didn't want to just walk away. I wanted to still hope that there might be some way to reach the heart of this high Baptist official.

As I stepped over to go talk with him, I remembered the words of my friend, Elana. On countless walks together, she had listened to me recount things Baptist leaders had said and done. She repeatedly heard my expressions of disbelief, and my statements of "Just when I thought I'd seen it all, they do this," or "Just when I thought they couldn't possibly stoop any lower, they do!" Elana had listened a lot, but recently, she had given voice to her own disbelief.

"Christa, I can't believe you still expect anything OTHER than low behavior from them. They have shown you what their true values are and they have shown you over and over again. When will YOU learn? Why do YOU keep expecting the best of them? What holds YOU to that belief?"

Elana was asking a good question, but I didn't have any answer. And there I was again, holding onto that same hope and going over to talk with Charles Wade, even though I had no basis grounded in reality for any belief that Wade would ever choose to help.

I stood there, trying to tell Charles Wade and Frank Fulmore about how desperately clergy abuse survivors need a safe place to report abuse – a place that is outside the church of the pastor-perpetrator. Wade said "maybe so" but insisted that, for Baptists to implement such a system "would make us into slaves." Baptists aren't subject to bishops, he explained. "What we lose in safety, we gain in freedom."

Apparently, this seemed like a fair trade-off to him – the safety of kids for the freedom of a free-wheeling religious polity that renders clergy unaccountable.

I realized then that we were having parallel conversations. His abstract words about religious slavery seemed meaningless to me as I tried to tell him about the real problems of real people who have been terribly wounded by real Baptist preachers. But from his vantage of religious nobility, it seemed that my talk about real people was equally meaningless to him.

"Look, even if you can't do anything else, can't you at least try to minister to the wounded?" I asked. "Why not try to bring in the lost sheep? Do you have any idea how much it would mean to them? There are so many who still hold some hope that the faith community will actually care about what happened to them. Help them. Help them keep that hope."

I felt my eyes welling up, and I hated myself for it. But even as I silently cursed my tears, I looked at Charles Wade's empty eyes and thought this was a man who could actually do with a little *more* emotion. Where was there any compassion or feeling in those eyes? It wasn't apparent to me, that was for sure.

"So many need help so badly," I said, trying to continue and still hoping to get some message across to him. I had reached the point that I was virtually pleading with him, and I hated hearing that sound of near-begging in my voice. But I kept on.

"My greatest wish for others is that they might be spared the misery of what I went through afterwards – *later* – in trying to report the abuse. That's where so much *more* harm is done."

The two men seemed to be just waiting for me to finish, and I suddenly felt the futility of it all.

"Look, I've seen and heard too much. I'm hopeless. But you could still reach out to so many others."

"Ohhhhh, you aren't hopeless, Christa." That was Frank's immediate, light-hearted response. But it was just a gauzy, feel-good reaction, sort of like the way so many of these men say, "We'll pray for you." Most of the time, it's just words. It's what they say to distance themselves from the pain that's in front of them. It's what they say to make *themselves* feel better.

After talking with the two of them, I got on the highway to drive the 90 miles back to my home, and I had to pull off the road a couple times because I was shaking and crying so much. The pain of that conversation weighed on me and merged into one big mess of misery. It brought back memories of all my prior talks with Texas Baptist officials Jan Daehnert and Sonny Spurger, and of all the dissembling and duplicity that I had encountered. The voices of other abuse survivors who had vainly sought help from the Baptist General Convention of Texas rang in my head . . . people who had sought help a decade ago and people who had sought help a few weeks ago.

I felt like a battered wife who, over and over again, keeps wanting to believe her husband when he says, "I promise it won't happen again – things will be different."

I knew I couldn't let myself keep hoping that officials at the Baptist General Convention of Texas would actually care about clergy abuse victims. I couldn't keep believing that they would choose to help abuse survivors, would do what they said they'd do, or would even honor the words in their own published booklet. It wasn't healthy for me. It was a psychological mistake.

At some point, the battered wife must look at the long pattern, must stop believing the promises of change, and must say "no more." That's how I felt about the Baptist General Convention of Texas.

I finally made it home, and I curled up on my bed and cried. I woke up the next morning and cried some more. I knew I could no longer be the same person I once was. I could no longer be the person I was before I heard so many other Baptist abuse survivors' stories and learned that the same heartlessness inflicted on me had been inflicted on many more. I could no longer be the person I was as recently as a couple years ago, when I still held some small belief that the Baptist General Convention of Texas stood for something. I wished I could. But once you've seen so many bodies, you can't unsee them.

A few months after that encounter with Charles Wade and Frank Fulmore, *EthicsDaily* reported that "media staff at a large, moderate Baptist state convention" referred to me as "THAT woman" while criticizing *EthicsDaily*'s coverage of Baptist clergy sex abuse.[209] I knew immediately that it had to be Frank Fulmore . . . and I was right. After talking with me face-to-face in San Antonio, and after acting as though he cared, he had turned around and made me into a nameless tabloid slur.

Fulmore was a professional media person and he was talking to a reporter when he said it. If that's the sort of thing Fulmore says when he's talking to a reporter, what does he say when he's just shooting the breeze with his buddy in the office next door? And if that's the sort of thing a Baptist *media* person says – i.e., a paid spokesperson who is trained to be careful with his words – what do some of the other men in that big Baptist building say? I figured it was pretty vile stuff. I didn't even want to imagine it.

209. Robert Parham, "Does EthicsDaily.com matter?" *EthicsDaily*, November 19, 2007.

44

The Guru Gets Ugly

I'm probably going to get a lot of flak for writing about Joe Trull. He's a tall, white-haired Southern gentleman and a former seminary professor. Among Baptists, he's considered one of their most knowledgeable people on the subject of clergy sex abuse. He's *very* well-respected.

And that's exactly why I'm writing about him.

If someone as knowledgeable and well-respected as Joe Trull couldn't see the clergy abuse cover-up that was going on in his own church, why do Baptist leaders persist in imagining that ordinary congregants will be able to see it when it happens in *their* church?

It's a case that wasn't intended to see the light of day. In November 2006, Pastor Reynolds of Southmont Baptist Church in Denton, Texas, paid "hush money" to settle a lawsuit that alleged his sexual abuse of a 14-year-old church girl.[210] The now 37-year-old woman, K. Roush, agreed to never talk about the case, except with a therapist.

I had heard about the case many months earlier, but after that, it went quiet. Then, one day, I was out in front of the Dallas Convention Center with several other Baptist abuse survivors, getting ready to do a SNAP press conference at the annual meeting of the Baptist General Convention of Texas.[211] One of the top things we were asking was that the Baptist General Convention adopt a policy against the use of "hush money" agreements with clergy abuse victims. Catholic bishops adopted a policy against such agreements in 2002, and we were asking the Baptist General Convention of Texas to do the same thing.

Three TV crews were there, and they were hoisting their cameras onto their shoulders just as my phone buzzed. I answered, thinking it might be another reporter who was having a hard time finding us.

---

210. Bob Allen, "Pastor reportedly settled lawsuit alleging sexual abuse of minor, *EthicsDaily*, November 20, 2006; Donna Fielder, "Suits allege clergy misconduct: Two Baptist ministers apologize after women bring forth accusations," *Denton Record-Chronicle*, December 17, 2006.

211. Bob Allen, "SNAP urges Texas Baptists to disclose list of sexual predators," *EthicsDaily*, November 13, 2006.

Instead, it was a woman talking fast and loud. She was so outraged that I could hardly understand what she was saying. Finally, I realized she was talking about the pastor at Southmont.

In between outbursts, she told me about how her friend had just signed a confidentiality agreement saying she would never again talk about what the pastor did to her when she was a kid.

"They shut her up fine and good," she raged. "Now she can't even talk to *me* about it anymore. But he gets to keep right on preaching."

The woman's voice was rising. She was on the verge of shouting. "All he's gonna have to do is stand up at a church service and say he engaged in 'inappropriate conduct.' That's all. And I bet you he's just going to mumble something. He's not going to really tell those people what he did."

She wanted to know what I could do about it, but mostly, I was just trying to get off the phone. I kept trying to tell her that I'd have to call her back because I could see the reporters waiting on me. But she just wouldn't let me go.

"Do you know what he did to her?" she kept demanding.

She wanted me to go to Denton and do a press conference outside the church. When I told her I couldn't, I heard that wail again: "Do you know what he did?"

"Yes ma'am. I know. I've got a copy of the court filing on that case. I've seen it. I know."

My words seemed to momentarily appease her, and so I quickly promised that I'd do what I could and hung up. With her voice of outrage still ringing in my ears, I turned to the cameras.

After the press conference, we moved to the inside of the convention center where we distributed flyers, urging people to "Protect Baptist Kids" by insisting that Baptist officials open their secret files and warn people about ministers reported by churches for sexual abuse. Joe Trull stepped up and introduced himself.

I was happy to meet him because I knew who he was. Joe helped the Baptist General Convention of Texas write its "Broken Trust" policy booklet about clergy abuse, and then he parlayed that into a chapter in his book on "Ministerial Ethics."[212] Ever since then, he had been the

---

212. Joe E. Trull & James E. Carter, *Ministerial Ethics* (Baker Academic 2004).

go-to guy for Baptists on the subject of "sexual misconduct." He was their expert.[213]

Of course, for Baptists, it might not take much. So many of them are so squeamish about sexuality that I wondered whether a minister might be considered in the vanguard of knowledge if he was simply willing to say the word "sex" out loud.

But Trull was obviously some steps beyond that. His book had some good language in it:

> The problem of clergy sex abuse is not just a Catholic issue – the problem extends to Protestant denominations as well. Studies have shown no differences in its frequency by denomination, region, theology, or institutional structure. . . .

> National policies regarding sexual misconduct have been adopted by most mainline denominations, including Methodists, Presbyterians and Lutherans. . . . Decentralized denominations such as the Southern Baptist Convention . . . have no national policies, leaving each individual church to establish its own guidelines. Sexual misconduct is routinely covered up in these settings.[214]

In other comments, Trull even acknowledged that "Baptist churches who have autonomous church government are *more* vulnerable" to clergy sexual abuse.[215] Because of the "lack of accountability," he explained, "most Baptists and nondenominational ministers know that 'If I get caught, I can move to California and start a new church'."[216]

Words like these gave me hope that Trull might be someone helpful. I even allowed myself to imagine that Joe Trull could become the Thomas Doyle of Baptists. I thought he might wind up being the courageous

---

213. Joe Trull describes himself as having extensive "experience, training and focus of study" on "clergy sexual misconduct." He sometimes speaks on the topic at Baptist conferences. Joe E. Trull, "The Haggard Affair: Overlooked Issues," *Christian Ethics Today*, issue 62, vol. 12, no. 5 (2006).
214. Joe E. Trull & James E. Carter, *Ministerial Ethics, supra* at p. 162.
215. Hannah Elliott, "Baptist churches more vulnerable to clergy sex abuse, experts say," *Associated Baptist Press*, January 23, 2007.
216. Hannah Elliott, "Baptist churches more vulnerable to clergy sex abuse, experts say," *supra*.

leader who would help Baptists lift their veil of denial and see the horror in their mishandling of clergy abuse reports.

Of course, that was just wishful thinking on my part. In hindsight, I see how desperately I wanted to believe in the possibility of some Baptist hero like that. But with Trull, clergy abuse seemed more of an academic topic. He wrote about it as an issue of ministerial ethics. I didn't sense that Trull had any genuine understanding of how sexual trauma affects the victims or of its soul-murdering impact when the perpetrator is a pastor.

I had observed a similar attitude in the comments of other Baptist preachers. Typically, they viewed the problem from the perspective of the minister rather than the perspective of the victim. They talked about it in terms of "sexual temptation," "sexual sin," "sexual immorality," "sexual ethics," and "sexual integrity." It was easy to see that, at root, most of them thought the problem was about sex. But of course, thinking clergy sex abuse is about sex is like thinking the Bataan Death March was about marching.[217]

Nevertheless, because of some of the good language in Joe Trull's book, I had taken the initiative to write to him, hoping to establish a dialogue. We went back and forth on the issue. He said the problem rested in "the ignorance of a few."[218]

"Where are those who are NOT ignorant?" I asked. "Where are the Baptist leaders who are not ignorant at best or hostile at worst?[219] When it's so extremely difficult to find a denominational leader who will treat seriously a substantiated report of a minister's sexual abuse of a minor – as it surely was for me – then the reality is that most clergy predators will easily remain hidden. And so long as it's that easy for a predator to remain hidden, kids will not be safe."

"Progress is being made," said Trull.[220]

"If the way I was treated constitutes progress," I replied, "then this denomination lives in very dark ages. Progress would mean working to protect others, but what I saw seemed more akin to an effort to stone me back into oblivion."[221]

Where Trull and I really went back and forth was on "predators" and "wanderers." These are categories he uses to describe ministers

---

217. Christa Brown, "It's not about sex," *EthicsDaily*, January 22, 2008.
218. Email correspondence from Joe Trull to Christa Brown dated July 21, 2006.
219. Email correspondence from Christa Brown to Joe Trull dated August 30, 2006.
220. Email correspondence from Joe Trull to Christa Brown dated July 21, 2006.
221. Email correspondence from Christa Brown to Joe Trull dated August 30, 2006.

who commit sexual abuse, and I told him I thought this academic dichotomy was being misused. I urged him to reconsider it in light of its real-world effect.

"As I see it," I explained, "your dichotomy between 'wanderers' and 'predators' helps to provide the architecture for the rationalization by which this denomination justifies its continued lack of action in protecting against this horrific crime."[222]

"*Even if* you are correct in recognizing two camps of offenders," I continued, "you and others are still making a huge and very damaging mistake in that you are effectively choosing to err on the side of 'restoring' the 'wanderers' rather than on the side of protecting against the 'predators'."[223]

Trull didn't give much credence to my concern. Instead, he told me about a man "who for years counseled ministers for the Baptist General Convention of Texas" and who "indicated he had NEVER had a 'predator' come for help, but he had worked with numerous persons who fit the category we describe as a 'wanderer'."[224]

I suppose Trull thought this bit of information might comfort me, as though it would prove how few in number the "predators" are because ALL the ministers who go through the Texas Baptist convention's ministerial counseling service are mere "wanderers."

But I didn't see it that way. I saw this bit of information as another horrifying piece of the puzzle. It makes the Texas Baptist convention's ministerial counseling service sound a lot like the sort of counseling that many Catholic bishops sent child molesting priests to. The bishops provided blind-eyed counselors who were easily conned. They quietly treated the priests and then sent them back out to parish churches.

I found myself wondering whether the same sort of thing had been happening for the past two decades with child molesting Baptist ministers who got counseling provided by the Baptist General Convention

---

222. Letter from Christa Brown to Joe Trull, sent in mid-July 2006.
223. See also Ken Camp, "Stepping over the line," *The Baptist Standard*, June 8, 2007 (quoting similar remarks).
224. Email correspondence from Joe Trull to Christa Brown, dated July 21, 2006. This same thought is expressed in the book by Joe Trull and James Carter, *Ministerial Ethics*, at p. 168 (Baker Academic 2004). ("A counselor of ministers who developed a restoration process for fallen ministers shared in a meeting that in his years of work not once did a predator come to him for help. On the other hand, he witnessed scores of wanderers who benefited from his recovery program.")

of Texas. Was every single one of them considered a mere "wanderer" who got restored to ministry?

As I stood there talking in person with Trull at the Dallas Convention Center, he himself brought up the predator/wanderer distinction, recalling that it was something we had discussed in correspondence. He went on and on, and I found myself marveling at how Baptist ministers are often such good talkers but such poor listeners. They're accustomed to being in control of conversations and to having everyone defer to them.

Finally, I interrupted and reminded him that I was a kid when a Baptist minister sexually abused me. Debbie was standing there with me, and I pointed out that Debbie also was abused as a kid.

"The 'wanderer' label cannot *ever* be appropriate for clergy who abuse kids," I told Trull. "That's predatory. Period. By definition."

Trull just looked at me. Actually, he seemed to look right through me. His eyes glazed over, and then he continued with his mini-sermon monologue. The fact that Debbie and I were abused as kids seemed to be a fact of no significance. I guess it just didn't fit with his abstract theory.

Trull ended things by telling me how I needed to be patient with my requests for denominational action on clergy abuse. He had a litany of reasons for why it wasn't a good time, including the fact that the Baptist General Convention of Texas was embroiled in a major financial scandal.[225]

I looked at him square in the eyes. "How should I be 'patient' when, even today, I'm hearing news about still another Baptist abuse victim who has been silenced while the pastor is still in the pulpit, and when I can readily see that the Baptist General Convention of Texas is part of it?"

I was recalling the outraged voice of the woman who had called me just an hour earlier right before the camera crews got rolling – the woman who had told me about the "hush money" agreement in the suit involving Southmont Baptist Church in Denton.

---

225. *See* Ken Camp, "No lawsuits planned," *Baptist Standard*, May 24, 2007; Marv Knox, "BGCT implements responses to church-starting scandal," *Baptist Standard*, March 2, 2007 (with a link to additional "Valleygate" articles). (A five month investigation revealed that about $1.3 million in church-starting funds were mismanaged and lost due to poor oversight and failure to comply with internal guidelines.)

I didn't know it then, but Southmont was Trull's own church. So there I was, telling Trull about his own church, without even realizing it.

To make matters even more ironic, the very next month, Trull had an article on "clergy sexual misconduct" in *Christian Ethics Today* titled "Overlooked Issues."[226] Yet, at the exact same time his article was going to press, his own church was engaged in a clergy sex-abuse cover-up. When that cover-up finally came to light, I wondered whether Trull was even capable of looking back and seeing how many issues he himself had "overlooked."

At least as far back as June 2006, other church and denominational leaders knew about the child molestation allegations against pastor Reynolds. They might have known sooner, but by then, they *had* to have known. That was when the lawsuit was served, both on Southmont and also on the Baptist General Convention of Texas. Yet, pastor Reynolds remained in the pulpit. He wasn't even required to step down pending investigation. Instead, it was all kept quiet.

But after the outraged woman's phone call, I got in touch with a couple reporters. In mid-November 2006, *EthicsDaily* published an article, reporting that Southmont's pastor Reynolds had paid "hush money" to end a suit alleging sexual abuse of a 14-year-old church girl.[227] Though *EthicsDaily* is a relatively small publication, it's read by many church and denominational leaders. So after the article came out, it was hard to imagine that there weren't still more Baptist officials who knew about the child molestation allegations against Reynolds. Yet, Reynolds remained in the pulpit.[228]

Apparently, the lawsuit's settlement agreement required Reynolds to make a public apology. So at a Thanksgiving church banquet on November 19, 2006, he stood up and said this:

---

226. Joe E. Trull, "The Haggard Affair: Overlooked Issues," *Christian Ethics Today*, vol. 12, no. 5 (2006).
227. Bob Allen, "Pastor reportedly settles lawsuit alleging sexual abuse of minor," *EthicsDaily.com*, November 20, 2006.
228. At the time, Southmont Baptist Church was affiliated, not only with the Baptist General Convention of Texas, but also with the Southern Baptist Convention and the Cooperative Baptist Fellowship. But despite the news reported in *EthicsDaily*, there was no indication that any of these organizations took steps to warn people in the pews or to preclude Reynolds from continuing to work as a Baptist minister.

Twenty years ago, I made a terrible mistake. I realize now that my lapse in judgment caused one of our parishioners great harm. I confess that proper boundaries were not kept. I am publicly apologizing to K. Roush for hurting her. I ask God for forgiveness, you for forgiveness, and Miss Roush for forgiveness.[229]

Though numerous church-members heard this apology, apparently no one insisted on knowing exactly what the "terrible mistake" was. And apparently no one insisted on more information about the "boundaries" that were crossed by their beloved pastor. And apparently no one in leadership was willing to tell the congregants that the "boundaries" involved a 14-year-old. It was all just "overlooked."

Not until there was a major article in the local newspaper was the issue finally brought out in the open with church-members. Reynolds couldn't hide anymore and he decided to "retire."[230]

But even up to the last minute, another Southmont minister still tried to keep things hushed up. He wrote to the newspaper, asking it not to run the story and telling them it would be destructive to "the cause of Christ."[231] Fortunately, despite the minister's chastening letter, the *Denton Record-Chronicle* didn't back down.

It was a shame that the people in that church had to read about their pastor in the newspaper rather than being told forthrightly by the people they trusted – the *other* leaders of their church. But apparently a lot of the church people weren't too troubled by it anyway. They gathered a $50,000 "love offering" to give to Reynolds when he left.[232]

229. Donna Fielder, "Suits allege clergy misconduct: Two Baptist ministers apologize after women bring forth accusations," *Denton Record-Chronicle*, December 17, 2006; Jim Avila, Bonnie Van Gilder and Matt Lopez, *ABC 20/20*, "Preacher Predators," April 13, 2007 (showing Reynolds' apology, filmed with a phone camera).

230. Bob Allen, "Bellevue pastor staying, Texas pastor leaving, over clergy sex-abuse scandals," *EthicsDaily.com*, December 22, 2006; Donna Fielder, "Southmont pastor plans to retire," *Denton Record-Chronicle*, December 21, 2006.

231. Donna Fielder, "Suits allege clergy misconduct: Two Baptist ministers apologize after women bring forth accusations," *Denton Record-Chronicle*, December 17, 2006.

232. Jim Avila, Bonnie Van Gilder and Matt Lopez, "Preachers accused of sins and crimes," *ABC 20/20*, April 13, 2007 (transcript) [http://abcnews.go.com/2020/Story?id=3034040&page=1].

After Reynolds "retired," and after a couple people told me that Southmont was Joe Trull's church, I decided to write to Trull again. I hoped the whole experience might have opened his eyes a little.

"I am wondering if you have any different thoughts now than you did when I spoke with you in Dallas," I asked him.[233]

I also told Trull how saddened I was by the turmoil that I knew many Southmont people were feeling. I wasn't just saying that; some Southmont people had contacted me. A couple of them admitted they had heard a bit of "gossip" about the lawsuit, but said they quickly put it out of their heads. Now they didn't know what to think.

One of the church deacons said he had heard about the lawsuit, but assumed that if there was anything to it, the Southern Baptist Convention wouldn't let Reynolds keep preaching. I told him that, in virtually all cases like this, denominational leaders don't intervene and don't exercise any oversight. "Bottom line – they do nothing," I said. Even though this man was a church official – a deacon – that news still seemed to surprise him.

As I continued my letter to Trull, I told him how, in hindsight, our conversation in Dallas seemed ironic since I was actually telling him about his own church without even realizing it. Then I got to the crux of what I was trying to communicate to him.

> You speak around the country on this subject. You write on this subject. And yet, even as someone who is a great deal more knowledgeable than most, you apparently didn't see the cover-up and collusion that was happening in your own church. The lawsuit had been on file for over six months. There *had* to have been people in the church, and also at the Baptist General Convention of Texas, who knew about it. . . . If someone as knowledgeable and in-sightful as yourself cannot see the collusion and cover-up going on in your own church until it's published in the newspaper, then why in the world does anyone imagine that ordinary victims are going to be able to get the real facts before a congregation? If church leadership doesn't turn to someone as respected as you when confronted with this sort of crisis, then why would anyone imagine that they would give any credence to a victim? Typically,

233. Email correspondence from Christa Brown to Joe Trull dated January 8, 2007.

we are outcasts – and if we weren't already outcasts, we become outcasts the moment we speak up.[234]

I ended my note with what I intended as a compliment. I pointed out to Trull that when I first contacted him, I said how I had often wondered "Where is the Thomas Doyle of Southern Baptists?"

"I still keep wondering that," I told Trull, "and I still ponder whether that person couldn't just as easily be you."[235]

Trull's response was brief. He said he hadn't seen the earlier *EthicsDaily* article and that he didn't know anything about the whole mess until the story broke in the *Denton Record-Chronicle*. He claimed there were only three church leaders who knew about it.[236]

I couldn't accept that. If nothing else, there had been Reynolds' public apology at the Thanksgiving banquet. After that, even if church-members didn't know all the details, they knew enough that somebody at that church should have been asking some questions.

And I couldn't begin to let the Baptist General Convention of Texas slide by as easily as Trull apparently could. They were put on formal notice of the child molestation allegations against Reynolds, and yet they didn't choose to warn people. In fact, the very same lawyer who tried to get *me* to sign a secrecy contract had also been the lawyer for the Baptist General Convention on this case, except that this time the victim actually wound up signing the church's hush-money agreement.

Why didn't leaders at the Baptist General Convention of Texas tell Trull about the fact that the pastor of his own church had been reported for child molestation? Trull was their own go-to guru on the clergy abuse subject, and yet they apparently chose to leave him in the dark when it involved the pastor of his own church. The whole matter would have faded quietly into the background if not for the righteous anger of K. Roush's neighbor, my own effort in contacting reporters, and the reporters' exemplary work of bringing the news into the light of day.

But Trull seemed willing to completely "overlook" the failure of the Baptist General Convention of Texas. What I saw then was a man whose long-time loyalty to the Baptist General Convention of Texas had blinded him to that organization's collusion in keeping quiet about clergy sex abuse. It was the same old pattern. People are blinded by

---

234. Email correspondence from Christa Brown to Joe Trull dated January 8, 2007.
235. Email correspondence from Christa Brown to Joe Trull dated January 8, 2007.
236. Email correspondence from Joe Trull to Christa Brown dated January 9, 2007.

what they *want* to believe when ugly news involves people they trust and religious institutions they love.

I kept it super-short when I wrote back to Trull. It was obvious that he wasn't seeing what I was seeing. "If you ever reach the point," I said, "that you're capable of seeing . . . the hideous collusion in how the Baptist General Convention of Texas is handling things in actual practice, you know how to reach me."[237]

Trull took offense at that. After all, in his eyes, he was the expert, not me.

"You seem to enjoy gunny-sacking every time a new episode emerges," he railed back at me.[238] "You seem to enjoy unloading all of your frustrations on others – perhaps it's time for you to listen a little bit and not be so quick to jump to conclusions and judge everyone else's motives. . . . If we are ever going to make any progress, it's going to take all of us working together, not constantly taking out our anger on each other." Then he proceeded to brag about how the Baptist General Convention of Texas was going to form a new committee on the subject.

I viewed that as Trull's way of telling me to "shut up." And it seemed obvious to me that *he* was the person who was doing the "unloading" and taking out his anger. I wondered if he realized how much his over-defensive reaction paralleled the sort of reaction that congregants usually have when their pastor is accused. Trull couldn't stomach my saying that his beloved organization – the Baptist General Convention of Texas – was colluding in keeping quiet about clergy sex abuse. And churchgoers typically can't stomach having an accuser say their beloved pastor committed abuse. In almost every instance, the reaction is to kick the messenger.

I tried to imagine whether Father Thomas Doyle would ever accuse a clergy abuse survivor of "gunny-sacking," and I knew he wouldn't. It's normal for people who have been victimized by this terrible crime to feel anguish when they see religious organizations covering-up for the abuse of still more kids. We aren't merely "gunny-sacking." We're grieving with the wounded, and we're trying to shine light on the problem in the hope that someone will actually do something so that other kids might be spared the pain of what we went through.

The more I thought about Father Doyle, the more I thought how

237. Email correspondence from Christa Brown to Joe Trull dated January 11, 2007 4:34 p.m.

238. Email correspondence from Joe Trull to Christa Brown dated January 11, 2007.

ironic it was that Trull didn't seem to realize what a compliment I had given him by suggesting a possible comparison. Maybe Trull didn't even know who Father Doyle was. That seemed unlikely for someone who cast himself as an expert on the subject of clergy sex abuse, but by now I had figured out that Trull might not be as much of an expert as I had once imagined.

I didn't care to engage Trull much more, but I also wasn't willing to meekly stay mute to his brag about the Baptist General Convention of Texas. I had experienced first-hand the pain of that organization's do-nothingness, and for me, it wasn't just an academic exercise. So, I wrote back to Trull and said this:

> I think the world of Father Thomas Doyle. The fact that I would even imagine that you might be someone who could potentially fill those shoes was a huge compliment. I guess you didn't realize that. The fact that I would still imagine that possibility even after all this time, even after talking with you in person, and even after learning that Southmont was your church, was an even bigger compliment. To the extent I jumped to any sort of erroneous conclusion or misjudged you, it was in that respect.[239]

Trull responded with still more praise for the Baptist General Convention of Texas.[240] Since I figured he was probably the sort of guy who liked to get the last word, I decided to let him have it. I didn't reply.

Just a few days after Trull's last email, news about the Davies case broke. It was reported as "Missouri's biggest sex abuse case to date," and the perpetrator was a Southern Baptist minister.[241]

At least 13 children in three states were sexually molested and abused by minister Davies, and investigators said there were probably others."[242]

---

239. Email correspondence from Christa Brown to Joe Trull dated January 11, 2007, 11:30 p.m.

240. Email correspondence from Joe Trull to Christa Brown dated January 12, 2007.

241. Hannah Elliott, "Missouri Baptist pastor sentenced to 20 years for child sex-abuse," *Associated Baptist Press*, January 18, 2007.

242. Erica Osborne, "Youth minister faces sex charges," *Georgetown News-Graphic*, June 30, 2006; Erica Osborne, "Former Baptist youth minister convicted in Kentucky," *Georgetown News-Graphic*, January 21, 2007.

Even though prior churches had expressed serious concerns,[243] Davies was allowed to move unchecked from one Baptist church to another, sexually assaulting young boys along the way.[244] His most recent church in Greenwood, Missouri, hired Davies even while he was under investigation in Kentucky. Then, according to police, the senior pastor even allowed Davies to continue working with children for four full months after police specifically told him about their investigation of Davies.[245]

As I thought about the horrible harm to so many young boys, and about how it could have been prevented, I sat at my desk and wept. And as I put the news articles about the case onto the StopBaptistPredators website, I wondered if Joe Trull would say that I was just "gunny-sacking."

Weeks later, I heard that Trull had left the Southmont church, and I couldn't help but think how easy it was for him. Baptist clergy abuse survivors don't have the luxury of simply being able to go to a different church when they're trying to report abuse and find themselves facing entrenched denial. They have to go to the church of the perpetrator and they have to figure out all on their own how to get that church to consider the allegation seriously.

It's an impossible task. Most clergy abuse survivors won't go to the den of the wolf who savaged them. They know it won't do any good, and they can't see why they should set themselves up to be stoned by people who don't want to hear what they've got to say. And they're right. If a much-respected leader like Joe Trull couldn't convince his own church of how inappropriate their $50,000 "love offering" for Reynolds was, how can Baptist leaders imagine that a child molestation victim – a person who has often been away from the church for many years – can go to the church as an outsider and convince members of the truth about the terrible thing their pastor did?

Southmont was a church that had more resources than most. It had a highly educated, affluent congregation, and it even had a professed clergy abuse expert as a member. Yet, Southmont leaders knew about

243. Bob Allen, "Clergy sex abuse case reveals flaws in SBC system, victims' advocate says," *EthicsDaily*, January 22, 2007.

244. Hannah Elliott, "Missouri Baptist pastor sentenced to 20 years for child sex-abuse," *Associated Baptist Press*, January 18, 2007; see also Greg Warner, "Betrayed trust: The recycle of abuse continues at Baptist churches," *Associated Baptist Press*, June 11, 2007 (describing Baptist churches as "unwitting accomplices to predator pastors who are recycled from one unsuspecting congregation to another").

245. Hannah Elliott, "Missouri police investigate molestation by minister in Baptist church," by Hannah Elliott, *Associated Baptist Press*, May 5, 2006.

the child molestation allegations against Reynolds. . . . and nothing happened. The Baptist General Convention of Texas knew about the child molestation allegations against Reynolds. . . . and nothing happened. Only the involvement of the press brought the information to the people in the pews.

45

The Do-Nothing Denomination

"Under pressure to fight child sex abuse, the Southern Baptist Convention's executive committee said . . . the denomination should not create its own database to help churches identify predators or establish an office to field abuse claims."[246] That was the lead in the Associated Press article that went out in over 200 newspapers and media outlets across the country in June 2008 when Southern Baptist officials reported back on their "study" and said they weren't going to do anything.

Their do-nothingness was a disappointment, but not a surprise. And despite their do-nothingness, I knew that we had made progress in our fight for clergy accountability among Southern Baptists. We hadn't succeeded in pushing Baptist officials to institute any changes, but we had succeeded in making a whole lot of people a whole lot more aware of the problem. Some people were suddenly seeing that the Southern Baptist emperor had no clothes.

Given that we never saw much of anything that resembled a real study, the committee's conclusions weren't much of a surprise. Their conclusions were essentially the same as what they had been saying all along, even before they purported to do a study. Augie Boto was the primary paid Southern Baptist official assigned to assist the committee, and Southern Baptist president Frank Page publicly identified Boto as the man "in charge" of it.[247] Boto had made his position clear from the get-go: "It is not possible for the denomination to create an independent sexual abuse review panel."[248] Nevertheless, despite his predetermined

---

246. Eric Gorski (Associated Press), "Southern Baptists reject sex-abuse database," *Washington Post*, June 10, 2008.
247. Elizabeth Ulrich, "What would Jesus say?" *The Nashville Scene*, February 14, 2008. (The actual chairman of the subcommittee was Stephen Wilson, vice-president of academic affairs at Mid-Continent University, but Southern Baptist president Frank Page's statement that Boto was "in charge" may have revealed a de facto reality about who was really wielding the most power.)
248. Adelle M. Banks, "Southern Baptist lawyer says independent abuse panel not possible," *EthicsDaily*, February 26, 2007; see also Gary Soulsman, "Keeping doors open," *Delaware News-Journal*, March 3, 2007.

point of view,[249] Boto was left "in charge" and so it wasn't surprising when the committee reached the same conclusion that Boto had spouted all along.

"Southern Baptists believe that the local church in New Testament times was autonomous, and thus our local churches are autonomous," said executive committee president Morris Chapman in his address to the convention.[250] "Local church autonomy rules out creating a centralized investigative body to determine who has been credibly accused of sexual abuse . . . and the convention has no authority to bar known perpetrators from ministry or start an office to field abuse claims," the committee said in its report.[251]

It was that same tired "autonomy" excuse that they had dished out a gazillion times before.[252] It was that same coded language for "not our problem." It was that same well-practiced rationalization for preserving a status quo in which leadership turns a blind eye to clergy abuse reports.

So the high-honchos in this behemoth of an organization – an organization that gets $200 million per year in contributions from local churches – decided not to help the local churches by providing them with information on credibly-accused clergy child molesters. And they decided not to help the victims of clergy child molesters by providing them with a safe place to report abuse. And they decided not to help the families in Baptist churches by providing any sort of record-keeping or tracking of credibly-accused clergy so as to prevent them from moving church to church in search of new prey.

Nope. This was to remain the do-nothing denomination.

Southern Baptist pastor Wade Burleson saw the irrationality in

---

249. *See* Bob Allen, "Clergy sex abuse survivor questions fairness of SBC executive committee study," *EthicsDaily*, September 21, 2007.

250. Drew Nichter, "SBC officials reject idea of sex-offender database," *Associated Baptist Press*, June 11, 2008; Bob Allen, "SBC leaders recommend against national database of clergy sex offenders," *EthicsDaily*, June 11, 2008.

251. Eric Gorski (Associated Press), "Southern Baptists reject sex-abuse database," *Washington Post*, June 10, 2008.

252. *See* Robert Parham, "Dismantle false wall of church autonomy that protects child predator preachers," *EthicsDaily*, April 9, 2007 (quoting various Southern Baptist officials on how "autonomy" prevented the SBC from taking action against clergy predators); Christa Brown, "Baptist autonomy ignored in investigating gays, but not clergy child molesters," *EthicsDaily*, November 20, 2006 (giving examples of how the Southern Baptist Convention's autonomy excuse is often phrased).

it.[253] "To argue that a list of Southern Baptist ministers who are sexual predators violates the self-government of a local church is illogical," he said.[254] "A database is only information . . . What a church does with that information is their decision."[255]

But however illogical it may have been, executive committee president Morris Chapman's speech was apparently a rousing one. He was interrupted six times by applause[256] as he made bold-sounding statements about "encouraging" churches to rout out predators.[257]

Chapman is a great preacher. But Southern Baptist woman Alyce Faulkner wasn't swayed by the sound of it. She saw the truth for what it was and flat-out grieved about it on her blog. "We rally around words – when will we rally around reality? Once again, we resolve to do nothing. God help us."[258]

Across the country, journalists also saw the irrationality of Southern Baptists' do-nothingness:

"The very fact that Baptist churches are autonomous signals that they need the information the convention could provide," wrote the *Tennessean*.[259]

"Baptists miss an opportunity," declared the *Dallas Morning News*.[260]

"Holy hypocrisy," said the *Winston-Salem Journal*.[261]

Not only was there hypocrisy in Baptist leaders' do-nothing conclusion, but there seemed to also be hypocrisy in their very pretense of

253. Wade Burleson, "Cost plays a role, child safety a priority," *The Tennessean*, June 10, 2008; Eileen Flynn, "Austin lawyer pushes Baptist churches to confront sexual abuse," *Austin American-Statesman*, June 9, 2008.
254. Wade Burleson, "Cost plays a role, child safety a priority," *supra*.
255. Eric Gorski (Associated Press), "Southern Baptists reject sex-abuse database," *Washington Post*, June 10, 2008.
256. Mark Kelly, "Stop sexual predators, Chapman urges," *Baptist Press*, June 10, 2008.
257. *See* Elizabeth Ulrich, "Save Yourselves," *Nashville Scene*, June 19, 2008.
258. Alyce Faulkner, "Moving from resolution to reality," *Miracle of Mercy* blog, June 10, 2008 [http://miracleofmercy.blogspot.com/2008/06/moving-from-resolution-to-reality.html].
259. Editorial, "Who should lead church on safety if not the SBC?" *The Tennessean*, July 10, 2008. (In an on-line readers' poll, 96 percent of *Tennessean* readers said Southern Baptists should create a database of clergy sex offenders among their ranks. *See* Bob Allen, "SBC official says relatively 'low' number of cases," *EthicsDaily*, May 14, 2007.)
260. Editorial: Hits and misses, "Baptists miss an opportunity," *Dallas Morning News*, June 14, 2008.
261. John Railey, "A little autonomy can be a scary thing in fighting predators," *Winston-Salem Journal*, June 22, 2008.

having done a study. When Catholic bishops finally decided to look seriously at clergy abuse, they commissioned a multimillion dollar two-part study from the John Jay College of Criminal Justice.[262] The first part of the study was released in 2004, and though it was a study with some flaws, it at least provided the beginning of a yardstick for assessment, and it was a whole heckuva lot more than Southern Baptist leaders did with their purported study.

When a reporter asked them about their budget for the study, "no one could provide one."[263] Finally, a Baptist official admitted that there wasn't any budget at all set aside for the "study".[264] Likewise, there weren't any transcripts of committee hearings with experts, and there wasn't any data compiled or presented. Their "study" appeared to be little more than a group of guys sitting in a room talking and reconfirming for one another what they already believed before they ever started the so-called "study."

Ironically, in the same year when Southern Baptist officials couldn't seem to come up with anything resembling a real study on clergy sex abuse, they nevertheless managed to conduct a survey and compile data for a study designed to provide churches with accessible online information about how to adequately compensate their ministers.[265] Baptist officials thought it was important for denominational entities to "work together to serve our churches with information to help them adequately compensate our ministers."[266] I couldn't help but wonder why it wasn't equally important for denominational entities to work together to provide churches with information about credibly-accused clergy child molesters.

The most troubling part, though, was the executive committee's explanation for *why* it wasn't going to create a database of credibly-accused Baptist clergy: It claimed a denominational database would be incomplete.[267] The committee told churches that they should instead

---

262. Rachel Martin, "The Aftermath: The Church Responds," *NPR.org*, January 11, 2007 [http://www.npr.org/templates/story/story.php?storyId=6799693]
263. Elizabeth Ulrich, "What would Jesus say?" *Nashville Scene*, February 14, 2008.
264. Elizabeth Ulrich, "What would Jesus say?" *supra.*
265. "Church compensation survey underway," *Baptist Press*, January 8, 2008.
266. "Church compensation survey underway," *supra.*
267. Bob Allen, "SBC leaders recommend against national database of clergy sex offenders," *EthicsDaily*, June 11, 2008.

208 — Christa Brown

conduct background checks using the U.S. Department of Justice's national database of convicted sex offenders.[268]

The way I saw it, this explanation could only be based on ignorance or disingenuousness. Either way, it was inexcusable. If the committee had conducted any sort of a study at all, the first thing they would have learned is what almost all experts in the field know – that over 90 percent of active sex offenders have no criminal record that will show up in a background check.[269] They aren't on sex-offender registries. So background checks, though an essential small step, can never be anywhere near enough.

This is why other faith groups now have their own denominational review processes for clergy.[270] They don't wait for a minister to be criminally convicted and show up on a sex offender registry before they'll undertake a review to see whether allegations of abuse are credible. Even if religious leaders can't put such men in jail, they can at least take away the weapon of ministerial trust and prevent them from using it to molest kids.

But Baptists still don't do this. It's why clergy child molesters can so easily slip through the cracks in Baptist churches.

I could understand that ordinary people in the pews might not realize that most child molesters aren't on sex offender registries. But leaders who supposedly conducted a "study" should have known this fact and they should have addressed the reality of it. To me, it looked as though Southern Baptist officials were essentially promoting ignorance as a strategy against clergy predators. In the process, they were devaluing the very people whom they purport to serve – the very people who look to them for leadership.

Law professor Marci Hamilton didn't mince words when she saw Southern Baptist officials' ridiculous rationalization. "The Southern Baptist Convention prevaricates," she declared. Then she explained why their reasoning was so lame as to be incredible.

---

268. Eric Gorski (Associated Press), "Southern Baptists reject sex-abuse database," *Washington Post*, June 10, 2008; Heather Hahn, "Southern Baptists rule out sex-offender list," *Arkansas Democrat-Gazette*, June 11, 2008.

269. Eric Tryggestad, "Sex abuse in churches preventable, say experts," *The Christian Chronicle*, June 1, 2007.

270. *See* Heather Hahn, "Southern Baptists rule out sex-offender list," *Arkansas Democrat-Gazette*, June 11, 2008.

The way SBC officials make it sound, the issue is now dead and individual churches should just do their own individual background checks. Never mind that such checks would be profoundly easier – and more likely to be thorough – if an intra-organizational database could be consulted.

There is a procedural answer to what the SBC has portrayed as an insuperable barrier – agree among all independent entities to coordinate. If Baptist churches cannot coordinate on a shared, national strategy in favor of children at risk, they rightly lose a great deal of moral capital.

Thus, the autonomy excuse is nothing more than that: an excuse.

The church-network database suggestion was visionary – and the suggestion that it would simply overlap with Megan's Lists or federal databases is dead wrong.[271]

Within mere days after Southern Baptist officials rejected the creation of a denominational database to help churches identify credibly-accused clergy child molesters, it was revealed that the Southern Baptist Convention's own ministerial registry included at least ten more men who had been convicted or charged with sex crimes involving children.[272] So, even as executive committee president Morris Chapman stood there telling the convention crowd that "our denomination . . . must condemn publicly this vile act,"[273] and even as convention-goers stood there applauding Chapman's fine preaching, known child-molesters were being publicly held forth as ministers on the Southern Baptist Convention's registry in Nashville.

---

271. Marci Hamilton, "The Southern Baptist Convention's unconvincing claims as to why it cannot report or prevent child abuse," *FindLaw*, June 12, 2008 [http://writ.news.findlaw.com/hamilton/20080612.html].

272. Bob Smietana, "Church website hasn't purged alleged predators," *The Tennessean*, June 24, 2008.

273. Bob Smietana, "Southern Baptists won't create a sexual predator database, *The Tennessean*, June 11, 2008.

Of course, it wasn't the first time Southern Baptist officials had been told about convicted child molesters on their ministerial registry. *EthicsDaily* had told them *several* times previously.[274] *ABC's 20/20* had told them.[275] And now the *Tennessean* was telling them about still more names.[276] One of the ten names that the *Tennessean* revealed was a name that *EthicsDaily* had pointed out more than a year earlier.[277] But in a years' time, no one at Southern Baptist headquarters had bothered to do anything about it.

The do-nothing reality of Southern Baptist leaders was obvious: Despite all their fine words, they couldn't manage to keep even criminally convicted child molesters off their own ministerial registry. And they weren't even considering doing anything about "credibly-accused" clergy in the way that other faith groups do.

I thought back on how Southern Baptist president Frank Page had railed against the media, claiming that Baptist officials were being wrongly portrayed as "uncaring and uninformed" about clergy sex abuse.[278] And once again, I found myself wondering how an intelligent man could possibly imagine that Southern Baptist officials should be portrayed in any other way. "Uncaring and uninformed" – the words fit.

Professor Marci Hamilton summed up the sad reality. "The Southern Baptist Convention has . . . proven why it is that children are at risk for sexual abuse in our society: It's easier *not* to protect them, and especially easy to issue ineffectual platitudes while looking the other way."[279]

Southern Baptist officials did what was easy. They did nothing.

---

274. Bob Allen, "Clergy sex abuse activist awaits response from SBC," *EthicsDaily*, October 11, 2006; Bob Allen, "Baptist minister, volunteer track coach charged with rape," *EthicsDaily*, March 28, 2007; Bob Allen, "SBC president says denomination looking into sex offender registry," *EthicsDaily*, April 16, 2007.

275. Bob Allen, "SBC officials criticize 'Preacher Predator' report on '20/20'," *EthicsDaily*, April 18, 2007.

276. Bob Smietana, "Church website hasn't purged alleged predators," *The Tennessean*, June 24, 2008.

277. Bob Allen, "Baptist minister, volunteer track coach charged with rape," *EthicsDaily*, March 28, 2007.

278. "Page says *20/20* segment one-sided," *Baptist Press*, April 16, 2007; Bob Allen, "SBC president labels sexual abuse critics as 'opportunists'," *EthicsDaily*, April 20, 2007.

279. Marci Hamilton, "The Southern Baptist Convention's unconvincing claims as to why it cannot report or prevent child abuse," *FindLaw*, June 12, 2008 [http://writ.news.findlaw.com/hamilton/20080612.html].

Part Five

A Free Spirit

Build thee more stately mansions, O my soul . . .
Til thou at length art free.

OLIVER WENDELL HOLMES,
"The Chambered Nautilus"

46

The Hurt of "God's Love"

"God loves you." Lots of people seem to want to tell me that, and I hate it when they do. It's a visceral response. Those words ring in my ears like a vile curse. I'd rather hear someone say "Go to hell" than "God loves you."

Perhaps God does indeed love me, but I will never sense it in the sound of those words. For me, those feel like words of hate.

People seem to also want to tell me that God will heal me if only I will put my faith in Him. I try to be polite, because they're usually well intentioned, but to me, those are also hurtful words. Faith is what got me into this. Faith is where the path turned terribly wrong.

For most people of faith, their faith is a source of solace. It gives them comfort and strength for all manner of life's travails. It's a powerful resource for healing. But for me, faith is neurologically networked with a nightmare. Sexual trauma and faith are inextricably seared together in my brain.[280]

This is what it means to be subjected to the force of faith unleashed by a clergy predator. It is not only physically, psychologically, and emotionally devastating, but it is also spiritually annihilating. It is soul-murder. It is why many experts talk about the unique nature of clergy abuse trauma and the devastation of its impact.[281]

When faith has been used as a weapon, it becomes almost impossible to use it as a resource for healing. You can't pick which edge of the faith

---

280. SNAP's National Director, David Clohessy, once described the difficulty of the faith/trauma link in this way: "No victim feels more alone than somebody abused by a religious figure or in a religious setting. The most universal source of comfort and solace in painful times is God. But if God is perceived to be an integral part of one's abuse and cover-up, victims are left with virtually nowhere to turn." Michelle Roberts (*Religion News Service*), "Abuse survivors struggle with loss of faith, confidence," *Baptist Standard*, November 7, 2008.

281. Shirley Ragsdale, "Sexual abuse by clergy leaves greater damage, experts say," *Desmoines Register*, April 4, 2004; *see also* Michelle Roberts, "Abuse survivors struggle with loss of faith, confidence, *supra*.

blade you use. It's all the same bloody sword. It's the sword I fell on when I was a church girl in Farmers Branch, Texas. It's the sword that eviscerated me.

For me, the most difficult encounters are the ones with people who want to tell me how wonderful it is that God is using me in this way. They say my current activism is the proof of how God had a plan all along, and they claim that, even though I couldn't understand that plan when I was a kid, God knew what He was doing and now we're seeing His will brought to fruition as he uses me to shine light on this terrible problem.

It's all I can do to keep from gagging when people say this kind of stuff. I know they don't mean any harm, but I have to rein myself in to even be polite.

Without realizing it, they're mimicking the talk of my perpetrator. All that talk about "God's will" and my predestined purpose was exactly the sort of talk that savaged me. I cannot allow myself to ever again believe such things. I won't. And it strikes me as a very hateful view of God to imagine that He pre-ordains certain kids to be the rape-toys of anointed clergy so that they can then be used to advance His will at some point in the future.

Of course, by the time the future arrives, a lot of those kids will have slit their wrists because the psychological and spiritual pain of clergy sex abuse is so great. I wonder if these people who posit such pre-ordained child-rapes also think that God takes into account the percentage that will be lost to suicide.

I can't even begin to go down the path toward that way of thinking. It would take me back to believing the things my perpetrator told me – that I was "chosen" – that it was all preordained – that God had a plan – that it wasn't for me to understand – that God wanted me to live by faith – that God would make all things work together for good – and that it would all happen in God's time and in God's way.

I understand that way of thinking. I was raised in that way of thinking. But I can't go there again. I can't even tiptoe around the edges of that terrain without getting nauseated.

People who tell me these things want me to believe that God is in control of everything that ever happens and that it's all part of some great master-plan. For them, that's a belief that helps them feel safer in the world. For me, that's religious terrorism.

I once tried to explain some of this to a friend who, with the best of intentions, wrote to tell me about God's love and about how God would restore me if I would put my faith and trust in Him. Most of the time, I let such talk slide and don't say much, but the strength of this woman's sincerity made me realize she was deserving of a more serious response.

Dear Susan,

When I read your email, my hands shook so much that I spilled my coffee. My chest began to pound. I started being short of breath. I felt literally sick. I had to get up and take a walk with headphones to try to shift my brain into a different mode. That's what talk of God's love can do to me. It's a physiological response.

I do not believe you intended to inflict any hurt on me, and to the contrary, I expect that you intended to offer some comfort and hope. But, from my perspective, it is as though your email brandished in front of me the very weapon that was used against me. It is as though you are telling me that I should pick up that very same sword that was once used to eviscerate me and should fall on it all over again. I can't do that. My love of God, my faith, my own extraordinary desire to live the will of God . . . those are the very parts of me that were transformed into weapons that savaged and destroyed me. As a result, that part of my brain, that part of me that was once able to turn to God, to surrender to God, to pour my heart out to God, to put things in God's hands, to believe that God would take care of me . . . all of that part of my brain is inaccessible. It is electrically charged and it is the land of the predator . . . it is a ravaged land that is there within my own head.

I think it is somewhat analogous to a person who has a stroke. The person's brain tissue is damaged by the physical trauma of oxygen deprivation, and because of that trauma, a part of their brain doesn't get the connections right anymore. It is as though it is short-circuited out and (depending on what part of the brain is affected) the result may be that they can't form words anymore even though their thought-making process is still intact. My brain has also been damaged by trauma, although it was a severe psychological trauma rather than a physical brain injury.

Sometimes, with rehab work, people who have had strokes can learn to attach words to thoughts again, but they do so consciously and with great effort. In effect, they work at rewiring their brains around the place of trauma. In some ways, I think I am engaged in an analogous process. . . . The extent to which I may or may not be able to do so remains to be seen . . . .

Another possibly useful analogy is to think about a victim of torture whose torturer always played Beethoven while he beat and brutalized the victim. Years later, that victim of torture is unlikely to much appreciate the music of Beethoven, and he may feel great anxiety when he hears the music even if he is merely at a shopping mall. And perhaps he won't even realize why he is becoming so short of breath or why he is feeling the need to leave the mall immediately. The music is just background noise. But on some level his brain is still processing it as something that is linked to degradation, pain and fear. The sort of talk of God's love that is in your email is the sort of talk that transports me to the torture chamber that is in my own head. . . .

47

Heart of a Missionary

As a kid, I wanted to be like Lottie Moon.[282] I dreamed of being a great missionary and thought I would shine the light of truth in the darkest corners of Africa. As it turned out, the darkest corners were closer to home.

In countless encounters with Baptist leaders, their words and deeds have left a legacy of hate. The lesson they taught said, "You are a creature void of any value – you don't matter." Endlessly and repetitively, in both my childhood and adulthood, Baptist leaders made that message absolutely clear.

It was a lesson first taught by Eddie Dunagan, the minister who molested and raped me as a kid. It was a lesson reinforced by the keep-it-quiet music minister, Jim Moore, and by the other leaders in my childhood church, who knew and stayed silent. In recent years, the same lesson was retaught by current ministers and deacons at First Baptist Church of Farmers Branch – men who chose to threaten recourse against *me* rather than doing anything about their own former minister who molested me.

Then, as though Baptists were afraid I hadn't adequately learned my lesson, it was retaught by men of the Baptist General Convention of Texas who, with double-faced dissembling, strung me along, did nothing to help me, and instead helped the church that was seeking to silence me. The lesson was repeatedly retaught yet again and again by men of the Southern Baptist Convention who misled me to think my perpetrator wasn't in ministry, who wouldn't even shake my hand, who did nothing to help me, and who said remarkably hurtful things.

In truth, if I were to recount all the misery of what I've encountered these past few years in Baptist-land, there would be no end to it. And how I wish my story were a rarity. But it's not. I've seen the effect of

---

282. Lottie Moon was a famous Southern Baptist missionary woman who went to China in 1873. *See* Susan M. Shaw, *God Speaks to Us, Too*, p. 140 (University of Kentucky Press 2008).

Baptist leaders' "you don't matter" message on many other clergy abuse survivors.

Despite what Baptist leaders may say publicly about "precious children," when they leave predators in their pulpits and do nothing to help clergy victims, the message they send is the "you don't matter" message. It is a terribly hateful lesson for religious leaders to teach and it betrays the very faith they purport to profess.

If I had fully believed the lesson that Baptist leaders taught, I would surely be dead by now. But I was graced to have other people in my life – people who worked hard to counter Baptist teachings and to constantly remind me that my life mattered. Thank God for non-Baptists and non-believers.

I realize how lucky I've been. Strangely, it is that sense of having been graced by goodness that makes me feel obligated to try to shed light in this land of darkness. At its core, that's an evangelical sort of thought, and I can't help but laugh at myself in the very thinking of it.

Perhaps a more rational person would run from this Baptist morass of hatefulness – as far and as fast as their legs could carry them. But though I am no longer Baptist, my self-identity still carries a strong link to them.[283]

The habits of evangelical thought beckon like siren songs. Deeply familiar, they call me home to a way of thinking that was once my own.

All those early years of scripture memorization, service projects and mission-field maps can't be easily erased. After all, I fulfilled enough good-Baptist-girl-tasks to rise to the highest rank in Girls' Auxiliary – Queen Regent in Service. It was sort of like being an uber-Eagle Scout of Southern Baptist girls. Once upon a time, that was me.

But now, the faith of my youth and every memory connected to it is a rocky land of treachery. I hear faith's siren call but I know it's not safe. My home is gone.

One of the strongest habits of Baptists' evangelical thinking is the habit of always asking "What does God want?" It's the "What am I called to do?" question. As a kid, it was the question that occupied my every prayer.

Nowadays, I feel a measure of revulsion for even the word "calling."

---

283. For many who are raised Baptist, they are as strongly bonded to their faith identity as to their family identity. *See* Susan M. Shaw, *God Speaks to Us, Too*, at pp. 6–8, 175 (University of Kentucky Press 2008).

Yet, there is no getting around the strange sense of being on a path that is not of my choosing. But I wish for a different word to describe it.

Besides, to the extent I feel something akin to a "calling," it is a calling that comes with the mere fact of being human. It is a calling that comes with being a mother. In fact, it is a calling that sounds for *every* mother, *every* parent, and *every* adult. We are *all* called upon to protect the young, and I will never understand how so many Baptist leaders can close their ears to that calling.

As a kid, I never imagined that I might come to view Southern Baptists themselves as a sort of mission field. When I said the Girls' Auxiliary pledge – "knowing that countless people grope in darkness" – I certainly never imagined that one day I would think those groping in darkness were Baptists themselves. And when I sang "This Little Light" in Sunday School, I never imagined that one day I would be trying to shine my "little light" into the dark continent of Baptist-land. But missions are a primary focus for anyone raised Baptist, and so I wound up becoming a mission-oriented sort of person. It's a way of thinking that has never quite left me.

Another habit of evangelicalism is the giving of personal testimony. It's how we were raised to persuade others. We tell our stories. We give our testimony. We bear witness. So I'm the sort of person who sees evangelical power in the stories and testimonies of Baptist abuse survivors. And I believe that the cumulative power of those stories will eventually compel the people of this in-the-dark denomination to convert to an ethical practice that prioritizes kid-protection ahead of institutional protection.

But whether or not Baptists *ever* convert, the stories of survivors should still be told. Silence perpetuates shame, and it is not our shame to bear. We give power back to ourselves in speaking our stories, and we refuse to cede power to evil.

The evil resides not only in the monstrous acts of the ministers who commit such foul deeds, but perhaps even more so in a denominational system that allows their foul deeds to be so easily ignored.

In my activist efforts these past few years, I have necessarily spent some time in the outer atmosphere of the Baptist system, and it has felt like a return to the land of bondage. For me, it now seems like a land without oxygen. I recognize the terrain, but I don't breathe the air. Thank God.

I often have dreams of desperate hovering. I'm trying to gain altitude, but I can't, and I barely stay out of reach of the giant swooping net. I can't see who or what holds that long-handled net. The holder is far below. I see only the net. It sweeps out at me, trying to capture me and pull me down. It grazes my underside. I am beating my wings frantically as I try to escape. But I can't. I can manage only to stay just barely, barely out of reach. I am never trapped, but I am never soaring free either.

"What does God want?"

Maybe it's the question itself that tethers me.

In writing this book, I have often felt as though I was trying to reach back in time to find that girl who vanished in the land of bondage – that girl whose faith was infinite. But more and more, I sense that the time travel went both ways. It's not merely me reaching backward in time. It's also the girl herself who reached forward.

As a child, she was under his spell, lost in a dark and tangled wilderness, unable to even conceive of escape. The fairy-tale forest of faith was all she knew. There was no world beyond.

"But you *did* escape," says my therapist. "You saved yourself. You told others. *You* made it end."

My therapist is right. That girl was the one who did it.

She is a stranger to me, but she is a stranger to whom I am indebted. In juvenile, inept, and uncomprehending ways, she tried to make the horror end. If it had not been for her efforts back then, I suspect that in the here and now, Baptist leaders may have flat-out called me a "liar." But despite so many other hateful words, they never hurled that one.

It was the girl who stymied them. By assuring the knowledge of others, the girl aided the adult. She reached forward through time to protect *me*.

I am grateful to her.

I see how scared she was. I see how alone she was. And I see how courageous she was.

Epilogue

At the end of 2008, *TIME* magazine listed Southern Baptists' rejection of a sex-offender database as one of the top under-reported news stories of the year.[284] It was on the same "top 10" list with stories about the deadly conflict in Sri Lanka, where 300,000 people were forced from their homes, and about the civil war in the Congo, where a million people were displaced. So this story about clergy sex abuse and cover-ups in Baptist-land is a story that keeps dreadful company. It is a story that will not go away anytime soon.

Southern Baptists have over 101,000 clergy in this country, and the denomination has no effective system of oversight for them. This means that children in Southern Baptist churches are not being afforded the same sorts of institutional safeguards as children in Catholic, Episcopal, Presbyterian, Lutheran and Methodist churches.

Clergy abuse can happen in any faith group, and there have been horrific failures and cover-ups in all faith groups. But as compared to the other major faith groups in the United States, Southern Baptists are far behind the curve in taking steps to systematically address the problem.[285]

This book presents only a few snapshots taken near the beginning of Baptists' journey toward clergy accountability. It should have been a faster journey because other faith groups have already cut rough pathways ahead of them. But Baptists are lost, and it looks as though their journey will be a long one.

---

284. Laura Fitzgerald, "Top 10 underreported news stories of 2008: Southern Baptists decide against pedophilia database," *TIME*, December 22, 2008; Bob Allen, "*TIME* ranks SBC rejection of sex-offender database as 'underreported' story," *Associated Baptist Press*, December 17, 2008; Bob Allen, "Former Southern Baptist pastor pleads guilty to sexual abuse, *Associated Baptist Press*, April 30, 2009.

285. In 2008, religion writer Terry Mattingly again noted the difficulty of cracking down on sexual abuse among Southern Baptist clergy and of even bringing attention to the problem. It is, he concluded, "an important – although frustrating – story worthy of more coverage." Terry Mattingly, "Sex scandals in free-church pews," *GetReligion.org*, May 18, 2008 [http://www.getreligion.org/?p=3512].

The denomination needs to provide (1) a safe and welcoming place for victims to report clergy sex abuse, (2) an objective, professionally trained panel for responsibly assessing victims' abuse reports, and (3) an efficient means of assuring that the assessment information reaches people in the pews – i.e., a database.[286]

There is little reason to believe that Southern Baptist leaders will be able to prevent the clergy child molesters they don't yet know about when, over and over again, they do nothing about the clergy child molesters they're specifically told about. Until they take on the burden of responsibly assessing clergy abuse reports, all their talk about "precious children," all their glossy brochures, and all their public-relations spin will amount to nothing but gauzy drapes in gale-force storms.

Clergy predators wreak hurricane havoc, and Southern Baptists are leaving the windows wide open.

---

286. These three specific needs were again set forth in the letter of November 14, 2008 from David Clohessy and Christa Brown of SNAP to the new Southern Baptist president Johnny Hunt. *See also* Adelle Banks (Religion News Service), "Southern Baptists elect president, reject database," *Christianity Today*, June 11, 2008 (quoting Christa Brown saying that "unless and until there is a safe place to which the victims themselves can report abuse with some reasonable expectation of being objectively heard, everything else will be window dressing").

Acknowledgments

With Thanks . . .

To "Dan," my love, my rock, and my mate. No words are adequate.

To "Emily" who, from her first breath, has been an inspiration.

To Elana, who listened relentlessly and gave me new ways of thinking.

To Bob Allen for cutting-edge journalism, an unyielding willingness to chronicle the stories, and a courageous ethics example.

To Mark Pinsky, religion writer extraordinaire, who pursued my story and first gave me a voice.

To Barbara Grant, who helped me find myself amidst the mass of toxic debris.

To my Texas SNAP friends who first started me on this road and who, with tired eyes, tolerated my desperate certainty that Baptist officials would react differently from Catholic bishops.

To every clergy abuse survivor who shared part of their story with me; I was inspired by your courage and honored by your trust.

To so many others who have helped me over and around the rocks in the road: Kaye Maher, Dee Ann Miller, Susan Hogan-Albach, David Clohessy, Jeri Massi, Brooks Egerton, Miguel Prats, Curt Cukjati, Barbara Garcia-Boehland, Tim Fischer, and many more.

I have been graced ten-thousand times over by the goodness of so many people who have crossed my path. My heart overflows with gratitude.

CPSIA information can be obtained
at www.ICGtesting.com
Printed in the USA
BVHW032055040620
580773BV00006B/104